CELEBRATE THE SEASONS OF CHILDHOOD

~ First Grade Curriculum ~
Winter Semester

Recommended for children Ages 6-7 ready for an academic, secular, art, and nature-based curriculum.

Little Acorn Learning | © 2020 ALL RIGHTS RESERVED

All rights reserved. No part of this book may be reprinted, copied, shared or reproduced in any form by print or electronic/mechanical means, including information storage and retrieval systems, without permission in writing from the publisher, except by a reviewer who may quote brief passages in a review.

TABLE OF CONTENTS

Daily Rhythm 1

Winter Festivals & Holidays 5

Week 13: *Trinkets, Treasures & Coins, Hope* 9

Week 14: *Winter Light, Helping Others* 47

Week 15: *Evergreen & Deciduous Trees, Feeling Joy* 83

Week 16: *Clocks, Time Travel & Telling Time, Recycling* 123

Week 17: *Nocturnal & Diurnal Animals, Warmth* 163

Week 18: *Kings & Queens, Peace in Our Homes* 205

Week 19: *Snow & Ice, Forgiveness* 241

Week 20: *Different Cultures, Religions, & Traditions, Tolerance* . 283

Week 21: *Music & Sounds, Listening* 323

Week 22: *Flames & Shadows, Cleansing* 363

Week 23: *Ocean, Waves & Water, Love & Affection* 401

Week 24: *Seeds, Self-Reflection* 447

Daily Rhythm

Use this daily rhythm as a compass while allowing yourself the freedom to add or let go of things as necessary. Small changes will make a big difference in your home and one day does not look like the other. It is important to be flexible while doing your best to maintain a steady flow and structure for the children and yourself.

The morning and bedtime verse should remain the same. All other items are covered in your weekly lessons specifically based on that week's program.

Morning Verse

Look out the window with your children – what do you see? Sunshine, clouds, rain or snow? After you've determined the weather – light a candle with your children, say the first verse – then choose the appropriate second verse:

> Good morning to the glad new day,
> Whatever the skies let fall,
> If storm or sunshine, it is sent,
> A loving gift to all.

For sunshine:

> Good morning to the sunshine fair,
> That lights this world of ours,
> Good morning to the singing birds,
> Good morning to the flowers!

For clouds or rain:

> Good morning to the friendly clouds
> That bring refreshing rain,
> Which patters out "Good morning, dears!'
> Against the window pane.

For snow:

Good morning to the lovely snow,
That lies so soft and deep
Above the little tender seeds
In mother earth asleep.

Good Morning Song

Use this verse to open your circle. Stand together or in a ring if possible and make motions that feel comfortable and flowing to you with your body. Be consistent with the way you present these movements each day. If you are teaching only one child, you can still hold this time together facing one another.

Good morning dear earth
(hands out)
Good morning dear sun
(hands above sun)
Good morning dear resting stones
(hold stones hands)
And beasts on the run
(move hands)
Good morning dear flowers
(hands bloom)
And birds in the trees
(birds hands flying)
Good morning to you
(hands out to children around)
Good morning to me
(hands folded on chest)

Circle, Songs and Movement
included in weekly lesson plans

Closing Circle Verse

The earth is firm beneath my feet
The sun shines bright above
And here I stand so straight and tall,
All things to know and love

Blackboard Drawing
specific ideas included in weekly lesson plans

Take time to make a simple blackboard drawing that relates to your story or verses for the week. This can be done on Sunday evenings or anytime the weekend before. Buy a small but sturdy blackboard and invest in a good set of colored chalk. Keep the drawing simple and colorful, using the sides of the chalk to make the color look smooth. Cover your drawing with a silk and unveil it for the children during circle time. This will become a much loved tradition in your home and the children will be so excited to see the drawing each week when they arrive.

Story Time
included in weekly lesson plans

Morning Lessons
included in weekly lesson plans

Short Morning Talk
included in weekly lesson plans

Morning Snack
see our seasonal childcare menus

Eat family style and help one another cut, chop and pass food. Light a candle, hold hands and say the following blessing.

Blessings on the blossoms
Blessings on the roots
Blessings on the leaves and stems
Blessings on the fruit
Blessings on our meal

Outdoor Time/Nature Walk

Lunch

Meals same as snack time with family style and blessing.

Afternoon Lessons
included in weekly lesson plans

Afternoon Snack

Meals same as snack time with family style and blessing.

Outdoor Time

Dinner

Bedtime Blessing

In the evening, when the dishes have been cleaned up and the children are in their pajamas bring your family together for a bedtime story and blessing. This would be a great time to reread the story of the week so it remains fresh in your child's mind. Children thrive on repetition and routine and will truly appreciate hearing a story retold.

After your story:

Light candle with your children

Say the following blessing together or one of your own:

Bless my pillow
Bless my bed
Bless me too from toes to head
Bless the earth, sun and air
Bless the children everywhere

Caregiver's Meditation
included in weekly lesson plans

Remember to take care of yourself. Working with children is extremely rewarding but takes a lot of energy. Each day find time for quiet reflection and meditation. We have provided a weekly Caregiver's Meditation and Caregiver's Focus for you. Going outdoors alone for even a few minutes a day is also very healing.

Winter Festivals & Holidays

~December Festivals & Holidays~

Advent (begins fourth Sunday before Christmas)
Saint Nicholas Day – December 6th
Saint Lucia Day – December 13th
Chanukah – (varies per year)
Winter Solstice/Yule – December 21st or 22nd
Christmas Day – December 25th
Kwanza – December 26th - January 1st
New Year's Eve – December 31st

December's Full Moon: The Full Cold Moon

The Full Cold Moon comes at a time when the nights are long and dark. The Full Cold Moon or Moon Before Yule signifies a time to go within and shed the light of the season onto any dark and secret places of our soul.

December's Stones: Turquoise, Blue Zircon & Tanzanite

Prosperity is the customary promise made to those born in December by these three lustrous blue birthstone gems. They range in color from the bright sky blue of ancient turquoise, to the glittering icy blue hue of biblical zircon, to the deep rich purple-blue of tanzanite, a new birthstone only discovered in 1967.

First Grade Curriculum | WINTER | Little Acorn Learning

~January Festivals & Holidays~

New Year's Day – January 1st
Martin Luther King Jr. Day – (third Monday of January)
Twelfth Night – January 5th
Three Kings Day/The Epiphany – January 6th

January's Full Moon: The Full Wolf Moon

This moon arrives at time when the winter cold has taken its toll on many of life's creatures and hunger has set in. The January full moon was named after the hungry cries of wolves that Native Americans often heard around their tribe at this time of year.

January's Stone: Garnet

Garnet is traditionally regarded as the gem offering consistency, faith, and truth for those of January birth. Garnet comes in a wide variety of brilliant colors, every color but blue.

~February Festivals & Holidays~

Chinese New Year – (varies per year)
St. Brigid's Feast Day – February 1st
Candlemas – February 2nd
Groundhog Day – February 2nd
Imbolc – February 1st or 2nd (depending on custom)
Valentine's Day – February 14th
President's Day – (third Monday in February)
Leap Day – February 29th (every four years)

February's Full Moon: The Full Snow Moon

The Full Snow Moon was called such by native tribes because of the heavy snows that would often fall during the month of February. This moon opens the passageway for renewal, soul searching, change and hope.

February's Stone: Amethyst

Amethyst can range from pale lilac to deep purple. It is the stone of transformation, healing and sobriety. It holds great energy and power in the protection of self and guards against unhealthy behaviors. This stone is a perfect companion for you this month as you work toward cleansing and self-reflection in your life and work.

Week Thirteen, Autumn
First Grade

Theme: Trinkets, Treasures & Coins, Hope

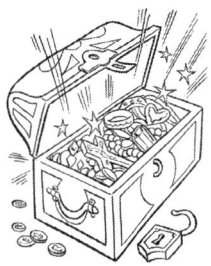

This Week's Lessons:

Language Arts:
Little Piccola Story
Letter M

Mathematics:
Number 13
Counting from 30 - 40
Learning About Money
Division, Budgeting and Math Facts

Social Studies, Geography, Weather, Time:
Learning About Currency: Bartering and Trading, Money and Banks
Appreciating Diversity in Holiday Traditions

Science, Nature Study, Earth Discovery:
Winter Scavenger (Treasure) Hunt

Teacher's Classroom Work:
Create a Special Hope Chest

For the Caregiver:
Caregiver Meditation: Hope
Caregiver Focus: Give an Anonymous Gift

Domestic Arts/Practical Life Skills:
Winter (or Advent) Spiral Bread
Caring for Houseplants
Lighting the Living Wreath or Advent Wreath

Music:
Trinkets, Treasures, Coins & Hope - Fingerplays & Songs
Beginning Recorder or Flute

Art/Handwork:
Handwork: Sewing, Simple Mitten Pattern
Beginner Knitting: Continue Practicing
Art: Coin Rubbings
Embroidery Letter M
Alphabet Card Letter M

Form Drawing:
Mountain and Hill Forms & Lines

Movement, Body Awareness & Health:
Making and Moving Mountains

Supplies Needed for Week Thirteen

Cooking List:

2 ½ Cups Unbleached Flour
1 Package Dry Yeast
1 ½ Cups Milk
½ Cup Water
3 Tbsp. Margarine or Butter
3 Tbsp. Brown Sugar
1 ½ Tsp. Salt
2 ½ Cups Whole Wheat Flour

Homeschooling List:

Felted or Toy Bird in Shoe
Blackboard
Chalk
Lesson Book
Stockmar Stick Crayons
Stockmar Block Crayons
Colored Pencils
Stockmar Beeswax Modeling Material
Knitting Needles
Super Bulky Single Ply 100% Wool Yarn
Embroidery Needle
Embroidery Floss
White Scrap Fabric
Embroidery Hoop (optional)
Scissors
Fabric or Felt
Thread
Needle
Pins
Penny
Nickel
Dime
Quarter
Heavy White Cardstock

First Grade Curriculum | WINTER | Little Acorn Learning

Week Thirteen Book Recommendations

Visit your local library the weekend before to check out books based on your theme for the week. Older children can help you look up the books by author and title. When setting up your play space for the week ahead, mindfully display these books in baskets for the children to enjoy.

Shelly's Stocking Goes Missing ~ Anitha Rathod
The Coin Counting Book ~ Rozanne Lanczak Williams
My Rows and Piles of Coins ~ Tololwa M. Mollel
Saint Nicholas and the Nine Gold Coins ~ Jim Forest
The Financial Fairy Tales: The Last Gold Coin ~ Mr. Daniel Britton
Lion, King, and Coin ~ Jeong-hee Nam
The Three Silver Coins: A Story from Tibet ~ Veronica Leo
The Penny Pot ~ Stuart J. Murphy
The Mystery of the Ancient Coins ~ Eleanor Florence Rosellini
The Baker's Dozen: A Saint Nicholas Tale ~ Aaron Shepard
A St. Nicholas Story: The Fiercest Little Animal In The Forest ~ Terri Reinhart
Nicholas St. North and the Battle of the Nightmare King ~ William Joyce
Christmas in the Big Woods ~ Laura Ingalls Wilder
Sleep Tight Farm: A Farm Prepares for Winter ~ Eugenie Doyle
Animals in Winter ~ Henrietta Bancroft
Walking in a Winter Wonderland ~ Richard B. Smith
Winter Is Coming ~ Tony Johnston
Winter's Gift ~ Jane Monroe Donovan
Hope: A Pig's Tale ~ Randy Houk
Mia's Story: A Sketchbook of Hopes & Dreams ~ Michael Foreman
Small Beauties: The Journey of Darcy Heart O'Hara ~ Elvira Woodruff
The Mitten ~ Jan Brett
The Treasure Tree: Helping Kids Understand Their Personality ~ John Trent
Pete the Cat and the Treasure Map ~ James Dean
Smells Like Treasure ~ Suzanne Selfors
All My Treasures: A Book of Joy ~ Jo Witek
Finding Treasure: A Collection of Collections ~ Michelle Schaub
Pattern-Tastic Treasure Hunt ~ Hvass & Hannibal
The Sea Glass Treasure ~ Shelly Peters
Those Shoes ~ Maribeeth Boelts
A Dollar for Penny ~ Julie Glass
The Happy Hollisters and the Secret of the Lucky Coins ~ Jerry West

First Grade Curriculum | WINTER | Little Acorn Learning

Week Thirteen Circle, Songs & Movement

The following songs and verses should be shared during circle time each day this week after you open your circle.

December Finger Play
(use fingers on your hands for each "bunny")

One, two little bunnies
Sitting on the ground.

Three, four little bunnies
Looking all around.

Five, six little bunnies
Standing in a row.

Seven, eight little bunnies
Waiting for the snow.

Nine, ten little bunnies
All ready to go.

Warm Mittens
(wiggle each as appropriate)

I wiggle my left hand,
I wiggle my right,

inside of my mittens,
so warm and so tight.

I wiggle my pinkie.
I wiggle my thumb,
so when I make snowballs,
my hands don't get numb.

Five Pirates on a Treasure Chest
(can be used as a fingerplay or puppet show)

Five pirates on a treasure chest,
One jumped off and four are left.

Four pirates on a treasure chest,
One slid off and three are left.

Three pirates on a treasure chest,
One fell down and two are left.

Two pirates on a treasure chest,
One was pushed off and one is left.

One pirate on the treasure chest,
He climbed down and none are left.

Ten little pirates stood in a row
(hold up all ten fingers)

They bowed to their captain so
(lower and raise fingers)

They marched to the left
(move hands to left)

They marched to the right
(move hands to right)

They shouted "Yo-Ho!"
(cup hands over mouth)

And gave their captain a fright
(act afraid, hands over mouth)

Coin Combinations

5 pennies make a nickel
2 nickels make a dime
2 dimes and a nickel
Make a quarter every time.

4 quarters make a dollar
and that is quite a lot.
And a dollar in my pocket
is exactly what I've got.

Three little nickels in a pocketbook new,
(hold up three fingers)

One bought a peppermint, and then there were two,
(bend down one finger)

Two little nickels before the day was done,
(two fingers up)

One bought an ice cream cone, and then there was one
(bend down another finger)

One little nickel I heard it plainly say,
(one finger up)

"I'm going into the piggy bank for a rainy day!"

A Little Candle
(sing to the tune of "I'm a Little Teapot")

Here's a little candle dressed in white,
Wearing a hat of yellow light.
When the night is dark, then you will see
Just how bright this light can be.

Here's a little candle straight and tall,
Shining it's light upon us all.
When the night is dark, then you will see
Just how bright this light can be.

Here's a little candle burning bright.
Keeping us safe all through the night.
When the night is dark, then you will see
Just how bright this light can be!

Kind old man Saint Nicholas, dear,
Come into our house this year.

Here's some straw and here's some hay
For your little donkey gray.

Pray put something into my shoe;
I've been good the whole year through.

Kind old man Saint Nicholas dear,
Come into our house this year.

The first light of Advent,
It is the light of Stones,
Stones that live in crystals,
Seashells and our bones.

Week Thirteen Blackboard Drawing

Drawing Ideas for This Week: Capital letter M as shown in the mountains the little swallow from our story went to live in the summer, the letter M in the stitches of the stockings Little Piccola knits, thirteen coins, a pair of warm mittens, Roman numeral XIII, THIRTEEN, 13, stockings on fireplace mantle, little shoe with bird inside, mountains with the sparrow nearby

Week Thirteen Teacher's Classroom Work

1. Create a Special Hope Chest

Traditionally, hope chests were created to store items for a young girl to have when she got married. These chests were often built by hand and filled with items the girl would be able to use upon marriage. This tradition goes way back to when marriages were often arranged, and the bride's family would collect material things as a dowry for their daughter's hand in marriage. They even were sometimes called a Dowry Chest!

Thankfully, we now live in a society where this is no longer a needed custom. However, the idea of collecting items in a special chest filled with family heirlooms, handmade items, and special memories is a beautiful way to inspire hope for the future. Both boys and girls alike can enjoy this special new tradition of putting loved items away for the future.

Ideas for your Hope Chest:

Create a Graduation Hope Chest

This special box can contain special milestone memories, items you work on together for your graduation ceremony, things needed after your child graduates, photos, scrapbooks, letters, poems, and books for inspiration.

Create a Craft Hope Chest

Little by little collect special art supplies, books, crafts, things you've made together and more. Keep them together in a special hope box and choose a milestone or celebration to open up your chest and use the supplies.

Create a Hope Chest of Your Own

The future is never promised to us but as adults we also have so much to look forward to. You may decide to make your very own hope chest. If you have items you made your child when they were small that you'd like to pass down to future generations, you can collect them in a special hope box for grandchildren or your own children to have one day. You may write letters to the future, include photos and scrapbooks, your wedding gown, jewelry, and other special items that you want to pass down and keep in your family.

Week Thirteen Caregiver Meditation

This Week's Reflection: <u>Hope</u>

"The very least you can do in your life is to figure out what you hope for. And the most you can do is live inside that hope. Not admire it from a distance but live right in it, under its roof." ~ Barbara Kingsolver

The funny thing about hope is that we often search for it at our very worst moments. When things are going well, we may not even know it is there. But it is.

The will and the hope to survive, to be happy and to live a good life is inside each and every living thing on this planet.

When you look to your future, what wishes do you have for yourself and your life? While many of these hopes and dreams likely include your children, what hopes and dreams do you have that are just for you?

To shift the focus from what you hope to obtain to who you hope to continue to become is the key to success and happiness. Who are you? What do you love to do? How can you make a difference? What parts of yourself do you hope to grow and nurture?

Think back to when you were young and free to explore, learn and just be. What activities did you gravitate toward? Did you love books, drawing, the outdoors, singing or dancing? How many of those things do you still enjoy? Can you make a promise to yourself to bring some of those passions back into your life?

Remember the young child within you, think about how much you have grown since then and all you have learned and experienced. So much of who we are and what we have today is what we could only have hoped for yesterday and we still have an entire lifetime ahead of us.

Week Thirteen Story

Little Piccola was able to find goodness and beauty in all that was around her even when she had so little. The story speaks to us of hope and faith in the goodness of the world around us. Little Piccola continued to believe that St. Nicholas would leave her a gift and she was so grateful for the little bird that found its way into her shoe.

The story reminds us that when we change our perspective, we can change our reality. Keep a small felted or stuffed bird tucked inside a shoe nearby and share it with your children when Piccola wakes up to find her gift in the story. If you celebrate St. Nicholas Day, you could even leave a little toy bird for your child in their shoe to be found on December 6th morning.

The Story of Little Piccola

In the sunny land of France there lived many years ago a sweet little maid named Piccola. Her father had died when she was a baby, and her mother was very poor and had to work hard all day in the fields for a small wage.

Little Piccola had no dolls and toys, and she was often hungry and cold, but she was never sad or lonely. She did not care that there were no children for her to play with. And, she did not worry if she did not have fine clothes and beautiful toys.

She was happy because in summer there were always the birds in the forest, and the flowers in the fields, mountains, and meadows. The birds sang so sweetly, and the flowers were so bright and pretty! She also enjoyed the winter when the ground was covered with snow. That is when she would help her mother and knit long stockings of blue wool. And, of course, the snowbirds had to be fed with crumbs if she could find any. But best of all was Christmas Day. So much to be joyous about!

But one year her mother was ill and could not earn any money. Piccola worked hard all the day long, and sold the stockings which she knit, even when her own little bare feet were blue with the cold.

As Christmas Day drew near, she said to her mother, "I wonder what the good Saint Nicholas will bring me this year. I cannot hang my stocking in the fireplace, but I shall put my wooden shoe on the hearth for him. He will not forget me, I am sure." "Do not think of it this year, my dear child," replied her mother. "We must be glad if we have bread enough to eat."

But Piccola could not believe that the good saint would forget her. On Christmas Eve she put her little wooden shoe on the hearth before the fire and went to sleep to dream of Saint Nicholas. As the poor mother looked at the little shoe, she thought how unhappy her dear child would be to find it empty in the morning, and wished that she had something, even if it were only a tiny cake, for a Christmas gift. There was nothing in the house but a few coins, and these must be saved to buy bread.

When the morning dawned Piccola awoke and ran to her shoe. Saint Nicholas had come in the night. He had not forgotten the little child who had thought of him with such faith.

Do you know what the good Saint Nicholas brought her? Within the wooden shoe lay a sweet little swallow looking up at her with its two bright eyes, chirping contentedly as she stroked its soft feathers. The little bird had flown into the chimney and down to the room and had crept into the shoe to get out of the cold.

Piccola danced for joy and clasped the shivering swallow to her breast. She ran to her mother's bedside. "Look, look!" she cried. "A Christmas gift, a gift from the good Saint Nicholas!" And she danced again in her little bare feet.

Then she fed and warmed the bird and cared for it tenderly all winter long; teaching it to take crumbs from her hand and her lips, and to sit on her shoulder while she was working.

In the spring she opened the window for it to fly away, but it lived in the beautiful mountains near by all summer and came often in the early morning to sing its sweetest songs at her door.

Monday Student Lessons – Week Thirteen

(Baking/Cooking – Purple Day)

As many of you may be using this Winter Semester curriculum during holiday times, we have worked hard to incorporate as many as we can. We believe it is extremely important to teach children tolerance, acceptance, and respect for all belief systems. You may like to spend a little extra time this month exploring the various holidays and festivals that are celebrated this time of year. Be sure to tailor your homeschool according to your own beliefs while teaching love and understanding for all. Some questions you can ask your child to inspire free discussion:

- Some people celebrate Christmas this time of year while others celebrate different holidays and festivals. What do we celebrate in our family?

- Can you think of some ways other families celebrate differently than us? Do you know any of those holidays? (Yule, Hanukah, Kwanza, etc.)

- How are some ways that we celebrate our holidays? (lighting candles, decorating a tree, shoes out on St. Nicholas Eve, etc.)

Language Arts

1. Begin your lesson time by reading (or telling) *Little Piccola* to your child. Let the children look at the sentences as you read as this visual will aid with their knowledge of letters, words, and sentences. If possible, use simple props to accompany the story as we have suggested.

2. When your story is finished, unveil your blackboard drawing that you have prepared ahead of time as suggested at the beginning of this week's curriculum. If your child has his or her own small blackboard and chalk, have them take a few moments to create their own drawing.

3. Review what your child worked on last week in their lesson book. Have them practice writing the capital letter L a few times on their blackboard or an extra piece of paper. Be sure they have a good grasp of this letter before moving onto the next.

4. In your child's lesson book, have them create a similar image of the mountains or the stockings from our story (or whatever depiction you used) with the letter M revealed inside. On the righthand side, have your child practice writing the capital letter M. Share this poem as you work to form the letter:

Make a line from the top and down,
Then connect a V without a sound.

Another line down and soon you'll see,
The letter M is two mountains majesty.

Mathematics

1. In addition to the Roman numeral XIII, write down the number 13 and word THIRTEEN in all capital letters for your child to see. Say each letter as you write: T, H, I, R, T, E, E, N, and the word out loud:

<pre>
T
H
I
R
T
E
E
N
</pre>

THIRTEEN

Tucked in the shoe, the swallow was unseen,

<pre>
T
H
I
R
T
E
E
N
</pre>

THIRTEEN

When the little girl woke, she thought it was a dream!

2. Have the child draw images of the number THIRTEEN. They may copy some of the items you made in your blackboard drawing for this week. Your child should then practice writing the number 13, Roman numeral XIII, and the word THIRTEEN in all capital letters on the opposite page of their book. If you feel they need extra time with writing, let them continue to practice as needed. Here is a verse to share when forming the number 13:

> *Thirteen is easy as can be,*
> *First write one and then a three!*

3. Now that your child is well versed in numbers 20-30, you can trust that they are able to move more quickly and practice their counting from 30-40. Count everything you can! If your child seems ready, you can expand your four processes math skills to include larger numbers up to 40 as well. Remember to go at your child's pace and pay close attention to how your child learns most effectively.

Domestic Arts/Practical Life Skills

Winter (or Advent) Spiral Bread

If you celebrate Advent, this is a lovely way to bring this spiritual time into your home learning. This bread can also represent the beginning of winter and be created in a spiral with candles to celebrate. Remember to always weave your own creativity, traditions, and beliefs into your homeschool program.

As always, use baking and cooking as ways to practice mathematics skills with your child.

Supplies Needed:
2 ½ Cups Unbleached Flour
1 Package Dry Yeast
1 ½ Cups Milk
½ Cup Water
3 Tbsp. Margarine or Butter

3 Tbsp. Brown Sugar
1 ½ Tsp. Salt
2 ½ Cups Whole Wheat Flour

In a large bowl, mix flour and yeast. Heat milk, water, margarine, brown sugar, and salt on low. Add to flour mixture. Stir several minutes (remember to let children help during this entire process…have them take turns and be patient. The goal is not to have bread, it is to enjoy the process of making the bread) Add whole wheat flour until dough forms. Knead on floured table until smooth and elastic (children love this part!). Place in greased bowl. Cover and let rise until it doubles in bulk.

After the dough has risen, you will need to punch down the dough. The best way to do this is to let children pound the dough with their fists. After you have done this, shape your dough into a spiral. If there seems to be too much, make more than one spiral!

If you have star shaped cookie cutters, have the children cut stars out of excess dough and decorate their spiral with it.

Cover and let rise to double.

Place the bread into the oven in a pan and set at 400°F for 30 minutes.

The smell of bread baking in the oven is a very soothing way for children to fall asleep, work on their afternoon lessons or do a quiet activity.

You can add candles to your Winter or Advent Spiral bread and light before saying your mealtime verse today.

Outdoor Time/Nature Walk

Take your children outside each day regardless of the weather. Invest in good rain gear, snow gear and wool undergarments if your location requires it. Do your lessons outdoors whenever possible.

Caregiver Focus

Anonymous Gifting

Give a gift to someone anonymously this week. You may do this by leaving a box of cookies at a neighbor's door, paying for the car behind you in a drive-thru or donating something to someone in need.

If you are working on this lesson in the beginning of December, this would be a nice way to acknowledge Saint Nicholas Day on December 6th (if your beliefs allow). Regardless of when this lesson falls in your homeschool year, it is ALWAYS the right time to give to others and practice being humble.

Afternoon Lessons

Handwork: Sewing, Simple Mitten Pattern

Supplies Needed:
Fabric or Felt
Thread
Needle
Scissors
Pins

Here is a very simple pattern that your child can work on to create a cute set of decorative mittens to hang during the winter months.

Pin template to fabric and cut out four mittens. A simple way to do this is by doubling fabric and cutting two sets.

You can also cut out four cuff patterns of different fabric or felt and sew them on the four separate mitten cut outs BEFORE sewing it all together (otherwise your opening won't be open!).

Match mitten cut outs together right sides facing.

Depending on your child's ability, you may choose to punch holes where they should sew and use yarn to lace or let your child practice their regular hand sewing skills with a needle and thread. Make sure you leave the top of the mitten open.

You can add a simple loop of fabric or yarn to hang your project.

Turn the item inside out and your stitches will be hidden inside. Experiment with different sizes and patterns. If your child wants to practice their embroidery before sewing together, they can add simple snowflakes, names, or other things. These would make lovely holiday presents, or you can make your own Advent/holiday count down with them and leave little trinkets or coins inside.

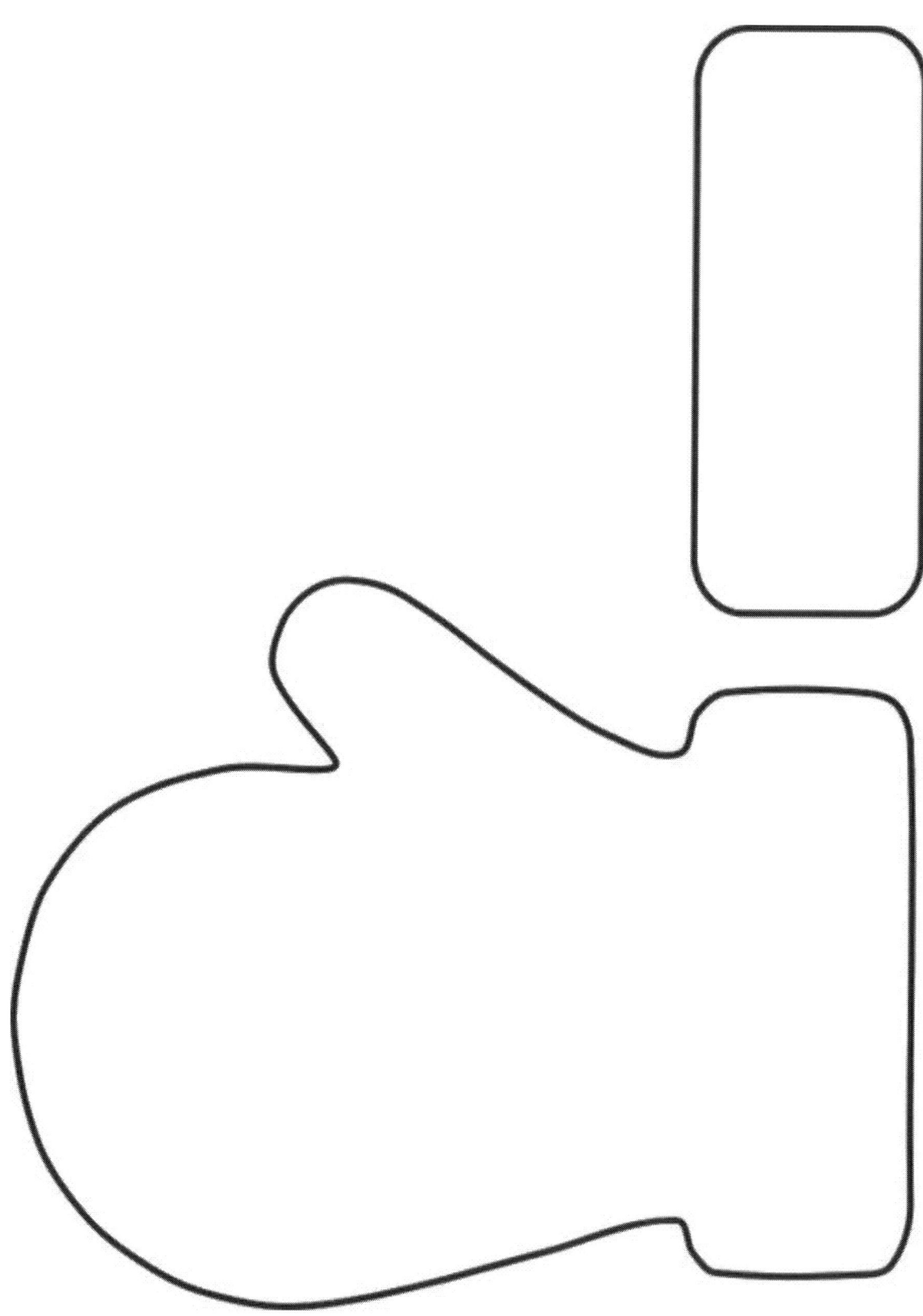

Tuesday Student Lessons – Week Thirteen
(Painting – Red Day)

Language Arts

1. Like yesterday, begin your lesson time by continuing to read (or tell) *Little Piccola*. Provide your child with a piece of beeswax modeling material as you read. Let them hold this piece of beeswax as they listen, warming it with their hands so it softens.

2. Have your child form the softened beeswax material into the letter M. Roll it into a long snake, form it just so and then put it back together again. Next, have them form it into the number 13.

3. Open your lesson book and review the work you did yesterday. Have your child trace the letter M number 13 and word THIRTEEN with their fingers.

4. Practice saying the sounds of the letter M. Notice how our mouth forms to make the sound. Bringing awareness to the way our body forms sounds and words is very important. This process helps us to notice the use of air and our body muscles as we communicate.

5. Today we will work on a tongue twister to practice and memorize with your child to help learn the letter M and its sound. Tongue twisters and rhymes are fun ways to learn and help with finding rhythm.

    To begin, say the following tongue twister to your child slowly and clap your hands and stomp your feet to the syllables the way we have listed below to create a pattern for memory:

    A man *(clap two hands over head)*
    with a nick-el *(stomp right foot, stomp left foot)*

    A sword *(clap two hands stretched out in front of you)*
    and a sick-le *(stomp right foot, stomp left foot)*

    A pipe *(clap regular)*
    and a pap-er *(stomp right foot, stomp left foot)*
    of pins *(clap regular)*

First Grade Curriculum | WINTER | Little Acorn Learning

Mathematics

Skip Counting by Tens

After your child has learned to count by fives in a confident way, it is time to introduce skip counting by tens.

1. Make an even number pile of coins no more than 40. Using your hands, group them into tens. Begin counting by tens placing one hand over each pile until you get to the final number. Let your child watch. Then, count the items regularly to show that the final number is the same. Repeat this and challenge your child to do it with you.

2. Skip Counting Coin Jump

   Make a very long row of coins in equal numbers of 10. Have your child skip count by ten and pull out every tenth coin. Use your coins to continue learning about skip counting.

3. Reinforce counting skills and count groups of 40 with various coins, also practice each coin's name and value. If possible, practice counting dollars up to 40 as well.

Outdoor Time/Nature Walk

Take your children outside each day regardless of the weather. Invest in good rain gear, snow gear and wool undergarments if your location requires it. Do your lessons outdoors whenever possible.

Social Studies, Geography, Weather, Time/Mathematics

Learning About Currency: Bartering and Trading

Your child likely has a good understanding of what trading is. When is the last time they traded a stick of gum for something else, swapped sporting cards with a friend or agreed to trade different color lollipops or toys with a sibling?

1. Ask your child if they can imagine a world without money. How would they be able to get things they needed? If they went into a store and the owner had beautiful books and your child wanted one, how would they be able to get the owner to agree to give it to them without money?

   They would have to ask the owner of the store if there is anything that they need or want in return for the book. The owner may need a warm sweater for her child, or she may need help stacking all the books. Before money was created, people would trade and barter for things in this way. It is a wonderful way to work together but it can become challenging when you do not have things the other person needs or wants. Because of this, eventually people created coins and paper money to use instead of always trading.

2. Play Store: Bartering

   Have your child set up a special store. They can fill their store with anything they want from the home: toys, books, pretend food, crafts, etc. Then have your child invite a sibling, friend or yourself to come "shop" at their store. When you find something that you want, work together to come up with a good trade. It is fine if this proves difficult in some situations as it will display how money has made things easier for our society.

3. Organize a book exchange with your child and other children. They can be siblings, cousins, homeschool co-op students or friends. Have each child pick a book they would like to trade and host a day and time to meet. Wrap your book and place in a pile. Each child then goes and picks a book they did not bring and has a lovely gift to take back home.

Afternoon Lessons

1. Music: Continue Practicing Flute or Recorder

2. Handwork: Beginner Knitting

   Continue working on your knitting and perfecting your craft. Explore various stitches and patterns.

Wednesday Student Lessons – Week Thirteen
(Coloring – Yellow Day)

Language Arts

1. Practice our Letter M tongue twister again. Keep working on this until you have it memorized together. Use the following verse and movement pattern:

    A man *(clap two hands over head)*
    with a nick-el *(stomp right foot, stomp left foot)*

    A sword *(clap two hands stretched out in front of you)*
    and a sick-le *(stomp right foot, stomp left foot)*

    A pipe *(clap regular)*
    and a pap-er *(stomp right foot, stomp left foot)*
    of pins *(clap regular)*

2. In your child's lesson book, have your child draw a picture of Little Piccola and her swallow. Let them express their creativity and illustrate the scene they imagine when they hear this story being told. On the other side, practice letters and words that pertain to the story depending on your child's ability. Some ideas:

    Bird
    Stocking
    Shoe
    Mountain
    Saint Nicholas

3. Tonight, at bedtime continue to tell your child the story of *Little Piccola*

4. When out and about, ask your child to find things that begin with the letter M. This can be done while shopping or when driving in the car. Throughout the week, ask your child to think of all the words they can that begin with the letter M. How many can they come up with? Make a list.

Mathematics

Value of Coins and Money

1. Show your child an example of a penny, nickel, dime, and quarter.

   Using your blackboard or a blank piece of paper, draw each coin and what value it equals.

   Penny ● = 1 cent

   Nickel ○ = 5 cents or 5 pennies

   Dime ○ = 10 cents - 10 pennies, or two nickels (5+5)

   Quarter ○ = 25 cents - 25 pennies, 2 dimes and one nickel (10+10+5) or 5 nickels (5 + 5 + 5 + 5)

2. Use these coins to practice your math facts. Experiment with repetitive addition, addition, subtraction, and multiplication. Have your child enter these equations and answers in their lesson book.

Outdoor Time/Nature Walk

Take your children outside each day regardless of the weather. Invest in good rain gear, snow gear and wool undergarments if your location requires it. Do your lessons outdoors whenever possible.

Social Studies, Geography, Weather, Time

Play Store: Shopping and Budgeting with Money

Have your child set up a special store. They can fill their store with anything they want from the home: toys, books, pretend food, crafts, etc. Then have your child invite a sibling, friend or yourself to come "shop" at their store. Give this customer a budget of only a certain amount of money. How will they spend their money wisely? Switch roles and let your child now be the customer. Make a list of more important things they must pay for first out of their budget and see what is left over for fun items.

Afternoon Lessons

Art: Coin Rubbings

Supplies Needed:
Penny
Nickel
Dime
Quarter
Paper
Beeswax Block Crayons

Using Beeswax Block Crayons, rub coins to see the image of each coin both front and back. Talk about the value of each coin. You can even talk about the Presidents on each coin.

This is a fun way to introduce young children to the basic concept of money. You can use these rubbings in mathematics lessons by dictating addition or subtraction facts and having them answer with the correct coin rubbings.

Thursday Student Lessons – Week Thirteen
(Crafting/Games – Orange Day)

Language Arts

1. Continue to tell your child the story of *Little Piccola*.

2. Alphabet Cards

   Supplies Needed:
   Heavy White Cardstock
   Beeswax Stick Crayons
   Scissors

   Spend time cutting cards out of cardstock with your child. Using beeswax crayons, continue to finish drawing each letter we have learned so far and include the letter M. Next to the letter, have your child draw an image that begins with it. Use scissors to round the corners of these cards and keep working on them throughout the year. You can use them in your lessons and for an upper case and lowercase match game later in the curriculum when we learn those as well.

3. Continue reading simple reader books together.

4. Print out or share the following photos and practice saying them together with your child. Your child may be ready to copy these words into their lesson book.

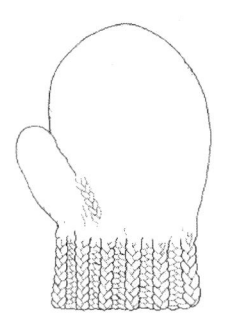

MITTEN

MOUNTAIN

MOUSE

MONEY

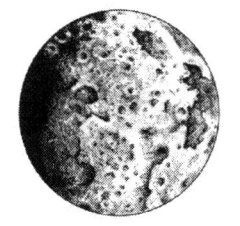

MOON

Mathematics

Learning About Money: Value of Coins and Money

1. Show your child an example of a one dollar bill, a five dollar bill, a ten dollar bill and a twenty dollar bill. (It is fine to create pretend bills out of paper for this lesson.)

   Using your blackboard or a blank piece of paper, draw each bill and what value it equals.

   One Dollar Bill ▭ = 1 dollar (four quarters, ten dimes, twenty nickels, one hundred pennies)

   Five Dollar Bill ▭ = 5 dollars (or 5 one dollar bills)

   Ten Dollar Bill ▭ = 10 dollars (or 2 five dollar bills, or 10 one dollar bills)

   Five Dollar Bill ▭ = 5 dollars (or 5 one dollar bills)

2. Use these dollars to practice your math facts. Experiment with repetitive addition, subtraction, and multiplication. Have your child enter these equations and answers in their lesson book.

Outdoor Time/Nature Walk

Take your children outside each day regardless of the weather. Invest in good rain gear, snow gear and wool undergarments if your location requires it. Do your lessons outdoors whenever possible.

Science, Nature Study, Earth Discovery

Winter Scavenger (Treasure) Hunt

Take your child out on a nature walk and talk about the season of winter. Here is a fun Winter Scavenger Hunt to bring along and check off as you and your child find each item (this is included in our First Grade Winter Semester).

Please note, this hunt has been created with very traditional winter items and weather. If you live in an environment that this would not pertain to, we hope you use it as inspiration to create your own.

Winter Scavenger Hunt

○ **FROZEN FLOWER**	○ **EVERGREEN NEEDLES**	○ **NUTS**	○ **WINTER BERRIES**
○ **ANIMAL TRACKS**	○ **BIRD IN WINTER**	○ **ROOTS**	○ **NEST**
○ **SPIDER WEB**	○ **MOSS**	○ **SQUIRREL IN WINTER**	○ **WINTER LEAF**
○ **HOLIDAY LIGHTS**	○ **FROZEN OR COLD FUNGI**	○ **ICICLE**	○ **SNOWFLAKE**

www.littleacornlearning.com

First Grade Curriculum

Movement & Body Awareness

Moving and Making Mountains

Have your child make big mountains out of various items inside and outside your home. They may use pillows, stuffed animals, blankets, bails of hay, snow, dirt, and many other things. Let them climb these mountains and move them from one place to another.

Go on a more difficult walk or hike with your child that requires managing some steep hills and inclines. Sing songs together. Here is a fun one that you may know from your own childhood:

The Bear Went Over the Mountain

The bear went over the mountain
The bear went over the mountain
The bear went over the mountain
To see what he could see

To see what he could see
To see what he could see
The bear went over the mountain
The bear went over the mountain
The bear went over the mountain
To see what he could see

The other side of the mountain
The other side of the mountain
The other side of the mountain
Was all that he could see

Was all that he could see
Was all that he could see
The other side of the mountain
The other side of the mountain
The other side of the mountain
Was all that he could see

Afternoon Lessons

1. Form Drawing/Art – Running Mountain Lines

   In our story of *Little Piccola*, she lived near beautiful mountains that the little swallow enjoyed so much. Today in your lesson book, have your child work to create running mountain lines. When doing this, talk about how the word mountain begins with the letter M and try to make the mountains with this in mind.

   Practicing these running lines and forms is wonderful for your child's fine motor skills and if you bring our story of the week into the lesson it takes on a beautiful life of its own. These "mountains" can later be enhanced and colored to create a colorful illustration.

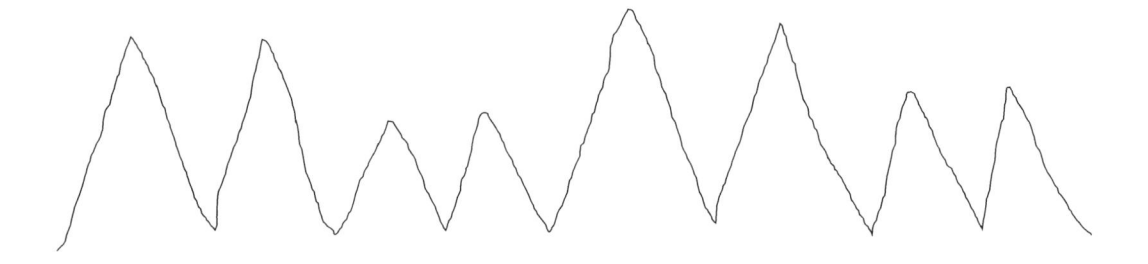

2. Handwork: Hand Stitching/Embroidery

   Supplies Needed:
   Embroidery Needle
   Embroidery Floss
   White Scrap Fabric
   Embroidery Hoop (optional)
   Scissors

   Using our embroidery instructions, work with your child to make a letter M embroidery piece. You can do this with a simple running stitch, or you may choose to learn more complicated stitches together.

Friday Student Lessons – Week Thirteen

(Modeling/Housework – Green Day)

Language Arts

1. Today have your child continue to practice writing the letter M in their lesson book on unlined paper.

2. In your child's lesson book, have them practice writing the alphabet from A-M copying each letter a few times on each line.

3. Have your child practice writing some of the following words in capital letters in their lesson book:

   MAN
   MINT
   MOW
   MULE
   MOON

4. Ask your child to tell YOU the story of *Little Piccola*.

Mathematics

Learning About Currency: Money and Banks

1. Your child likely has a good understanding of what money is and after this week of lessons, they are starting to understand the value of coins and bills. Be sure to include your child whenever you use money at stores, while using vending machines, etc.

   Show them how the cash register is used and pay attention to when you get change back from a purchase. Ask your child to count the change and make sure it is correct. If your child seems ready, you can briefly explain how cards can be used to use the money you hold in your bank accounts. This does not need to be a heavy lesson at this young age. Just a basic understanding. Take a trip to your bank and show your child how you deposit and withdraw your money and use the bank to keep it safe.

2. Ask your child to go back to our lesson earlier in the week when they imagined a world without money. Visualize the store again with beautiful books. Instead of working to come up with a trade with the owner, now have them imagine paying for the book with their own money.

Talk to your child about how money is obtained. People must work hard to make money by doing a job. Discuss your job or the jobs of other members of your family and they get paid sometimes by the hour, week, or specific project they work on. They must then budget their money carefully and make sure they have enough to buy certain things. A book may be something special to buy but other things must come first like paying for shelter, food, education, gas and more.

Outdoor Time/Nature Walk

Take your children outside each day regardless of the weather. Invest in good rain gear, snow gear and wool undergarments if your location requires it. Do your lessons outdoors whenever possible.

Domestic Arts/Practical Life Skills

1. Caring for Houseplants

   Buy a new plant this week and have your child help care for it. Teach your child how to make sure it has enough light, water, good soil, and proper care. If you have other plants in your home, watering the plants is simple job that children of this age can do each week.

2. Light a Candle on Your Living Wreath

   If your family celebrates Advent and you are doing this lesson during that time of year, you can light the candle on your living wreath as your first Advent candle. If you do not celebrate Advent, lighting a candle on your Living Wreath is still a beautiful way to welcome winter. Here is a simple verse to share when doing so:

   Color – Purple
   Theme – Hope

The hope inside my soul so deep,
Ignites the fire my spirit keeps,
Awake at night,
Alive all day,
Burns bright within to lead the way.

Allow the candle to burn as you enjoy your meal, and then snuff your candle out when you are done.

Afternoon Lessons

Use the afternoon hours today to review areas from this week's afternoon lessons that you feel may need a bit more attention. Bring these into your weekend as you find time.

Week Fourteen, Winter
First Grade

Theme: Winter Light, Helping Others

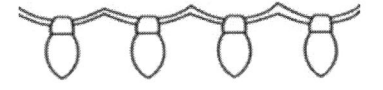

This Week's Lessons:

Language Arts:
The Elves and The Cobbler Story
Letter N
Learning About Syllables
Rhyming Words
Introducing Silent Letters

Mathematics:
Number 14
Counting from 40 - 50
Skip Counting Expanded
Explore Additional Three Dimensional Shapes
Measuring Length: Shortest, Longest & Distance
Ordinal Numbers

Social Studies, Geography, Weather, Time:
Weather Around the World: Hemispheres and Climate
Climate Charting

Science, Nature Study, Earth Discovery:
Ice Lanterns

Teacher's Classroom Work:
Helping & Kindness Tracker

For the Caregiver:
Caregiver Meditation: Helping Others
Caregiver Focus: Extending a Hand to Others in Need

Domestic Arts/Practical Life Skills:
Bake Lussekatter (St. Lucy Buns)
Grow Christmas Wheat
Living Wreath, Light a Candle

Music:
St. Lucia, Light and Winter Fingerplays & Songs
Beginning Recorder or Flute

Art/Handwork:
Beginner Knitting: Fingerless Gloves
Embroidery Letter N
Alphabet Card Letter N
Beeswax Modeling St. Lucia Figure
Masking Tape Letter N Painting

Form Drawing:
Form Drawing/Art – 'Spiral' Squares

Movement, Body Awareness & Health:
Game of Light
Number Movement Exercise

Supplies Needed for Week Fourteen

Cooking List:

For Lussekatter (St. Lucy Buns):
1 Cup Heavy Cream
1 Cup Scaled Milk
1/3 Cup Butter
2/3 Cup Sugar
6 Packages of Dry Active Yeast
Dash of Salt
2 Eggs, Beaten
6 - 8 Cups Sifted Flour
1/3 Cup Raisins

Homeschooling List:

Small Toy Shoe(s), Silk, Leather or Felt Cutouts, Small Figure for Elf with Silk or Handkerchief for Clothing
Blackboard
Chalk
Lesson Book
Stockmar Stick Crayons
Stockmar Block Crayons
Colored Pencils
Stockmar Beeswax Modeling Material
Knitting Needles
Super Bulky Single Ply 100% Wool Yarn
Yarn Needle
Embroidery Needle
Embroidery Floss
White Scrap Fabric
Embroidery Hoop (optional)
Heavy White Cardstock
Watercolor Paper
Masking Tape
Scissors
Watercolor Paints
Brush

Two Buckets or Tin Cans – One Smaller to Fit Inside Larger One
Duct Tape
Rocks
Greenery, Cranberries, Food Coloring, Glitter or Other Decorations
Electric Tea Lights
Flashlights
Small Flowerpot
Potting Soil
Grains of Wheat

Week Fourteen Book Recommendations

Visit your local library the weekend before to check out books based on your theme for the week. Older children can help you look up the books by author and title. When setting up your play space for the week ahead, mindfully display these books in baskets for the children to enjoy.

Lucia and the Light ~ Phyllis Root
The Light of Christmas ~ Richard Paul Evans
Celebrations Of Light: A Year of Holidays Around the World ~ by Nancy Luenn
OH, Yes You CAN!: A Book About Celebrating Our Differences By Helping Others ~ Tina McNeill
Arc of Light ~ Linda Jane Roberts
A Prairie Boy's Winter ~ William Kurelek
Dash's Week: A Dog's Tale About Kindness and Helping Others Hardcover ~ Nicole M. MacDonald
My Hands Were Made For Helping ~ Jacquelyn Stagg
How Can I Help?: A Book about Caring ~ Robin Nelson
Be Kind ~ Pat Zietlow Miller
Helping Daisy Grow ~ Layla Ford
Dandy the Lion: Helping Others ~ Kasey Shaver
Light The Lights! A Story About Celebrating Hanukkah And Christmas ~ Margaret Moorman
Winter Lights: A Season in Poems & Quilts ~ Anna Grossnickle Hines
Winter's Eve: Love and Lights ~ Lisa Sferlazza Johnson
Lights of Winter ~ Heather Conrad
Winter Is Coming ~ Tony Johnston
A Loud Winter's Nap ~ Katy Hudson
Share Some Kindness, Bring Some Light ~ Apryl Stott
Winter Dance ~ Marion Dane Bauer
SkySisters ~ Jan Bourdeau Waboose
Winter Candle ~ Jeron Ashford
Red and Lulu ~ Matt Tavares
Listening with My Heart ~ Gabi Garcia
Can a Cookie Change the Word? ~ Rhonda Bolling
Sophie and Little Start ~ Amber Hendricks
We'll Paint the Octopus Red ~ Stephanie Stuve-Bodeen
Ella's Night Lights ~ Lucy Fleming
Sprout Helps Out ~ Rosie Windstead

Week Fourteen Circle, Songs & Movement

The following songs and verses should be shared during circle time each day this week after you open your circle.

Awake, awake the sun shines bright.
Awake to greet the morning light.

The stars beyond the deep blue sky,
Now take their sleep for night is night.

Awake, dear light, in hands and feet!
Awake, dear light in every deed!

Awake in my own heart!

St. Lucia Verse

Night goes with silent steps
Round house and cottage
Over earth that sun forgot
Dark shadows linger
Then on our threshold stands
White clad, in candlelight
Santa Lucia, Santa Lucia

The light that shines away up high,
Likes to weave the colors bright;
A little of this light am I,
Like a candle in the night.

Santa Lucia

Santa Lucia, thy light is glowing
Through darkest winter night,
comfort bestowing.
Dreams float on dreams tonight,
Comes then the morning light,
Santa Lucia, Santa Lucia.

Pick Up Helping Song
(sing to Twinkle, Twinkle)

Pick up, pick up, pick up toys,
Every little girl and boy.
Look around and you will see,
All the things that shouldn't be.
Pick up, pick up, pick up toys,
Every little girl and boy.

Little Dwarves

Little dwarves so short and strong
Heavy footed march along
Every head is straight and proud
Every step is firm and loud

Pick and hammer each must hold
Deep in earth to mine the gold
Ready over each one's back
Hangs a little empty sack

When their hard day's work is done
Home again they march as one
Full sacks make a heavy load
As they tramp along the road

We are truthful and helpful
And loving in trust
For our heart's inner sun
Glows brightly in us

We will open our hearts
To the sunbeams so bright
And we'll fill all the world
With our heart's inner light

Here we are with joyful hearts
Working well and working hard
Helping gladly, quick and bold
Bringing joy to young and old

Week Fourteen Blackboard Drawing

Drawing Ideas for This Week: Capital letter N as shown in the stitching of the shoes or the little elves hats. Roman numeral XIV, FOURTEEN, 14, girl child with wreath with candles on head, Advent wreath with candles, Cobbler making shoes, starboy with cap and star

Week Fourteen Teacher's Classroom Work

1. Helping & Kindness Tracker

Cut out small hand shapes from construction paper. Each time someone in your home displays an act of kindness or helps others in some way, write down what they did and display it in your home.

2. Review any handwork before working on any projects with your child.

Week Fourteen Caregiver Meditation

This Week's Reflection: Helping Others

"I sought my soul, but my soul I could not see. I sought my God, but my God eluded me. I sought my brother and I found all three. ~ *Unknown*

We are all on a journey of self-discovery. Many of us have traveled long and difficult paths yet feel as if we are somehow still searching.

We work hard to dig deep within our souls, and we discover and grow so much by doing so. We may read self-help books, meditate, focus on healthy habits and learning more about ourselves. This can help us develop and become more conscious beings and is very important work.

Some of us also seek outside of our individuality through spiritual practice, religion, earth reverence and other ways of connecting to something greater than ourselves. Seeing ourselves as part of something bigger, whatever that may mean for you, is so very important as we develop and move toward higher consciousness together.

While we do this important work of seeking within ourselves and seeking outside of ourselves toward a higher power or purpose, we must not forget to seek out our brothers and sisters on this earth as well. If you have done the work and feel still that something is missing, it could very well be that you need to now put your energy into helping and giving to others to fulfill this void.

When we connect with other human beings with empathy, love, and kindness, we find ourselves in them. We realize that we are connected not only to ourselves and our universe but to one another. We are one. We belong to each other.

Spend time this week thinking of ways you can be of service and care to others who need you. You need not look too far out of your own homes or communities to do this. You can make the biggest impact right where you already are.

Week Fourteen Story

The Elves and The Cobbler is a very old tale of selflessness, helping others, and gratitude. How often do we do good deeds for the deed itself without want of recognition or praise? Do we stop to show our thanks to those who give to us selflessly? Before telling your story, set up a simple scene with small shoes hidden under a silk and leather or felt oval cut outs. As the cobbler leaves out his leather, do the same. As morning comes in your story, reveal the shoes under your silk. If you have a small figure to use as an elf, dress it at the end of your tale with doll clothing or a simple cape tied made of a silk or handkerchief.

The Elves and The Cobbler
A Grimm's Fairy Tale

Once upon a time there lived a cobbler. He was honest and hardworking, but he was very poor. Times were bad and he grew poorer and poorer. At last he only had enough leather to make one pair of shoes. This he cut out one night. "Now," he said, "I am all ready to begin work in the morning. I will get up early and make these shoes." Then he said his prayers and went to bed and slept in peace.

In the morning he got up early to begin his work. How surprised he was to find the shoes lying finished on the table! He looked carefully at them, but there was not a bad stitch in the work. Who had done it? He could not even guess. Soon a man came in to buy some shoes. The pair was so well made that he bought it for a good price. With this money the shoemaker got leather to make two pairs. That night he cut them out. But he did not have to make them next day. The work was done for him in the night. He sold these two pairs of shoes and bought leather for four pairs. These he cut out that night and found finished the next morning.

So, it went on. The work which he began one day, he found finished the next. He had only to buy leather and cut out shoes. One winter night the shoemaker cut out several pairs of shoes. Then, instead of going to bed, he said to his wife: "My dear, I should like to find out who helps us every night. Suppose we sit up and watch." His wife agreed. So, they left the candle burning. They hid themselves in a corner of the room. As the clock struck twelve here came into the room two little naked elves. They sat down on the shoemaker's table and began to work. They sewed so well and so fast that the shoes were soon finished. Then they skipped down and away they went.

The next morning the wife said: "Husband, these little men have helped us, and I should like to do something for them. Hear my plan! They must be cold, running about with not a rag upon their backs. I will make them some clothes and knit them some stockings. Do make a pair of shoes for each." "That I will and gladly, too," said her husband.

So, they set to work and made the clothes and shoes. That night they did not put any work on the table. Instead, they laid there the gifts. Then they hid to see what the little men would do. At midnight in they came. They jumped up on the table, expecting to find leather cut out for them to make into shoes. There was nothing but the beautiful little clothes. The elves looked at them in wonder. They felt the soft cloth and put their hands in the little pockets. At last they dressed themselves and jumped and danced for joy. Over stools and chairs they went, singing:

"Who will wonder at our glee?
Happy little men are we,
Well dressed now, as you may see."

At last they danced out of the room and they never came back anymore. But the shoemaker who had been kind to those who had helped him was never again in want. As long as he lived, he and his wife lacked nothing.

Monday Student Lessons – Week Fourteen

(Baking/Cooking – Purple Day)

Language Arts

1. Begin your lesson time by reading (or telling) *The Elves and The Cobbler* to your child. Let the children look at the sentences as you read as this visual will aid with their knowledge of letters, words, and sentences. If possible, use simple props to accompany the story as we have suggested.

2. When your story is finished, unveil your blackboard drawing that you have prepared ahead of time as suggested at the beginning of this week's curriculum. If your child has his or her own small blackboard and chalk, have them take a few moments to create their own drawing.

3. Review what your child worked on last week in their lesson book. Have them practice writing the capital letter M a few times on their blackboard or an extra piece of paper. Be sure they have a good grasp of this letter before moving onto the next.

4. In your child's lesson book, have them create a similar image of the elf's hat or the stitches in the shoe from our story (or whatever depiction you used) with the letter N revealed inside. On the righthand side, have your child practice writing the capital letter N. Share this poem as you work to form the letter:

    Go down and hit the ground
    and then be sure to stop
    Make a slanted line down from above
    and the last line up to the top

5. Without saying so, we have been practicing syllables all along. Talk about how words have a certain pattern of sound. These small groups of sound that make up a word we call syllables. To demonstrate this, have your child hold their hand under their chin, palm side down. Have them say a word slowly and count how many times their jaw pushes their hand down to count the syllables. Here are a few N words to experiment with:

- Neighbor
- Never
- Nine
- Nobody
- Number
- Nicholas
- Noodle
- Nightmare
- Napkin

Try this with many different words beginning with all letters. Next, do this same activity by clapping the syllables. Keep this practice going for the next week or two until your child feels confident in recognizing the amount of syllables in each word.

Mathematics

1. In addition to the Roman numeral XIV, write down the number 14 and word FOURTEEN in all capital letters for your child to see. Say each letter as you write: F, O, U, R, T, E, E, N, and the word out loud:

F
O
U
R
T
E
E
N

FOURTEEN

Now the night is nigh its noon,

F
O
U
R
T
E
E
N

FOURTEEN

Nimble gnomes beneath the moon.

2. Have the child draw images of the number FOURTEEN. They may copy some of the items you made in your blackboard drawing for this week. Your child should then practice writing the number 14, Roman numeral XIV, and the word FOURTEEN in all capital letters on the opposite page of their book. If you feel they need extra time with writing, let them continue to practice as needed. Here is a verse to share when forming the number 14:

   Write a one
   And then a four
   That's all it takes
   There's nothing more!

3. Now that your child is well versed in numbers 30-40, you can trust that they are able to move more quickly and practice their counting from 40-50. Count everything you can! If your child seems ready, you can expand your four processes math skills to include larger numbers up to 40 as well. Remember to go at your child's pace and pay close attention to how your child learns most effectively.

Domestic Arts/Practical Life Skills

If when you are using this program it is close to December 13th, you may wish to tie in the celebration of St. Lucia Day. This festival is popular in Sweden and the tale tells of a young girl who would secretly bring food to the persecuted Christians who lived in hiding. She would wear a wreath on her head of candles to light the way so she could carry things in. An ancient pagan festival of lights fell on December 13th which is why this day was eventually turned into St. Lucia Day during the uprising of Christianity.

Presently, this festival is often celebrated by girls dressing in a white dress and a crown of candles on their heads. Sometimes only the oldest daughter will wear the candles and serve the family breakfast in bed. Boys often like to dress as Stjarngossar (star boys) with a cone hat with a star on top.

Whether you are Christian or not, making Lussekatter (St. Lucy Buns) is a fun way to bake with your children this time of year. These are sweet buns that are often shared during St. Lucia Day celebrations.

As always, be sure to tie mathematics in when you measure and cook with your child.

Lussekatter (St. Lucy Buns)

Supplies Needed:
1 cup heavy cream
1 cup scaled milk
1/3 cup butter
2/3 cup sugar
6 packages of dry active yeast
dash of salt
2 eggs, beaten
6 - 8 cups sifted flour

1/3 cup raisins

Mix butter, cream and salt and stir. Mix yeast, milk and two tablespoons of the sugar. Leave aside for ten minutes or more until it foams.

Mix both butter mixture and yeast mixture along with one of the beaten eggs and remaining sugar. Gradually stir in the flour until a stiff dough forms. Put the mixture on a floured surface and knead ten minutes.

Add more flour if necessary. Place dough into a greased bowl, cover and let it rise until it doubles in bulk. Divide dough into 5" strips about 1" wide. Shape the strips into an 'S' shape and decorate with raisins. Brush with the remaining beaten egg and place on greased baking sheet.

Cover and let rise for one hour. Bake at 400 degrees approximately ten minutes (until lightly brown, check buns often).

Outdoor Time/Nature Walk

Take your children outside each day regardless of the weather. Invest in good rain gear, snow gear and wool undergarments if your location requires it. Do your lessons outdoors whenever possible.

Caregiver Focus

Extending a Hand to Others in Need

We've talked much about caring for ourselves and tending to our own needs. It is also important for you to find connection outside of yourself, your home life, and your family. Extending yourself by helping others in need outside of your home is not only fulfilling because of the good work that you are doing but it also helps you to form connections and a sense of community that can create a warmth inside that you may feel is missing. Consider how you can help in your community by volunteering at a library, school, church, shelter, or by offering your time to help an elder or a friend in need.

Afternoon Lessons

Beeswax Modeling

Supplies Needed:
Beeswax Modeling Material

Spend time today working with beeswax. Make small hearts to add to your nature table. Make a small figure with crown and candles to represent St. Lucia to place on your nature table.

Tuesday Student Lessons – Week Fourteen
(Painting – Red Day)

Language Arts

1. Like yesterday, begin your lesson time by continuing to read (or tell) *The Elves and The Cobbler*. Provide your child with a piece of beeswax modeling material as you read. Let them hold this piece of beeswax as they listen, warming it with their hands so it softens.

2. Have your child form the softened beeswax material into the letter N. Roll it into a long snake, form it just so and then put it back together again. Next, have them form it into the number 14.

3. Open your lesson book and review the work you did yesterday. Have your child trace the letter N number 14 and word FOURTEEN with their fingers.

4. Practice saying the sounds of the letter N. Notice how our mouth forms to make the sound. Bringing awareness to the way our body forms sounds and words is very important. This process helps us to notice the use of air and our body muscles as we communicate.

5. Today we will work on a tongue twister to practice and memorize with your child to help learn the letter N and its sound. Tongue twisters and rhymes are fun ways to learn and help with finding rhythm. As we have begun bringing awareness to syllables, pay careful attention with your child to be sure they get it correctly.

    To begin, say the following tongue twister to your child slowly **and tap one finger on the palm of your other hand to some of the syllables** to create a pattern for memory:

    > I need *(tap)* not your needles *(tap, tap)*,
    > They're needless *(tap, tap)* to me *(tap)*.
    > For the needling *(tap, tap)* of needles *(tap, tap)*
    > Is needless *(tap, tap)*, you see *(tap)*.

Mathematics

1. Skip Counting Expanded

   After your child has learned to count by tens in a confident way, you should explore skip counting with other numbers such as 3, 4, 6, 8 and onward. Take your time and do this in a way that is fun for your child. This is laying the foundation for many mathematical solutions to come that include multiplication and other formats.

2. Practice subtraction and addition of larger numbers (10-50) with your child today by using this sweet little rhyme. Again, go slowly and if your child needs to write it out on paper that is perfectly acceptable. If this proves to be too challenging, do the same activity with smaller numbers. For example:

   14 little birds on a branch one day,
   Then with the wind some flew away.
   7 little birds on a branch did stay,
   How many birds flew away?

   $14 - 7 = 7$

20 little birds on a branch one day,
Then with the wind some flew away.
8 little birds on a branch did stay,
How many birds flew away?

20 − 12 = 8

10 little birds on a branch one day,
Then with the wind some flew away.
4 little birds on a branch did stay,
How many birds flew away?

10 − 6 = 4

3. Explore additional three dimensional shapes with your child such as a cube, cone, cylinder, and sphere. Explore drawing these and recognizing them in nature and around your home.

Outdoor Time/Nature Walk

Take your children outside each day regardless of the weather. Invest in good rain gear, snow gear and wool undergarments if your location requires it. Do your lessons outdoors whenever possible.

Social Studies, Geography, Weather, Time

1. Weather Around the World: Hemispheres and Climate

   If you live in the Northern Hemisphere, the Winter Solstice may be drawing near and winter may be approaching. Depending on where you live, you may experience colder temperatures or maybe even snow.

   Individuals who live in the Southern Hemisphere, however, are likely experiencing warm temperatures leading into summer!

   Even within the same hemisphere, the weather can differ greatly depending on where you live. A family that lives in Florida may not see snow in the winter at all, while children in Vermont may see a lot of snow.

Take time to look at a globe with your child and do some research. Explain how there are two parts of the earth (hemispheres) and depending on how close that hemisphere is to the sun, it has summer and the other has winter. They experience opposite seasons.

2. Climate Charting

Do you have family members or friends that live in different areas? Give them a call with your child and ask them what the weather is like where they live. You can also look online or research at the library. Your child may wish to create a climate chart and mark down all the different locations you research and what the current weather and season is.

Afternoon Lessons

Art: Masking Tape Letter Painting

Supplies Needed:
Watercolor Paper
Masking Tape
Scissors
Watercolor Paints
Brush

Have your child cut the tape to create the capital letter N on their watercolor paper. Carefully wet the paper area around your tape. With brush and paints, have your child paint the paper (they can go over the tape).

When dried, pull off the tape and a beautiful letter N will appear.

Wednesday Student Lessons – Week Fourteen
(Coloring – Yellow Day)

Language Arts

1. Practice our tongue twister again. Keep working on this until you have it memorized together. Say the following tongue twister to your child slowly **and tap one finger on the palm of your other hand to some of the syllables** to create a pattern for memory:

    > I need *(tap)* not your needles *(tap, tap)*,
    > They're needless *(tap, tap)* to me *(tap)*.
    > For the needling *(tap, tap)* of needles *(tap, tap)*
    > Is needless *(tap, tap)*, you see *(tap)*.

2. In your child's lesson book have them draw a photo of the elves sewing the shoes for the cobbler. On the opposite page, your child is likely ready to write simple sentences (do not worry about punctuation at this time). Provide your child with a simple sentence on the blackboard to copy such as:

    THE SHOES WERE MADE AT NIGHT

3. Tonight at bedtime, continue to tell your child the story of *The Elves and The Cobbler*.

4. When out and about, ask your child to find things that begin with the letter N. This can be done while shopping or when driving in the car. Throughout the week, ask your child to think of all the words they can that begin with the letter N. How many can they come up with? Make a list.

5. We have been telling our children rhymes and fairy tales since they were very small. Spend extra time this morning discussing what a rhyme is. Begin by sharing a nursery rhyme or verse and each time you get to the rhyming word, stomp or clap and say that word louder. Here are some examples:

    Twinkle, twinkle, little **star**,
    How I wonder what you **are**!
    Up above the world so **high**,
    Like a diamond in the **sky**.

Christmas is coming, the geese are getting **fat**
Please to put a penny in the old man's **hat**;
If you haven't got a penny, a half penny will **do**,
If you haven't got a half penny then God bless **you**!

Pease porridge **hot**!
Pease porridge **cold**!
Pease porridge in the **pot**
Nine days **old**.

Some like it **hot**,
Some like it **cold**,
Some like it in the **pot**
Nine days **old**!

6. In your child's lesson book on the left side, have them either draw a picture of one of the nursery rhymes or write it out by copying it off the blackboard. On the right side, have them write the corresponding rhyming words. For example:

   FAT HAT

   DO YOU

   or

   HOT POT

   COLD OLD

   Think of other words that rhyme. Make up silly rhymes and made up words.

Mathematics

1. Measuring Length: Shortest and Longest

Go outside together and gather as many sticks as you can find. Have your child put them in piles of like sizes. Next, put them in order from shortest to longest.

2. Measuring Length: Distance

   Explore further outside and have your child use steps to determine distance. Starting from one spot, ask your child to count his or her steps to another area. Your child may choose to record these findings. Continue doing this with various scenarios. Next, ask your child to tell you which distance is further, and which is shorter than one another.

   We will not yet be exploring the detailed units of measurement this year, but you may like to introduce the simple concept of a ruler or measuring tape to your child. This will be a welcome tool for your child's play and be sure to let them enjoy it and pretend.

Outdoor Time/Nature Walk

Take your children outside each day regardless of the weather. Invest in good rain gear, snow gear and wool undergarments if your location requires it. Do your lessons outdoors whenever possible.

Afternoon Lessons

1. Music: Continue Practicing Flute or Recorder

2. Handwork: Beginner Knitting, Fingerless Gloves

   Supplies Needed:
   Yarn
   Knitting Needles
   Yarn Needle

   So many things can be made with simple knitted squares and rectangles. For this project, your child can knit two rectangles that fit the shape of their hand from knuckle to above the wrist. Carefully sew the long ends together leaving a small hole where the thumb can fit. Make another just the same.

Thursday Student Lessons – Week Fourteen
(Crafting/Games – Orange Day)

Language Arts

1. Continue to tell your child the story of *The Elves and The Cobbler.*

2. Alphabet Cards

    Supplies Needed:
    Heavy White Cardstock
    Beeswax Stick Crayons
    Scissors

    Spend time cutting cards out of cardstock with your child. Using beeswax crayons, continue to finish drawing each letter we have learned so far and include the letter N. Next to the letter, have your child draw an image that begins with it. Using scissors, round the corners of these cards and keep working on them throughout the year. You can use them in your lessons and for an upper case and lowercase match game later in the curriculum when we learn those as well.

3. Continue reading simple reader books together.

4. Print out or share the following photos and practice saying them together with your child. Your child may be ready to copy these words into their lesson book.

NEST

NAIL

NOSE

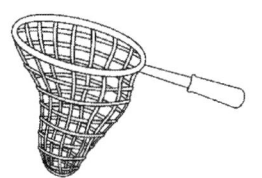

NET

NUT

NEEDLE

First Grade Curriculum | WINTER | Little Acorn Learning

Mathematics

Ordinal Numbers

An ordinal number is a number that describes a number's position, such as: first, second, 3rd, 10th, etc.

Spend time today going over these numbers. Tell stories that include ordinal numbers in description and text. Over the next few weeks, practice these with tangible items and work at your own pace in your lesson book to both write the numerical format and the written format as follows:

1st	FIRST
2nd	SECOND
3rd	THIRD
4th	FOURTH
5th	FIFTH
6th	SIXTH
7th	SEVENTH
8th	EIGHTH
9th	NINTH
10th	TENTH

Outdoor Time/Nature Walk

Take your children outside each day regardless of the weather. Invest in good rain gear, snow gear and wool undergarments if your location requires it. Do your lessons outdoors whenever possible.

Science, Nature Study, Earth Discovery

Ice Lanterns

Supplies Needed:
Two Buckets or Tin Cans – One Smaller to Fit Inside Larger One
Duct Tape
Rocks
Greenery, Cranberries, Food Coloring, Glitter or Other Decorations
Electric Tea Lights

Pour a small amount of water (about ½ cup) inside the large bucket. Put the smaller tin can or bucket inside the larger one. It will be floating slightly. Fill with rocks to keep from floating and make tops level. Using duct tape strap the smaller container to the larger container on four sides to keep it centered.

Put decorations (greenery, cranberries, etc.) in between the two cans. Add water between the large can and small can to about ½" below the tops of containers. Use this opportunity to talk about how water expands when it freezes, and therefore you are leaving space.

If it is cold enough where you live outside, leave this outdoors to freeze. Otherwise, place it carefully in your freezer.

After frozen, run warm water on the outside of the larger container and inside the small container filled with rocks until you can loosen them and pull your ice lantern right out.

Place an electric tea light (you can also try a regular candle) inside and light up the winter night!

Movement, Body Awareness & Health

1. Game of Light

    Supplies Needed:
    Flashlights

    This is a very simple but fun game to play either indoors or outside (if it is evening). Choose an item to hide. Have the children leave so they cannot see where you are placing it. Put the item somewhere it can be found easily when a flashlight is shone upon it.

    Give each child a flashlight and have them begin looking for the item. When a player sees the item, they must sit down. Everyone continues searching until all players are sitting down.

    The child that sat down first is the one to hide the item for the next game.

2. Number Movement Exercise

   This exercise is good for your child to practice balance and coordination. Holding a bean bag in one hand, have your child do the following motions according to the poem with the free hand. Then do the same holding the bean bag in the other hand.

   Number one,
   Touch your tongue.

   Number two,
   Touch your shoe.

   Number three,
   Touch your knee.

   Number four,
   Touch the floor.

   Number five,
   Reach up high.

   Number six,
   Grab some sticks.
   (pretend to grab from ground)

   Number seven,
   Back up to heaven.
   (reach up high again)

   Number eight,
   Stand up straight.

   Number nine,
   Touch your spine.

   Number ten.
   That's the end.

Afternoon Lessons

1. Form Drawing/Art – 'Spiral' Squares

   Have your child experiment with making 'spirals' in a square shape. First begin by walking the shape with your child on the ground. Begin in the center and build your square outward. Then, do the reverse and try to walk from the outside to the inside of your square.

   In your child's lesson book, let them draw various 'spiral' squares with different colors. They may even explore further and create a maze for you to solve!

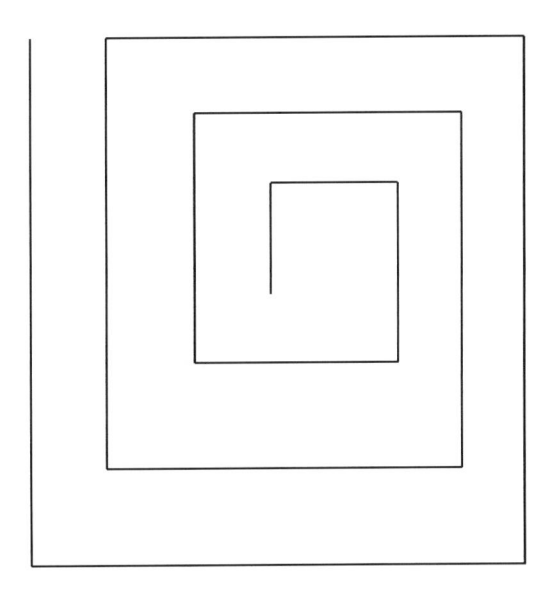

2. Handwork: Hand Stitching/Embroidery

   Supplies Needed:
   Embroidery Needle
   Embroidery Floss
   White Scrap Fabric
   Embroidery Hoop (optional)
   Scissors

Using our embroidery instructions, work with your child to make a letter N embroidery piece. You can do this with a simple running stitch, or you may choose to learn more complicated stitches together.

Friday Student Lessons – Week Fourteen
(Modeling/Housework – Green Day)

Language Arts

1. Today have your child continue to practice writing the letter N in their lesson book on unlined paper.

2. In your child's lesson book, have them practice writing the alphabet from A-N copying each letter a few times on each line.

3. Ask your child to tell YOU the story of *The Elves and The Cobbler*.

4. As your child may have come across, there are some letters when placed in a certain way that remain silent. This can become a bit confusing for an emerging reader as there are often no real explanations as to why this is. The history of the word, the language it derived from, changes in grammar and sound changes, are various reasons this exists in the English language. It is not our job as teachers to present this concept in a confusing way. The best way a child will truly be able to learn the "rules" of silent letters is by becoming an avid reader. Be sure to inspire a love of reading in your child and let them explore our language naturally.

Today you can explore some words that have silent letters inside. Make a point to point them out to your child when you see them in your everyday activities and while reading together. Here are some examples to put on your blackboard and ask your child to circle the letter that remains silent:

Gnome
Clim**b**
Nam**e**
Two
Why
Knock
Ghost

Can you imagine how difficult it must be for a non-native speaker to learn our language?

Mathematics/ Social Studies, Geography, Weather, Time

Card Game Math

Pull out the ace through 10 of a traditional set of cards. Explain to your child that ace equals one. Shuffle your cards and have your child pull two cards at a time. Alternate between the following mathematical challenges as your child pulls each set:

Subtract the lowest card from the highest.
Add the two cards.
Multiply the numbers.
Taking the largest number, divide as evenly as possible by the smallest number.

Continue playing this game to practice. You may wish to teach your child the value of the suit cards and explore other card games together.

Outdoor Time/Nature Walk

Take your children outside each day regardless of the weather. Invest in good rain gear, snow gear and wool undergarments if your location requires it. Do your lessons outdoors whenever possible.

Domestic Arts/Practical Life Skills

1. Christmas Wheat

   There is a Hungarian custom of growing wheat during this time of year. The wheat seeds are planted on St. Lucia Day are a reminder of spiritual rebirth at this time.

   Supplies Needed:
   Small Flowerpot
   Potting Soil
   Grains of Wheat

   Fill pot with soil. Lay grains on top of soil and gently press down until they are covered. Water daily and keep warm on your nature space. The children will enjoy watching the wheat grow as the holidays approach.

2. Light a Candle on Your Living Wreath

   If your family celebrates Advent and you are doing this lesson during that time of year, you can light the candle on your living wreath as your second Advent candle. If you do not celebrate Advent, lighting a candle on your Living Wreath is still a beautiful way to welcome winter. Here is a simple verse to share when doing so:

   Color – Purple
   Theme – Love

   Slowly creeping toward the day
   As the winter paves its way
   Love as fresh and pure as snow
   Guides us toward a loving glow

   Allow the candle to burn as you enjoy your meal, and then snuff your candle out when you are done.

3. Shoveling

   If you have snow in your area, allow your child to help you to shovel walkways, driveways, and other areas outside your home. Your child can still experience shoveling without snow. Provide them with a safe space to dig and shovel outdoors. Let them make holes, bury things, and enjoy this experience. If you have a garden, they can help put this skill to task there as well.

Afternoon Lessons

Use the afternoon hours today to review areas from this week's afternoon lessons that you feel may need a bit more attention. Bring these into your weekend as you find time.

Week Fifteen, Winter
First Grade

Theme: Evergreen & Deciduous Trees, Feeling Joy

This Week's Lessons:

Language Arts:
Why Evergreens Keep Their Leaves Story
Letter O
Silent Letters

Mathematics:
Number 15
Counting from 50 - 60
Counting Backwards
Ollie the Octopus Math
Winter Tree Division Dice Roll
Math Gnomes & Four Processes

Social Studies, Geography, Weather, Time:
Learning About Time: Introduction to Clocks

Science, Nature Study, Earth Discovery:
Bird Treat Ornaments & Holiday Tree for the Birds
Learning About Winter Trees: Evergreen & Deciduous

Teacher's Classroom Work:
Plan a Visit to a Tree Farm

For the Caregiver:
Caregiver Meditation: Joy
Caregiver Focus: Finding Joy in Your Work

Domestic Arts/Practical Life Skills:
Cooking Bird Treats
Living Wreath, Light a Candle

Music:
Trees and Joy Fingerplays & Songs
Beginning Recorder or Flute

Art/Handwork:
Handwork: Beginner Knitting, Knitted Beanbags
Art: Beeswax Modeling, Winter Trees and Animals
Embroidery Letter O
Alphabet Card Letter O
Art: Evergreen Discovery Jar

Form Drawing:
Form Drawing/Art – Touching Zig Zags

Movement, Body Awareness & Health:
Yoga for Children: Mountain & Tree Poses

Supplies Needed for Week Fifteen

Cooking List:

For Bird Treat Ornaments:
4 Cups Oatmeal
1 lb. Melted Suet or Shortening
1 Small Jar Peanut Butter
4 Cups Cornmeal
3 Cups Cream of Wheat
Popcorn
Stale Bread
Cookie Cutters
Yarn or Raffia
Birdseed
Melted Butter or Suet
Orange
Peanut Butter or Jelly
Raffia or Yarn

Homeschooling List:

Blackboard
Chalk
Small Felted Toy Bird, Houseplants, Small Tree
Lesson Book
Stockmar Stick Crayons
Stockmar Block Crayons
Colored Pencils
Stockmar Beeswax Modeling Material
Knitting Needles
Super Bulky Single Ply 100% Wool Yarn
Embroidery Needle
Embroidery Floss
White Scrap Fabric
Embroidery Hoop (optional)
Two Knitted Squares of Same Length
Nylon Stocking
Beans

First Grade Curriculum | WINTER | Little Acorn Learning

Thread/Yarn
Needle
Samples of Pine Needles, Evergreen Branches, Etc.
Pinecones
Nature Notebooks or Journal
Pen/Pencils
Magnifying Glasses (optional)
Heavy White Cardstock
Dice
Winter Tree Division Printouts
Clear Jars with Lids
Water
Gathered Nature Items

Week Fifteen Book Recommendations

Visit your local library the weekend before to check out books based on your theme for the week. Older children can help you look up the books by author and title. When setting up your play space for the week ahead, mindfully display these books in baskets for the children to enjoy.

Where Would I Be in an Evergreen Tree? ~ Jennifer Blomgren
Evergreens Are Green ~ Susan Canizares
Winter Trees ~ Carole Gerber and Leslie Evans
A Walk in the Deciduous Forest ~ Rebecca L. Johnson
Deciduous Forest Food Chains ~ Julia Vogel
Biome Beasts Deciduous Forest Animals ~ Lisa Colozza Cocca
The Woodland Trust: Into The Forest ~ Christiane Dorion
Night Tree ~ Eve Bunting and Ted Rand
Tell Me, Tree: All About Trees for Kids ~ Gail Gibbons
The Happiness Tree: Celebrating the Gifts of Trees We Treasure ~ Andrea Alban Gosline and Lisa Burnett Bossi
Christmas Farm ~ Mary Lyn Ray
Mr. Willowby's Christmas Tree ~ Robert Barry
Coniferous Forests ~ Donna Latham
Amazing Biome Projects: You Can Build Yourself ~ Donna Latham
Coniferous Forests: An Evergreen World ~ Jeanne Nagle
Why Christmas Trees Aren't Perfect ~ Richard H. Schneider
The Year of the Perfect Christmas Tree: An Appalachian Story ~ Gloria Houston
The Legend of the Christmas Tree ~ Rick Osborne, Pat Matuszak, and Bill Dodge
Uncle Vova's Tree ~ Patricia Polacco
A Wish to Be a Christmas Tree ~ Colleen Monroe
Learning About Trees ~ Catherine Veitch
The Tree Book ~ Gina Igoglia
Tree: A Peek-Through Picture Book ~ Britta Teckentrup
The Giving Tree ~ Shel Silverstein
The Hugging Tree ~ Jill Neimark
The Magic and Mystery of Trees ~ Jen Green
The Treasure Tree ~ John Trent
When Grandma Gives You a Lemon Tree ~ Jamie L.B. Deenihan
The Busy Tree ~ Jennifer Ward
A Tree is Nice ~ Janice May Udry
Tap the Magic Tree ~ Christie Matheson

Week Fifteen Circle, Songs & Movement

The following songs and verses should be shared during circle time each day this week after you open your circle.

Light a Candle
(if you celebrate Advent, you can replace the word Winter with Advent and Solstice with Christmas in the lyrics)

Light one candle winter's here
Light one candle winter's here
Light one candle winter's here
Solstice time is near. (*clap, clap*)

Light two candles winter's here
Light two candles winter's here
Light two candles winter's here
Solstice time is near. (*clap, clap*)

Light three candles winter's here
Light three candles winter's here
Light three candles winter's here
Solstice time is near. (*clap, clap*)

Light four candles winter's here
Light four candles winter's here
Light four candles winter's here
Solstice time is near. (*clap, clap*)

Outside there is a Pine Tree
Standing straight and tall

It needs no decorations
Nature's done it all

Pinecones on its branches
With icicles glistening bright

Snow upon its needles
And birds at rest from flight

I see it from my window
And take the time to say

Thank you for your beauty, tree,
On this winter day

The Trees' Rebellion

Dame Nature said to her children the trees,
In the days when the earth was new,
"It's time you are putting your green leaves on,
Take them out of your trunks, dears, do."

"The sky is a soft and beautiful blue,
The snow went away long ago,
And the grass some time since popped up its head,
The crocuses all are ablow."

"Now hurry and get yourselves dressed, my dears,
All ready for summer weather."

But the trees tossed their heads from side to side,
And grumbled out altogether:

"We really would like to alter our dress,

We are quite tired of wearing green;
Each year our new suits are just like our old,
Can we not have a change between?"

Dame Nature said to her children the trees,
"I'm astonished I must confess,
To hear you are tired of your robe of green;
I think it's a beautiful dress."

"But wear it always in summer you shall,
(I've said it and will be obeyed).
However I'll see when the winter comes,
If some little change can be made."

"Your Uncle John Frost comes to visit me
from his home in the polar seas,
And I'll ask him to bring for each of you
A dress any color you please."

Merry little snowflakes falling to the ground,
(fingers flutter like falling snow)

They're landing on the treetops, covering our town.
(fingers flutter)

They softly fall on noses
(touch nose)

And make our hair look white.
(touch hair)

They seem to call, 'Come out and play!'
('come here' motion)

As they fall throughout the night.
(repeat first action)

First Grade Curriculum | WINTER | Little Acorn Learning

Week Fifteen Blackboard Drawing

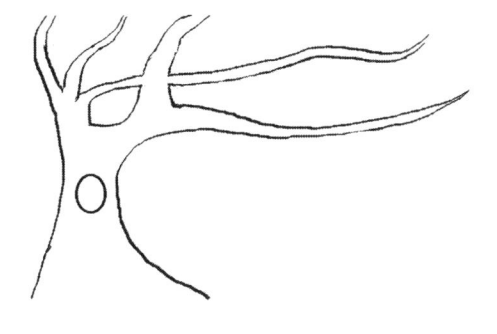

Drawing Ideas for This Week: Capital letter O as shown in the Big Oak Tree from our story (you can make a hole in the tree in the shape of an O), little bird traveling from tree to tree, evergreen and bare trees in winter, pine needles, wind blowing through forest trees, outdoor holiday tree decorated for birds, Roman numeral XV, FIFTEEN, 15

Week Fifteen Teacher's Classroom Work

1. Plan Visit to a Tree Farm

   This week visit a tree farm with your children. Many of these farms offer fun sleigh rides as well as tours of their facilities. Call the farm ahead of time to see what they have to offer this month. Many families may decide to purchase their own tree to decorate at home from the farm. While you are visiting, take time to learn about the various types of trees that are located in your area. Have the children bring along a nature notebook to journal and collect samples of what they see.

2. Get Tree Identification Book for Evergreen/Coniferous Tree Study

   Before doing the Evergreen/Coniferous Tree Study this week, you may wish to prepare yourself with a tree identification book from your local library to easily identify evergreens that are common to your neighborhood.

3. Review any handwork before working on projects with your child.

Week Fifteen Caregiver Meditation

This Week's Reflection: Joy

"Joy does not simply happen to us. We have to choose joy and keep choosing it every day." ~ Henri Nouwen

Caring for children is one of the most important duties in the world. Each moment you share yourself with a child, you feed their soul. And because young children learn primarily through imitation, the responsibility you have is immense. Having respect and reverence for even the most mundane parts of your job is the secret to finding true joy in your work.

You are helping to create a more peaceful planet with each child you care for. Your work is sacred. Take time this week to focus on finding joy in the simple and daily tasks that are required of you.

Week Fifteen Story

This is a sweet little story that teaches the children that evergreens keep their leaves during winter while other trees let their leaves go. A simple felted bird toy would make a nice prop as it visits 'trees' along its way such as a toy tree or two, a houseplant or your Christmas tree. You can even tell this story outdoors and travel from tree to tree.

Why Evergreens Keep Their Leaves
An Old Tale

The north wind was blowing. It was a cold, cold day. Winter was coming soon. Almost all of the birds had gone to the sunny South. But one tiny little bird had a broken wing and could not fly. When he saw all the other birds going away he was sad and lonesome. "What can I do?" he said, as he shivered and shivered in the cold wind. "How can I keep warm all the long, snowy winter?" I know. I'll ask a tree to help me. I'll ask a tree to keep its leaves all winter, and let me live in its warm branches. That's what I'll do."

So the poor little bird hopped away to the big oak tree. "O great, strong oak tree," he said, "I am a poor little bird with a broken wing. Will you keep your leaves all winter and let me live in your warm branches? If you will, I'll sing and sing and sing, And forget my broken wing. I'll sing and sing and sing. In the spring! In the spring!"

"Dear me! Dear me!" said the great, strong oak tree. "I can't keep my old leaves all winter. I must get ready to make new leaves. No, no; you can't live in my branches. I can't take care of a bird with a broken wing. Go away, go away." And the poor little bird hopped away, so sad, so lonesome, so cold.

By the brookside was a beautiful willow tree. Its leaves were turning to gold. "O beautiful willow tree," said the poor little bird with the broken wing, "will you keep your leaves all winter and let me live in your warm branches? If you will, I'll sing and sing and sing, And forget my broken wing. I'll sing and sing and sing. In the spring! In the spring!"

"Dear me! Dear me!" said the willow tree. "I can't keep my leaves all winter. I must rest. I must rest. No, no. You can't live in my branches. I can't take care of a bird with a broken wing. Go away, go away." The sad, cold little bird hopped away.

On a hill near by was a spruce tree. The spruce tree saw the little bird and said, "What's the trouble, little bird? Why don't you go south, where it's warm? Why are you here this cold, snowy day?" "O spruce tree, I have broken my wing, and I can't fly. I have asked the birch, the oak, and the willow trees to help me, but they won't keep me warm. I don't know what I shall do all the cold winter."

"You may live in my branches," said the spruce tree. "I'll keep you warm, poor little bird." "And may I live with you all winter, spruce tree? If I may, I'll sing and sing and sing, And forget my broken wing. I'll sing and sing and sing. In the spring! In the spring!"

"Yes, yes; you may live in my warm branches all winter. I shall be glad to take care of a little bird with a broken wing."

A big, strong pine tree that stood near by said, "I will keep the wind off the little bird." "I will give him berries to eat," said a juniper tree. So the tiny little bird with the broken wing lived in the branches of the spruce tree and ate juniper berries all winter long.

When North Wind and the Frost King came they blew all the leaves off the birch, the oak, and the willow trees. But they said, "We'll be good to the spruce, the pine, and the juniper trees. They took care of the little bird with the broken wing. Their leaves shall be ever green. Their leaves shall be green all summer and all winter."

And their leaves have been green every winter ever since.

Monday Student Lessons – Week Fifteen

(Baking/Cooking – Purple Day)

Language Arts

1. Begin your lesson time by reading (or telling) *Why Evergreens Keep Their Leaves* to your child. Let the children look at the sentences as you read as this visual will aid with their knowledge of letters, words and sentences. If possible, use simple props to accompany the story as we have suggested.

2. When your story is finished, unveil your blackboard drawing that you have prepared ahead of time as suggested at the beginning of this week's curriculum. If your child has his or her own small blackboard and chalk, have them take a few moments to create their own drawing.

3. Review what your child worked on last week in their lesson book. Have them practice writing the capital letter N a few times on their blackboard or an extra piece of paper. Be sure they have a good grasp of this letter before moving onto the next.

4. In your child's lesson book, have them create a similar image of the Old Oak from our story (or whatever depiction you used) with the letter O revealed inside. On the righthand side, have your child practice writing the capital letter O. Share this poem as you work to form the letter:

Circle round
Very slow
That is how
We make the O

5. Talk about how words have a certain pattern of sound. These small groups of sounds we call syllables. To demonstrate this, have your child hold their hand under their chin, palm side down. Have them say a word slowly and count how many times their jaw pushes their hand down to count the syllables. Here are a few O words to experiment with:

- Olive
- Otter
- Octopus
- Outside
- Ox
- Onto
- Ohio
- Oatmeal
- Oval

Try this with many different words beginning with all letters. Next, do this same activity by clapping the syllables. Keep this practice going for the next week or two until your child feels confident in recognizing the number of syllables in each word.

Mathematics

1. In addition to the Roman numeral XV, write down the number 15 and word FIFTEEN in all capital letters for your child to see. Say each letter as you write: F, I, F, T, E, E, N, and the word out loud:

F
I
F
T
E
E
N

FIFTEEN

The little bird flew through a winter scene

F
I
F
T
E
E
N

FIFTEEN

The pine tree's leaves were safe and green

2. Have the child draw images of the number FIFTEEN. They may copy some of the items you made in your blackboard drawing for this week. Your child should then practice writing the number 15, Roman numeral XV and the word FIFTEEN in all capital letters on the opposite page of their book. If you feel they need extra time with writing, let them continue to practice as needed. Here is a verse to share when forming the number 15:

> *First a one*
> *And then a five*
> *Number fifteen*
> *has come alive*

3. Now that your child is well versed in numbers 40-50, you can trust that they are able to move more quickly and practice their counting from 50-60. Count everything you can! If your child seems ready, you can expand your four processes math skills to include larger numbers up to 60 as well. Remember to go at your child's pace and pay close attention to how your child learns most effectively.

Domestic Arts/Practical Life Skills

As always, be sure to tie mathematics in when you measure and cook with your child.

1. Bird Treat Ornaments

A CHRISTMAS TREE FOR BIRDS AND ANIMALS

Set up your workspace to make bird treat ornaments. These ornaments will be hung on a special Holiday Tree for the birds that you and your children will decorate today during outside time. Each ornament will be an edible treat for the birds in your neighborhood. Be sure to continue to leave food out during the cold weather when the treats are done. The birds will come to depend on the food source. This is a good lesson to the children on how to be consistent and responsible caregivers.

Ornament #1 – Balls for Birds

Supplies Needed:
4 Cups Oatmeal
1 lb. Melted Suet or Shortening
1 Small Jar Peanut Butter
4 Cups Cornmeal
3 Cups Cream of Wheat

Combine all ingredients and mix well. Allow children to shape into balls. Wrap balls with ribbon and/or raffia and hang to trees. Balls can also be placed in empty onion bags and hung for birds to enjoy.

Ornament #2 – Popcorn Garland

Have children string popcorn on needle and thread to create long garland for decorating.

Ornament #3 – Stale Bread Ornaments

Supplies Needed:
Stale Bread
Cookie Cutters
Yarn or Raffia
Birdseed
Melted Butter or Suet

Have children cut shapes out of the stale bread with cookie cutters. Dip shapes into melted butter or suet. Sprinkle with birdseed and poke a hole in top for hanging with raffia or yarn.

Ornament #4 – Orange Peanut Butter Treats

Supplies Needed:
Orange
Peanut Butter or Jelly
Raffia or Yarn

Cut orange in half and hollow out (great snack while working). Punch a hole on each side and run raffia or yarn across and above to form a loop. Fill inside of orange with peanut butter or jelly. When hanging make sure the hollow part is facing up.

2. Holiday Tree for the Birds & Animals

After you have finished your ornaments, gather them in a container or box and take a walk outside to a tree you have chosen to be your Holiday Tree for Birds and Animals. Choose a tree that can be seen from a window in your home or program. Share the verses and songs from this week as you and the children decorate the tree together. Try your hand at storytelling and make up a simple tale about some of the small hungry animals that come to discover the tree with all the glorious treats hanging from each branch. You may also wish to scatter bread and birdseed under the tree. Check your tree every day to see what is missing. The children can document this information in their Nature Notebooks or a special journal.

Outdoor Time/Nature Walk

Take your children outside each day regardless of the weather. Invest in good rain gear, snow gear and wool undergarments if your location requires it. Do your lessons outdoors whenever possible.

Caregiver Focus

Finding Joy in Your Work

We can easily fall into a slump of feeling frustrated, annoyed, and unfilled with the tasks we have in front of us each day. A conscious shift in attitude and perspective is all that is needed to rediscover the joy in our work and remember why we decided to walk this journey in the first place.

This week, be extra mindful to truly absorb each moment, find gratitude and joy in each moment and task. When washing dishes, instead of focusing on the pile in front of you: feel the warm water on your hands, watch the soap form and rinse each item, remember where you purchased or received your dishes from, sing a song or listen to music, think of how lucky you are to have clean, running water, etc. While in line at a store, instead of getting trapped into feeling a lack of patience and frustration about the next place to be: use the time to slow down and breathe, talk to someone next to you, think about what you must do with the rest of your day and simply be content just being where you are.

Afternoon Lessons

Handwork: Beginner Knitting, Knitted Beanbags

Supplies Needed:
Knitting Needles
Super Bulky Single Ply 100% Wool Yarn
Two Knitted Squares of Same Length

Nylon Stocking
Beans
Thread/Yarn
Needle

Working with beanbags is a wonderful way to practice your body & movement exercises and also use with language art and mathematics lessons. Your child can make a bunch of these for your homeschool classroom in all different shapes and sizes that you can use together with your lessons.

Have your child knit two squares of equal length and shape. Join the squares together on three of the sides with an overcast stitch. Fill a nylon stocking that is cut to fit inside of your beanbag with hard beans. Be sure to check the amount of beans so that it fills just the way you like. Finish off the fourth side with more overcast stitching and end off.

Tuesday Student Lessons – Week Fifteen
(Painting – Red Day)

Language Arts

1. Like yesterday, begin your lesson time by continuing to read (or tell) *Why Evergreens Keep Their Leaves*. Provide your child with a piece of beeswax modeling material as you read. Let them hold this piece of beeswax as they listen, warming it with their hands so it softens.

2. Have your child form the softened beeswax material into the letter O. Roll it into a long snake, form it just so and then put it back together again. Next, have them form it into the number 15.

3. Open your lesson book and review the work you did yesterday. Have your child trace the letter O number 15 and word FIFTEEN with their fingers.

4. Practice saying the sounds of the letter O. Notice how our mouth forms to make the sound. Bringing awareness to the way our body forms sounds and words is very important. This process helps us to notice the use of air and our body muscles as we communicate.

5. Today we will work on a tongue twister to practice and memorize with your child to help learn the letter O and its sound. Tongue twisters and rhymes are fun ways to learn and help with finding rhythm. As we have begun bringing awareness to syllables, pay careful attention with your child to be sure they get it correctly.

   To begin, say the following tongue twister to your child slowly **and tap one finger on the palm of your other hand to the syllables** to create a pattern for memory:

   Ollie the octopus
   Offered the otter
   Organic oranges

   Organic Oranges
   The Otter was Offered
   By Ollie the Octopus

Mathematics

Counting Backwards

1. Using tangible items, begin counting backwards with your children today. Start simple from 10 to 1.

2. Write numbers 1 – 20 on your blackboard. Using your finger point to 20 and count backward to the number one. Have your child do this with you.

3. In your child's lesson book, have them draw 30 items on the left side. This could be 30 little trees, buttons, hearts or even simply sticks. Count them together first in order and then backward. Next, on the right side of your child's layout, have them write the number 30 and downward to the number 1. You can help them if they are struggling.

4. Continue these types of exercises over the next week or two aiming to be able to increase the amount of numbers your child can count backwards.

Outdoor Time/Nature Walk

Take your children outside each day regardless of the weather. Invest in good rain gear, snow gear and wool undergarments if your location requires it. Do your lessons outdoors whenever possible.

Social Studies, Geography, Weather, Time

Learning About Time: Introduction to Clocks

1. Regular family life has likely exposed your child to clocks as a method of telling time. Show your child the difference between an analog and digital clock this week. On your analog clock practice counting the 1–12 hour numbers both forward and backward.

2. Have your child draw an analog clock by copying one in their lesson book. Have them focus only on adding the hour numbers and one long and short hand. We will learn more about how these hands work next week.

3. When out and about, have your child find as many clocks as they can. For digital clocks, have them tell you the numbers they see. You can explain what

time that translates to. For analog clocks have them point out which numbers the big and little hands are closest to. You will have an opportunity next week to explain how to begin telling time in more detail.

Afternoon Lessons

Art: Beeswax Modeling, Winter Trees and Animals

Supplies:
Beeswax Modeling Material

Have your child work with brown and green beeswax modeling material to create winter trees for your nature table. Make some trees without leaves and some with leaves. Your child may also wish to make a few small winter animals to include in the scene.

Wednesday Student Lessons – Week Fifteen
(Coloring – Yellow Day)

Language Arts

1. Practice our tongue twister again. Keep working on this until you have it memorized together. Say the following tongue twister to your child slowly **and tap one finger on the palm of your other hand to the syllables** to create a pattern for memory:

    Ollie the octopus
    Offered the otter
    Organic oranges

    Organic Oranges
    The Otter was Offered
    By Ollie the Octopus

2. In your child's lesson book have them make a drawing of Ollie the Octopus. How many legs does an octopus have? (eight) Now draw another octopus so he has a friend. If we add up all the legs, how many do we have now? (sixteen) Ask your child to draw a few more friends and continue to use this as a way to add and multiply. Ask your child what would happen if one or two of the friends left? How many legs would there be then?

3. On the opposite page, your child is likely ready to write simple sentences (do not worry about punctuation at this time). Remember we are still writing in all capital letters. Provide your child with a simple sentence on the blackboard to copy such as:

    OLLIE IS AN OCTOPUS
    THE OTTER ATE THE ORANGES

4. Tonight, at bedtime continue to tell your child the story of *Why Evergreens Keep Their Leaves*.

5. When out and about, ask your child to find things that begin with the letter O. This can be done while shopping or when driving in the car. Throughout the week, ask your child to think of all the words they can that begin with the letter O. How many can they come up with? Make a list.

Mathematics

Winter Tree Division Dice Roll

Supplies Needed:
Dice
Tree Printouts (or the examples we've provided)

Present your child with a number of winter tree printouts (this is the dividend). Have them roll the dice (your answer is the divider). Next, have them work to color the trees in groups of the dice number divider. How many groups could they make (this is the quotient). Are there any remainders?

You do not have to bring these division definitions to the children yet. We will do that at a later time.

Winter Tree Division Dice Roll

How many winter trees are there? ☐

Roll the dice.
What number did you get? ☐

Group (divide) the trees by the number you rolled by coloring them into groups in different colors.

How many groups were you able to make? ☐

How many winter trees are remaining that couldn't be evenly grouped? ☐

Write the division equation:

☐ ÷ ☐ = ☐

Remainders? ☐

Winter Tree Division Dice Roll

How many winter trees are there? ☐

Roll the dice.
What number did you get? ☐

Group (divide) the trees by the number you rolled by coloring them into groups in different colors.

How many groups were you able to make? ☐

How many winter trees are remaining that couldn't be evenly grouped? ☐

Write the division equation:

☐ ÷ ☐ = ☐

Remainders? ☐

Outdoor Time/Nature Walk

Take your children outside each day regardless of the weather. Invest in good rain gear, snow gear and wool undergarments if your location requires it. Do your lessons outdoors whenever possible.

Science, Nature Study, Earth Discovery

1. Learning About Winter Trees: Evergreen & Deciduous

   Supplies Needed:
   Samples of Pine Needles, Evergreen Branches, Etc.
   Pinecones

   Facts and Questions for Your Children:

   Evergreen trees do not lose their leaves in the winter. They keep them all year round. Evergreens usually have leaves that are shaped like needles, or they have different leaves that are waxy in texture. Evergreen leaves are able to withstand the very cold months and still produce enough food for the tree to survive.

Evergreen trees stay green all year round – that's why we call them ever-green.

Can you find other things around the house that are green?

Deciduous trees have leaves that turn red, yellow or brown in the autumn and eventually fall off for the winter. In the spring, new leaves grow. Deciduous trees usually have big leafy leaves. These big leaves make food from the sun to feed the tree. In the winter, there isn't enough sunlight to make enough from these type of leaves so deciduous trees make a chemical that keeps the trees from growing leaves in the winter. If the tree has no leaves, it needs less food to survive. Deciduous trees store food to live through the winter, almost like winter animals store food to make it through the cold months.

Can you tell me what tree this belongs to? (pass around samples of leaves)
Would you say these are leafy leaves or needles? (they are pine needles)

Do you know what this is? (pass around pinecone)

This is a pinecone. The seeds of the tree are tucked inside the cone and protected.

What type of tree do you think Christmas trees are? (evergreen)

What type of tree do you think a maple tree is? (deciduous)

Continue this learning with your children and take them outdoors to look at all of the different types of trees in your neighborhood.

2. Learning About Winter Trees: Evergreen/Coniferous Tree Study

Supplies Needed:
Nature Notebooks or Journal
Pen/Pencils
Magnifying Glasses (optional)

Bring the children outside and observe the different types of evergreen trees in your neighborhood.

Study the tree as a whole first. How is it compared to the other types of trees? Which direction do the branches fall? What types of animals are using the tree for shelter? Can you describe the barks texture?

Then study the smaller parts of the tree. Use your magnifying glasses if you wish. What are the branches like? What types of needles does the tree have? Does the tree have cones? Can you find a few for the nature table? Take a sample of the needles and keep them in your nature notebooks.

Allow them to hold a branch of each tree. Touch the needles. What do they smell like? Allow them to hold the magnifying glass and look through to see the object closely. Draw a picture of the tree.

You can share the names of each species. Explain that evergreen trees are coniferous, and they stay green all year long. Encourage them to research the topic in more depth at home. Make a sketch of the various parts of the tree in your nature notebooks or a nice journal.

Afternoon Lessons

Music: Continue Practicing Flute or Recorder

Thursday Student Lessons – Week Fifteen
(Crafting/Games – Orange Day)

Language Arts

1. Continue to tell your child the story of *Why Evergreens Keep Their Leaves*.

2. Alphabet Cards

    Supplies Needed:
    Heavy White Cardstock
    Beeswax Stick Crayons
    Scissors

    Spend time cutting cards out of cardstock with your child. Using beeswax crayons, continue to finish drawing each letter we have learned so far and include the letter O. Next to the letter, have your child draw an image that begins with it. Using scissors, round the corners of these cards and keep working on them throughout the year. You can use them in your lessons and for an upper case and lowercase match game later in the curriculum when we learn those as well.

3. Continue reading simple reader books together.

4. Today begin to introduce the difference between long o and short o sounds. An easy way to remember if a vowel sound is long is if it sounds exactly like its letter is pronounced. For example:

    Long O sounds like (oh) – just like the actual letter O is pronounced
    examples: h**o**pe, r**o**se, t**o**e

    Short O sound is more like (ahh or awe). It is the sound we hear in words like: cl**o**ck, m**o**p, l**o**ck, st**o**p

    While we are learning about vowels by sight and sound, we are going to wait to learn more about how these special letters assist the consonants in spelling. Later in the year, we will introduce the vowels as characters in story. For now, we are creating letter and sound recognition only.

5. Practice saying the sounds of both the long O and the short O. Notice how our mouth forms to make the sound. Bringing awareness to the way our body forms sounds and words is very important. This process helps us to notice the use of air and our body muscles as we communicate.

6. Print out or share the following photos and practice saying them together with your child. Your child may be ready to copy these words into their lesson book. If you can, sort them into piles of short O and long O as well.

CLOCK

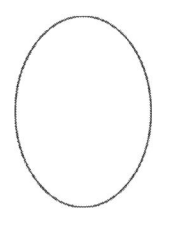

OVAL

OWL

OAK

ROSE

Mathematics

1. Math Gnomes & Four Processes

In the beginning of our first grade year, we created little math gnomes and our own story to teach the children the four processes. How are these little gnomes doing? Take them out and once again tell your story. The children will remember the learning you did together. Spend time using these gnomes to practice repetitive addition, addition, subtraction, multiplication and division with tangible items. If your child is able, work up to the number 60 with these math facts. Your child can write the equations in their lesson book along with a photo of each lesson.

2. Review Ordinal Numbers

Last week we learned that an ordinal number is a number that describes a number's position, such as: first, second, 3rd, 10th, etc.

We will once again review these numbers with the children. Tell stories that include ordinal numbers in description and text. Over the next few weeks, practice these with tangible items and work at your own pace in your lesson book to both write the numerical format and the written format as follows:

1st	FIRST
2nd	SECOND
3rd	THIRD
4th	FOURTH
5th	FIFTH
6th	SIXTH
7th	SEVENTH
8th	EIGHTH
9th	NINTH
10th	TENTH

Outdoor Time/Nature Walk

Take your children outside each day regardless of the weather. Invest in good rain gear, snow gear and wool undergarments if your location requires it. Do your lessons outdoors whenever possible.

Movement, Body Awareness & Health

Yoga for Children: Mountain & Tree Pose

The mountain and tree poses are two of the first and easiest yoga poses we can teach our children. Yoga is a wonderful way to support balance, posture and mindfulness and is just as beneficial for you as it is for your child.

1. Mountain Pose – *Tadasana*

   This is the foundation for all standing yoga poses and while it may seem like you are just standing there, it is actually a very active pose.

   - Stand with feet together and arms at your sides.
   - Breath steady and press your weight evenly across both feet.
   - Focus on the present moment and draw your attention inward.
   - Straighten your legs.
   - Press big toes together, then lift your toes up off the mat and spread them apart. Place them back down on the mat.
   - Next, keeping firm with your toes lift the heels of your feet and squeeze your shins together. Place them back down on the mat.
   - Inhale and straighten out through your torso. Exhale and release your shoulders away from head.
   - Keep neck elongated.
   - With each breath feel your spine stretch and straighten.

2. Tree Pose – *Vrksasana*

   This pose is a wonderful way to practice balance and coordination. Do not give up. It can take some practice but is well worth the effort.

   - Begin in Mountain Pose with arms at sides.
   - Shift weight to one foot.
   - Bend the knee of the opposite leg.
   - Carefully reach down and grab your inner ankle of the bent leg.

- Using your hand, pull your foot up and place it on the inner thigh of the sturdy leg. This takes some balancing. Go slow and be anchored in your other leg.

- If you cannot get your foot high enough to be over your knee, place it below the knee (not on the knee).

- Adjust your weight and carefully straighten up.

- Focus eyes on one spot and stay steady. Putting hands in a prayer position on your chest can help with balance. As you improve, you may be able to gently raise your hands above your head as you stand in tree pose.

- Inhale and exhale.

- Do again with other leg.

Afternoon Lessons

1. Form Drawing/Art – Touching Zig Zags

We have already practiced making zig zag lines. Now, have your child experiment with drawing two zig zag lines that touch points together and make diamonds. Then have them create two zig zag lines that cross over each other to do the same as below:

2. Handwork: Hand Stitching/Embroidery

   Supplies Needed:
   Embroidery Needle
   Embroidery Floss
   White Scrap Fabric
   Embroidery Hoop (optional)
   Scissors

   Using our embroidery instructions, work with your child to make a letter O embroidery piece. You can do this with a simple running stitch, or you may choose to learn more complicated stitches together.

Friday Student Lessons – Week Fifteen
(Modeling/Housework – Green Day)

Language Arts

1. Today have your child continue to practice writing the letter O in their lesson book on unlined paper.

2. In your child's lesson book, have them practice writing the alphabet from A-O copying each letter a few times on each line.

3. Ask your child to tell YOU the story of *Why Evergreens Keep Their Leaves.*

4. Today you can explore more words that have silent letters inside. Make a point to point them out to your child when you see them in your everyday activities and while reading together. Here are some examples to put on your blackboard and ask your child to circle the letter that remains silent:

Knit
Lam**b**
Chris**t**mas
S**w**ord
Wrist
Knee
Write

Mathematics

Winter Tree Division Dice Roll

Continue to play the division dice roll game with your child with various scenarios:

Winter Tree Division Dice Roll

How many winter trees are there? ☐

Roll the dice. What number did you get? ☐

Group (divide) the trees by the number you rolled by coloring them into groups in different colors.

How many groups were you able to make? ☐

How many winter trees are remaining that couldn't be evenly grouped? ☐

Write the division equation:

☐ ÷ ☐ = ☐

Remainders? ☐

Outdoor Time/Nature Walk

Take your children outside each day regardless of the weather. Invest in good rain gear, snow gear and wool undergarments if your location requires it. Do your lessons outdoors whenever possible.

Science, Nature Study, Earth Discovery

1. Learning About Winter Trees: Evergreen Nature Display

Today take the children on a nature walk and have them gather branches of the various evergreens that you come across. When you return indoors, place the branches in a vase of water (or moist moss) and display it on your Winter Nature Space. Save a good amount for the next activity today below. Here is a nice verse you can share as you walk or work together:

The pine's new dew has frozen still.
It stands alone upon the hill.

With arms at length to reach the snow
Its silence speaks from down below.
It tries to reach us with its sight
Among the white and star-filled night

The pine's new dew has frozen still.
It stands alone upon the hill.

2. Learning About Winter Trees: Evergreen Discovery Jar

Supplies Needed:
Clear Jars with Lids
Water
Gathered Nature Items

Go on a nature walk with your child and collect different species of evergreen samples. You might also wish to gather a few winter berries, small pinecones, acorns and other items. Back at home fill up an old spaghetti jar with your items and add a few other holiday trinkets. We used simple beads and sparkly pipe cleaners cut up into pieces. You may also wish to add a bit of glitter. When you have it just right, fill your jar with water and close it up. The water will work as a magnifying glass and makes the most beautiful holiday display.

Domestic Arts/Practical Life Skills

Light a Candle on Your Living Wreath

If your family celebrates Advent and you are doing this lesson during that time of year, you can light the candle on your living wreath as your third Advent candle. If you do not celebrate Advent, lighting a candle on your Living Wreath is still a beautiful way to welcome winter. Here is a simple verse to share when doing so:

Color – Rose
Theme – Joy

Burning with our Joy inside,
Candles glow on old Yuletide,

Warmth and light beneath the flame,
Brighten as we speak its name.

Allow the candle to burn as you enjoy your meal, and then snuff your candle out when you are done.

Afternoon Lessons

Use the afternoon hours today to review areas from this week's afternoon lessons that you feel may need a bit more attention. Bring these into your weekend as you find time.

Week Sixteen, Winter
First Grade

Theme: Clocks, Time Travel & Telling Time, Recycling

This Week's Lessons:

Language Arts:
The Prince and The Pea Story
Letter P

Mathematics:
Number 16
Counting from 60 – 70
Counting Backwards
Learning About Time: Calculating the Hour, Minutes & Flip Clock Practice

Social Studies, Geography, Weather, Time:
Learning About Time: Past, Present & Future

Science, Nature Study, Earth Discovery:
Making Potato Paper
Create a Family Time Capsule

Teacher's Classroom Work:
Create a Home Recycling System
Plan a Waste Free Day

For the Caregiver:
Caregiver Meditation: Recycling
Caregiver Focus: Reduce, Reuse and Recycle

Domestic Arts/Practical Life Skills:
Making Vegetable Soup
Waste Free Day
Light Last Candle Living Wreath
Holiday Home Clean Up

Music:
Time, Clocks, Recycling Fingerplays & Songs
Beginning Recorder or Flute

Art/Handwork:
Handwork: Beginner Knitting, Winter Cowl
Art: Recycled Noisemakers
Embroidery Letter P
Alphabet Card Letter P

Form Drawing:
Form Drawing/Art – Stars

Movement, Body Awareness & Health:
Time Travel Game
Sorting Recyclables Game

Supplies Needed for Week Sixteen

Cooking List:

For Vegetable Soup & Potato Paper:
7-9 Large Potatoes, Peeled and Washed
4 Carrots
1 Large Onion
Celery
Additional Vegetables for Soup (i.e. zucchini squash, etc.)
Vegetable or Chicken Broth
Water
Bread or Rolls
Butter

Homeschooling List:

Blackboard
Chalk
A Dried Pea or Bean, Layers of Fabric
Lesson Book
Stockmar Stick Crayons
Stockmar Block Crayons
Colored Pencils
Stockmar Beeswax Modeling Material
Knitting Needles
Super Bulky Single Ply 100% Wool Yarn
Embroidery Needle
Embroidery Floss
White Scrap Fabric
Embroidery Hoop (optional)
Chunky Yarn
Large Knitting Needles (Size 15 or close)
Old Tin Cans with Lids
White Cardstock or Construction Paper
Dried Beans, Macaroni, Pasta and/or Rice
Watercolor Paints
Paintbrush
Glue
Scraps of Old Paper torn into Small Pieces

First Grade Curriculum | WINTER | Little Acorn Learning

Old Newspapers
Blender
Large Bowl
Grater
Water
Staple Gun
Large Rags or Cloths 16x16 or Bigger
Metal Clothing Hanger
Rubber Band
Old Panty Hose
Rolling Pin
Iron
Spray Starch
Plastic Dishpan
Heavy Duty Scissors
Big Bag or Box
Items from Past, Present & Future
Container or Box for Time Capsule
Items to Include in Capsule of Present Time
Four Bins
Photos to Represent Paper, Plastic, Glass and Metal
Sidewalk Chalk

Week Sixteen Book Recommendations

Visit your local library the weekend before to check out books based on your theme for the week. Older children can help you look up the books by author and title. When setting up your play space for the week ahead, mindfully display these books in baskets for the children to enjoy.

Garbage and Recycling ~ Rosie Harlow and Sally Morgan
Why Should I Recycle? ~ Jen Green
Where Does the Garbage Go? ~ Paul Showers and Randy Chewning
Recycle Every Day! ~ Nancy Elizabeth Wallace
Recycle!: A Handbook for Kids ~ Gail Gibbons
EcoArt! ~ Laurie Carlson
The Wartville Wizard ~ by Don Madden
Cecil's New Year's Eve Tail ~ Marie Fritz Perry
Re-Cycles ~ Michael Elsohn Ross
A Box Can Be Many Things ~ Dana Meachen Rau
George Washington's Socks ~ Elvira Woodruff
The Journey Through Time ~ Geronimo Stilton
A Wrinkle in Time ~ Madeleine L'Engle
Almost Time ~ Gary D. Schmidt
Outlaws of Time: The Legend of Sam Miracle ~ N.D. Wilson
A Moment in Time ~ Jennifer Butenas
Telling Time with Big Mama Cat ~ Dan Harper
It's About Time! ~ Stuart J. Murphy
Bunny Day: Telling Time from Breakfast to Bedtime
The Clock Struck One: A Time-Telling Tale ~ Trudy Harris
About Time: A First Look at Time and Clocks ~ Bruce Koscielniak
Two Girls, a Clock and a Crooked House ~ Michael Poore
The Story of Clocks and Calendars ~ Betsy Maestro & Giulio Maestro
The Secret of the Old Cock ~ Carolyn Keene
Clocks and More Clocks ~ Pat Hutchins
The Spaniel Family's Time Capsule Mystery ~ Sharon Ellsberry

Week Sixteen Circle, Songs & Movement

The following songs and verses should be shared during circle time each day this week after you open your circle.

Light a Candle
(if you celebrate Advent, you can replace the word Winter with Advent and Solstice with Christmas in the lyrics)

Light one candle winter's here
Light one candle winter's here
Light one candle winter's here
Solstice time is near. *(clap, clap)*

Light two candles winter's here
Light two candles winter's here
Light two candles winter's here
Solstice time is near. *(clap, clap)*

Light three candles winter's here
Light three candles winter's here
Light three candles winter's here
Solstice time is near. *(clap, clap)*

Light four candles winter's here
Light four candles winter's here
Light four candles winter's here
Solstice time is near. *(clap, clap)*

Old Father Time

Old Father Time is passing by,
His cheeks are ruddy, he's bright of eye;
His beard is white with the snows of time.
His brow is hoary with frost and rime.
It's little he cares for the frost and the cold,
For Old Father Time he never grows old.

Garbage

Pick up garbage and throw it in the bin!
Push it down and stomp it in!

Carry the cans to the street
for the garbage trucks to eat.

When the truck comes roaring by,
workers lift the cans up high.

Garbage falls into the back.
Crush it, mash it, smash it flat!

Set the cans down with a thump.
Now drive that garbage to the dump!

Down at the Dump
(sing to Down by The Station)

Down at the dump, early in the morning,
See the dump trucks standing in a row.

See them dump the garbage
In a great big pile,
Dump, dump, dump, dump,
Watch them go.

Pretty soon our dumps will all be full,
We had better figure out something to do.

We could all recycle
Some of our garbage,

Recycle, recycle,
Watch us go.

The Clock Song
(sing to Wheels on the Bus)

The hands on the clock go round and round,
round and round, round and round
The hands on the clock go round and round,
All through the day.

The short hand on the clock goes from hour to hour,
hour to hour, hour to hour
The short hand on the clock goes from hour to hour
All through the day.

The long hand on the clock goes minute to minute
minute to minute, minute to minute
The long hand on the clock goes minute to minute
All around by fives.

Five Little Garbage Trucks
(a fingerplay – start with five)

Five little garbage trucks, painted green,
Picking up trash to keep the town clean.
They work and they work until they fill up.
Now one of the garbage trucks drives to the dump!

Four little garbage trucks, painted green…

Three little garbage trucks painted green…

Two little garbage trucks painted green…

One little garbage truck painted green…

Hickory, dickory, dock
The mouse ran up the clock
The clock struck one
The mouse ran down
Hickory, dickory, doc

Hickory, dickory, dock
The mouse ran up the clock
The clock struck two
The mouse said, boo
Hickory, dickory, dock

Hickory, dickory, dock

The mouse ran up the clock
The clock struck three
The mouse went, whee
Hickory, dickory, dock

Week Sixteen Blackboard Drawing

Drawing Ideas for This Week: Capital letter P as shown in the prince's cloak over his head or on his clothing, a pea in the bed with 16 blankets, the princess from the story, PRINCE, PRINCESS, PEA, clocks, watches, Father Time, bins of recycling, Roman numeral XVI, SIXTEEN, 16

Week Sixteen Teacher's Classroom Work

1. Create a Home Recycling System

   Spend time this week setting up containers for recycling in your home. If you have a garbage service that will pick up recycling at your residence, check their policy on how they want you to package your recyclables. If you do not have a service, you can take a field trip to your local recycle center to deliver the items. Typically, items should be sorted as follows:

   Newspapers, Magazines and Cardboard – Bundle and Tie
   Plastic, Metal and Glass – Bin or Bag

2. Waste Free Day

   Plan one day this week to spend the entire day as a waste-free day. Here are some ideas:

- Replace disposable products with cloth (napkins, toweling, diapers, etc.)

- Try to find alternatives to using paper

- Get creative with leftover food

- Turn off all lights and unplug all gadgets for as long as possible (candlelight dinner?)

3. Review any handwork before working on projects with your children

Week Sixteen Caregiver Meditation

This Week's Reflection: *Recycling*

"The ultimate test of man's conscience may be his willingness to sacrifice something today for future generations whose words of thanks will not be heard." - Gaylord Nelson, former governor of Wisconsin, co-founder of Earth Day

Making wise choices for our planet now, even though the result may not directly benefit you, is the ultimate way to send love back to the life force that sustains and provides for you. The future of our earth is in our hands. We are raising little children who will inherit this place and live in it. How we teach them to care for this planet is of utmost importance and young children learn best through example. What can you do today to make it a better place for future generations?

Week Sixteen Story

You may remember the tale of The Princess and The Pea. We have adapted it to now be The Prince and The Pea. As an adult, how does it feel reading this story from a different perspective? Does it seem more unkind the way the prince is judged by his appearances? Consider the messages our society sends to our children about gender roles. Dig within yourself and tailor your stories, your example, and your messages in the way you feel most appropriate for the lessons you wish to teach your family and your child.

As we were developing our curriculum, we (and many of our testers) struggled with how often women were being portrayed as helpless, how often they were required to be attractive, and how it seemed the story always was focused on the happy ending being when a man would save her. While the traditional stories are lovely to share, we decided to put a bit of a twist on some of these classic fairy tales to create more balance. In this particular story, our princess is the one who knows just what she wants, as many of our daughters do!

You can enhance this story with simple pieces of fabric and a pea. Layer them one by one as the queen does over the pea.

The Prince and The Pea
`Adapted from the original Princess and The Pea
by Hans Christian Andersen

Once upon a time there was a princess who decided she wanted to marry a prince; but he would have to be a real prince if she was to marry him. She told her brothers and they travelled all over the world to find one, but nowhere could they find a prince worthy of their sister. There were princes enough, but it was difficult to find out whether they were real ones. There was always something about them that was not as it should be. So, the princess was disappointed but kept herself interested in other things, although she would have liked very much to have a real prince for her own.

One evening a terrible storm came on; there was thunder and lightning, and the rain poured down in torrents. Suddenly a knocking was heard at the city gate, and the old king and his sons went to open it.

It was a prince standing out there in front of the gate. But, good gracious! What a sight the rain and the wind had made him look. The water ran down from his hair and clothes; it ran down into the toes of his shoes and out again at the heels. And yet he kept insisting that he was a real prince.

"Well, we'll soon find that out." thought the old queen. But she said nothing, went into the bedroom, took all the bedding off the bedstead, and laid a pea on the bottom; then she took twenty mattresses and laid them on the pea, and then twenty eiderdown beds on top of the mattresses.

On this the prince had to lie all night. In the morning he was asked how he had slept.

"Oh, very badly!" said he. "I have scarcely closed my eyes all night. Heaven only knows what was in the bed, but I was lying on something hard, so that I am black and blue all over my body. It's horrible!"

Now they knew that he was a real prince because he had felt the pea right through the twenty mattresses and the twenty eiderdown beds.

Nobody but a real prince could be as sensitive as that.

So, the princess agreed to take him for her husband, for now she knew that she had a real prince for her own; and the pea was put in the museum, where it may still be seen, if no one has stolen it.

Monday Student Lessons – Week Sixteen

(Baking/Cooking – Purple Day)

Language Arts

1. Begin your lesson time by reading (or telling) *The Prince and The Pea* to your child. Let the children look at the sentences as you read as this visual will aid with their knowledge of letters, words, and sentences. If possible, use simple props to accompany the story as we have suggested.

2. When your story is finished, unveil your blackboard drawing that you have prepared ahead of time as suggested at the beginning of this week's curriculum. If your child has his or her own small blackboard and chalk, have them take a few moments to create their own drawing.

3. Review what your child worked on last week in their lesson book. Have them practice writing the capital letter O a few times on their blackboard or an extra piece of paper. Be sure they have a good grasp of this letter before moving onto the next.

4. In your child's lesson book, have them create a similar image of the Prince from our story (or whatever depiction you used) with the letter P revealed inside. On the righthand side, have your child practice writing the capital letter P. Share this poem as you work to form the letter:

> *Pull down your pencil*
> *Then pick it up off the ground*
> *Go back to the top*
> *A half circle nice and round*

5. Once again practice noticing syllables with your child. Have your child hold their hand under their chin, palm side down. Have them say a word slowly and count how many times their jaw pushes their hand down to count the syllables. Here are a few P words to experiment with:

- Play
- Princess
- Prince
- Pea
- Playground
- Perfect
- President
- Peace
- Playmate

Try this with many different words beginning with all letters. Next, do this same activity by clapping the syllables. Keep this practice going for the next week or two until your child feels confident in recognizing the number of syllables in each word.

Mathematics

1. In addition to the Roman numeral XVI, write down the number 16 and word SIXTEEN in all capital letters for your child to see. Say each letter as you write: S, I, X, T, E, E, N, and the word out loud:

S
I
X
T
E
E
N

SIXTEEN

The pea lay flat beneath the sheets

S
I
X
T
E
E
N

SIXTEEN

16 layers down so very deep

2. Have the child draw images of the number SIXTEEN. They may copy some of the items you made in your blackboard drawing for this week. Your child should then practice writing the number 16, Roman numeral XVI, and the word SIXTEEN in all capital letters on the opposite page of their book. If you feel they need extra time with writing, let them continue to practice as needed. Here is a verse to share when forming the number 16:

> *First a one*
> *And then a six*
> *Number sixteen*
> *Is a simple trick*

3. Now that your child is well versed in numbers 50-60 you can trust that they are able to move more quickly and practice their counting from 60-70. Count everything you can! If your child seems ready, you can expand your four processes math skills to include larger numbers up to 70 as well. Remember to go at your child's pace and pay close attention to how your child learns most effectively.

Domestic Arts/Practical Life Skills

As always, be sure to tie mathematics in when you measure and cook with your child. You can present the following comments and questions to inspire free discussion during your cooking time:

When we cook, we often have a lot of food scraps and leftovers. What are some things you can think of that often get tossed away when we prepare meals?

How can we reuse some of the things we do not use in our recipe? (eat again, use in a different recipe, compost, make something new, etc.)

Today we are making vegetable soup. We will keep some of the food scraps that we do not use for a craft we are doing this week.

It's good for our earth to try hard not to waste things.

Making Vegetable Soup

Save leftover potatoes, carrot peelings and onion skins for this week's Potato Paper craft. Potatoes can be kept fresh covered in a bowl of water in the refrigerator. Carrot peels as well as onion skins can be kept in a sealed container in the refrigerator

Supplies Needed:
2-3 Large Potatoes, Peeled and Washed
4 Carrots
1 Large Onion
Celery
Additional Vegetables for Soup (i.e. zucchini squash, etc.)
Vegetable or Chicken Broth
Water
Bread or Rolls
Butter

Allow children to help wash and dice the vegetables.

Put broth into large pot with ¼ mixture of water. Place vegetables into the pot and simmer until tender.

When the vegetables are tender, salt and pepper to taste and serve with bread and butter. The soup will be very hot – be careful!

Outdoor Time/Nature Walk

Take your children outside each day regardless of the weather. Invest in good rain gear, snow gear and wool undergarments if your location requires it. Do your lessons outdoors whenever possible.

Caregiver Focus

Reduce, Reuse and Recycle

Being mindful requires us to slow down and pay close attention to our words, our thoughts, and our actions. It is the practice of both being still, and also taking action with more intention. Throughout this week, pay close attention to how you use things. Are you grabbing paper products because you are in a rush? Do you take the time to reuse things when possible and not waste? Can you spend time putting leftovers away rather than scraping plates quickly? Are you using too much plastic?

What changes can you make in your home to be more mindful of these things?

Social Studies, Geography, Weather, Time

Learning About Time: Reviewing Introduction to Clocks

1. Review the difference between an analog and digital clock this week. On your analog clock practice counting the 1–12 hour numbers both forward and backward.

2. Review your child's drawing of an analog clock in their lesson book. Copying a real clock, have them now add the four minute lines inside each of the hour spaces on their drawing. Count them with your child and help make the right number of minutes in between each.

3. When out and about, have your child find as many clocks as they can. For digital clocks, have them tell you the numbers they see. You can explain what time that translates to. For analog clocks have them point out which numbers the big and little hands are closest to. You will have an opportunity later in the week to explain how the minute hand position works.

Afternoon Lessons

Handwork: Beginner Knitting, Winter Cowl

Supplies Needed:
Chunky Yarn
Large Knitting Needles (Size 15 or close)

Cast on 20 stitches. Knit first and second row.
Continue onward in garter stitch until piece is approximately 50" long.
Lay flat and twist once in the center. Sew ends together to make circle with twist inside.

Tuesday Student Lessons – Week Sixteen
(Painting – Red Day)

Language Arts

1. Like yesterday, begin your lesson time by continuing to read (or tell) *The Prince and The Pea.* Provide your child with a piece of beeswax modeling material as you read. Let them hold this piece of beeswax as they listen, warming it with their hands so it softens.

2. Have your child form the softened beeswax material into the letter P. Roll it into a long snake, form it just so and then put it back together again. Next, have them form it into the number 16.

3. Open your lesson book and review the work you did yesterday. Have your child trace the letter P number 16 and word SIXTEEN with their fingers.

4. Practice saying the sounds of the letter P. Notice how our mouth forms to make the sound. Bringing awareness to the way our body forms sounds and words is very important. This process helps us to notice the use of air and our body muscles as we communicate.

5. Today we will work on a tongue twister to practice and memorize with your child to help learn the letter P and its sound. Tongue twisters and rhymes are fun ways to learn and help with finding rhythm. As we have begun bringing awareness to syllables, pay careful attention with your child to be sure they get it correctly.

   To begin, say the following tongue twister to your child slowly **and tap one finger on the palm of your other hand to the syllables** to create a pattern for memory:

   > *Peter Piper picked a peck of pickled peppers.*
   > *Did Peter Piper pick a peck of pickled peppers?*
   > *If Peter Piper picked a peck of pickled peppers,*
   > *Where's the peck of pickled peppers Peter Piper picked?*

Mathematics

Counting Backwards

1. Using tangible items continue counting backwards with your children today. This week start from 20 to 1.

2. Write numbers 1 – 30 on your blackboard. Using your finger point to 30 and count backward to the number one. Have your child do this with you.

3. In your child's lesson book, have them draw 40 items on the left side. This could be 40 little dots, trees, buttons, hearts or even simply sticks. Count them together first in order and then backward. Next, on the right side of your child's layout, have them write the number 40 and downward to the number 1. You can help them if they are struggling.

4. Continue these types of exercises over the next week or two aiming to be able to increase the amount of numbers your child can count backwards.

Outdoor Time/Nature Walk

Take your children outside each day regardless of the weather. Invest in good rain gear, snow gear and wool undergarments if your location requires it. Do your lessons outdoors whenever possible.

Social Studies, Geography, Weather, Time

Learning About Time: Hours

1. Explain to your child that the small hand on a clock is the hour hand and this is how we know what hour it is. Show your child an analog clock and which hand is the hour hand. Draw a few analog clocks without hands or minutes and have your child create the hour hand to show various times you dictate. You can also use the template we have provided below.

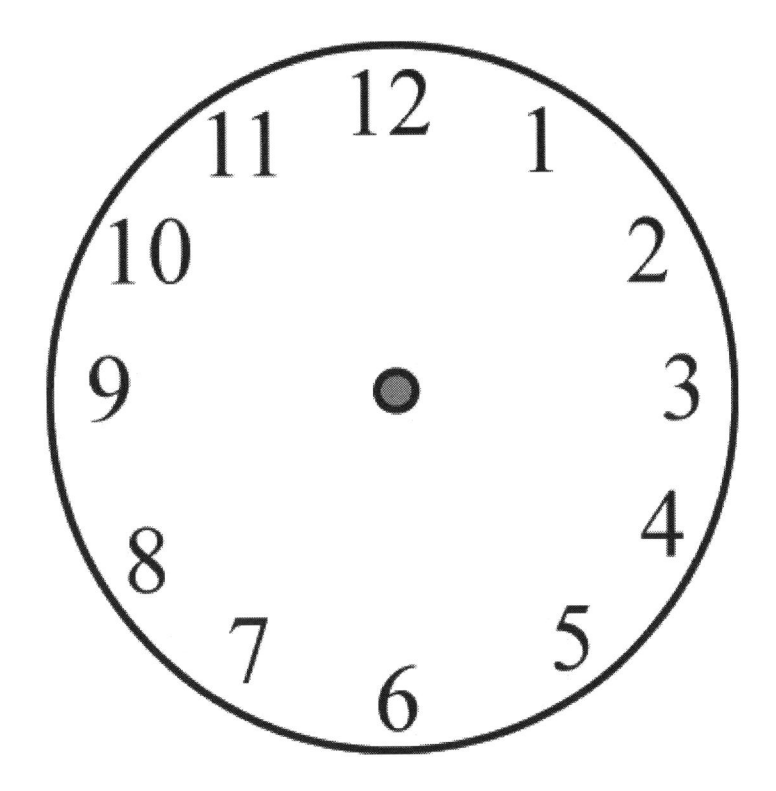

2. Next, draw the hand in between two of the numbers. Ask your child what hour they think it is now. Explain to them that it is still the hour shown <u>before the arrow</u> until it <u>actually hits</u> the next number. Practice this a few times around the clock.

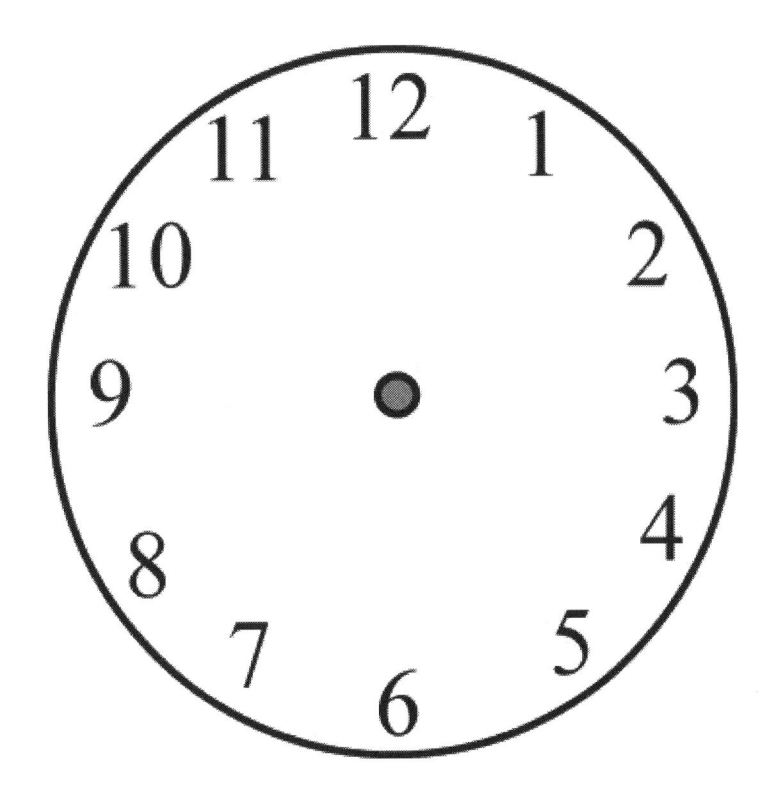

First Grade Curriculum | WINTER | Little Acorn Learning

3. Show your child a digital clock. Have them identify the hour position.

4. Use your lesson book to practice drawing the hours on a clock and different times.

5. Explain that an hour is made up of 60 minutes. We will learn more about minutes in another lesson.

Outdoor Time/Nature Walk

Take your children outside each day regardless of the weather. Invest in good rain gear, snow gear and wool undergarments if your location requires it. Do your lessons outdoors whenever possible.

Afternoon Lessons

Art: Recycled Noisemakers

If you happen to be working on this lesson during the beginning of a new year, these noisemakers would be a great way to celebrate! If not, they can be used as musical instruments and your children can create their own band.

Supplies Needed:
Old Tin Cans with Lids
White Cardstock or Construction Paper
Dried Beans, Macaroni, Pasta and/or Rice
Watercolor Paints
Paintbrush
Glue

Cut a strip that will cover the outside around your tin can. Watercolor paint this strip a beautiful color such as light purple or blue. Let dry. With a different color such as orange or red, watercolor paint another piece of paper. Let dry then have the children cut out small shapes such as stars, moons, the sun, etc. Glue the strip of paper around your tin can. Decorate the strip by gluing the shape cut outs on. Fill the container with beans, pasta and/or rice. Put a layer of glue around rim where lid meets the can. Close lid and let dry.

Wednesday Student Lessons – Week Sixteen
(Coloring – Yellow Day)

Language Arts

1. Practice our tongue twister again. Keep working on this until you have it memorized together. Say the following tongue twister to your child slowly **and tap one finger on the palm of your other hand to the syllables** to create a pattern for memory:

    Peter Piper picked a peck of pickled peppers.
    Did Peter Piper pick a peck of pickled peppers?
    If Peter Piper picked a peck of pickled peppers,
    Where's the peck of pickled peppers Peter Piper picked?

2. In your child's lesson book have them make a drawing of the prince laying on top of the blankets with the pea underneath. You may wish to make SIXTEEN layers of blankets.

3. On the opposite page, your child is likely ready to write simple sentences (do not worry about punctuation at this time). Remember we are still writing in all capital letters. Provide your child with a simple sentence on the blackboard to copy such as:

    THE PRINCE LAID ON THE PEA
    THE PEA WAS UNDER THE PRINCE
    THE PEA IS GREEN
    HE WAS A REAL PRINCE

4. Tonight at bedtime, continue to tell your child the story of *The Prince and The Pea*.

5. When out and about, ask your child to find things that begin with the letter P. This can be done while shopping or when driving in the car. Throughout the week, ask your child to think of all the words they can that begin with the letter P. How many can they come up with? Make a list.

Mathematics

Learning About Time: Calculating the Hour

When your child has a good understanding of how to identify what hour it is, have them work on writing the time down after looking at examples. You can use a real clock, draw them on your blackboard or use this template below. Showing the hour hand the same color as the hour numbers helps with identification.

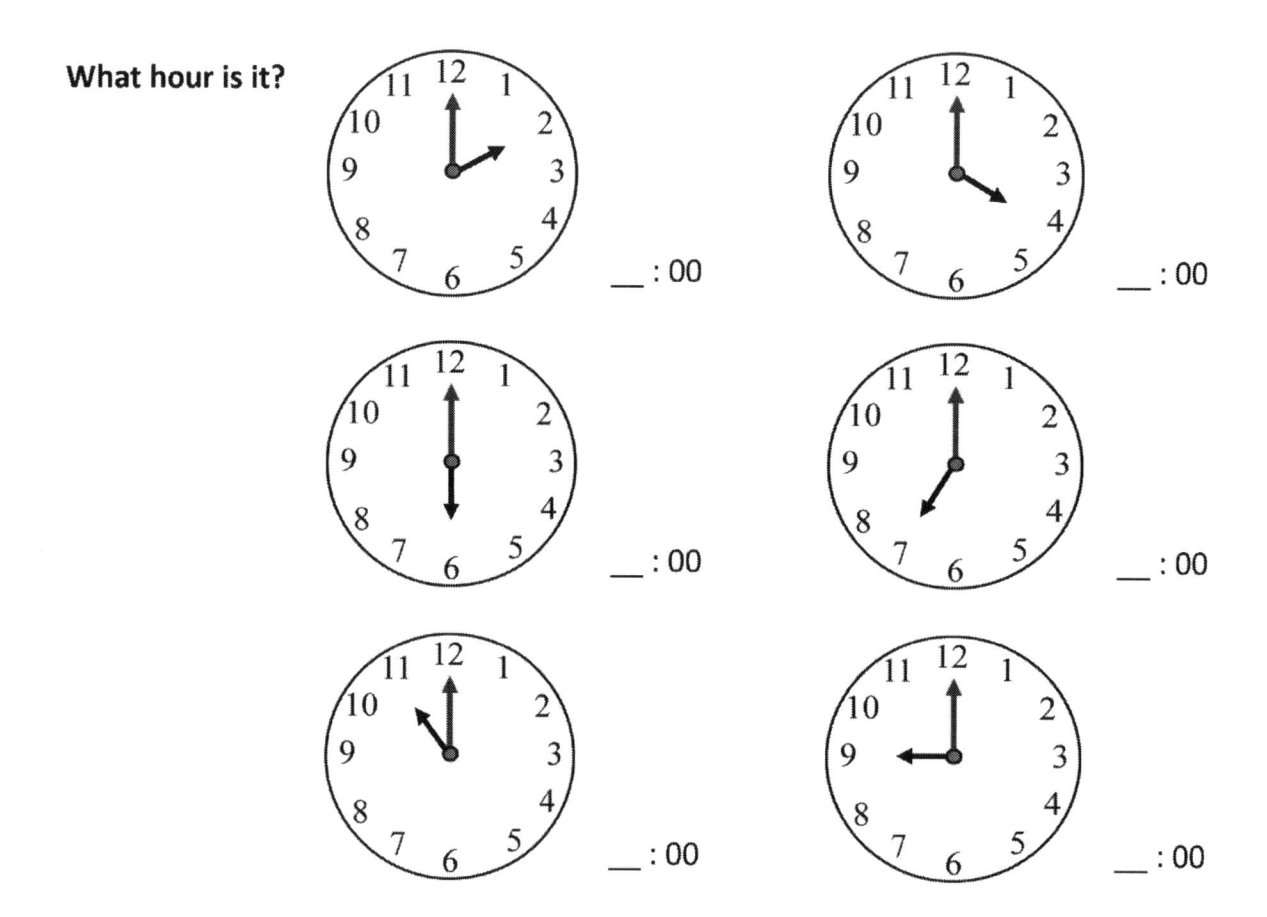

What hour is it?

_ : 00   _ : 00

_ : 00   _ : 00

_ : 00   _ : 00

Outdoor Time/Nature Walk

Take your children outside each day regardless of the weather. Invest in good rain gear, snow gear and wool undergarments if your location requires it. Do your lessons outdoors whenever possible.

Science, Nature Study, Earth Discovery

Making Potato Paper

Have the children help you set up your workspace to make Potato Paper with the leftover potatoes, carrot peelings and onion skins from your Vegetable Soup this week.

This craft is messy and will take up a good amount of time. Take your time and enjoy the process. Cover your workspace with old newspapers and be sure to cover the children's clothing with smocks or aprons.

Here are some questions to inspire free discussion as you work together:

Have you ever wondered where paper comes from?
Paper comes from trees. We need paper for many things, but we also need the trees on our planet, so we have clean air.
Can you tell me how we could make more trees? (plant seeds)
Can you think of a way we can reuse paper?
Old paper can be turned into new paper. This is another way to recycle.

Supplies Needed:
6 Large Peeled Potatoes
Scraps of Old Paper torn into Small Pieces
Old Newspapers
Blender
Large Bowl
Grater
Water
Staple Gun
Large Rags or Cloths 16x16 or Bigger
Metal Clothing Hanger
Rubber Band
Old Panty Hose
Rolling Pin
Iron
Spray Starch
Plastic Dishpan
Heavy Duty Scissors

Have children grate the potatoes into a large bowl. Add an equal amount of torn paper to the bowl. Add water until mixture is covered. Leave to soak.

Make your own framed screen by shaping the wire hanger into a square. Place the square inside the panty hose and secure the top with a rubber band, then cut off excess fabric with heavy duty scissors.

Have children take turns squishing the mixture in the bowl until it is mixed thoroughly.

Add some mix to blender until it is about half full. Add one cup of water and blend until smooth. Add more water as necessary to get mixture smooth. Have children add a few potato skins, onion skins and carrot peels to mixture. Add a little bit of water, as necessary.

Pour some mixture into your plastic dishpan until approximately 6" in the tub. Have children dip the framed screen into the mush. Gently shift the frame side to side under the mixture to get an even layer over the frame.

Slowly lift the frame out of the pan. Let water drain out over the tub. Be sure there are no holes. If there are holes, dip the frame back in.

Lay a clean rag over the top of the frame and mixture. Gently press to release any extra water. Turn the frame and rag upside down onto a flat surface with newspaper. Lift off the frame. Cover the mixture with another rag. Roll the rags with rolling pin to release excess water and flatten paper.

Carefully peel off the top rag and turn the bottom layer over onto a smooth surface, glass, or mirror – this can be a vertical surface, the mixture will stick until it dries. Carefully peel off the remaining rag. Leave to dry overnight.

To smooth paper, spray with starch and iron on warm until smooth.

Use your Potato Paper for card making, writing, drawing or other crafts.

Afternoon Lessons

Music: Continue Practicing Flute or Recorder

Thursday Student Lessons – Week Sixteen
(Crafting/Games – Orange Day)

Language Arts

1. Continue to tell your child the story of *The Prince and The Pea.*

2. Alphabet Cards

    Supplies Needed:
    Heavy White Cardstock
    Beeswax Stick Crayons
    Scissors

    Spend time cutting cards out of cardstock with your child. Using beeswax crayons, continue to finish drawing each letter we have learned so far and include the letter P. Next to the letter, have your child draw an image that begins with it. Using scissors, round the corners of these cards and keep working on them throughout the year. You can use them in your lessons and for an upper case and lowercase match game later in the curriculum when we learn those as well.

3. Continue reading simple reader books together.

4. Practice saying the sound of P. Notice how our mouth forms to make the sound. Bringing awareness to the way our body forms sounds and words is very important. This process helps us to notice the use of air and our body muscles as we communicate.

5. Print out or share the following photos and practice saying them together with your child. Your child may be ready to copy these words into their lesson book.

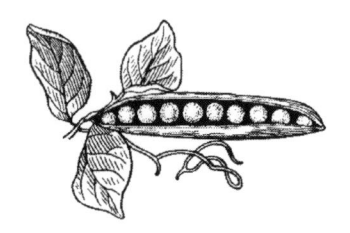

PEA

PRINCE

PRINCESS

PENNY

PIZZA

First Grade Curriculum | WINTER | Little Acorn Learning

Mathematics

1. Math Gnomes & Four Processes

   Spend time using your gnomes to practice repetitive addition, addition, subtraction, multiplication, and division with tangible items. If your child is able, work up to the number 70 with these math facts. Your child can write the equations in their lesson book along with a photo of each lesson.

2. Review Ordinal Numbers

   We will review ordinal numbers for the last time this week with the children. Tell stories that include ordinal numbers in description and text. Practice these with tangible items and work at your own pace in your lesson book to both write the numerical format and the written format as follows:

1st	FIRST
2nd	SECOND
3rd	THIRD
4th	FOURTH
5th	FIFTH
6th	SIXTH
7th	SEVENTH
8th	EIGHTH
9th	NINTH
10th	TENTH

Outdoor Time/Nature Walk

Take your children outside each day regardless of the weather. Invest in good rain gear, snow gear and wool undergarments if your location requires it. Do your lessons outdoors whenever possible.

Social Studies, Geography, Weather, Time

Learning About Past, Present & Future

Spend time talking with your child about past, present and future today. Explain that where we are now is the present. What happened before is in the past and the future is yet to come. Show photos of the past to your child. Ask your child how they imagine themselves to be in the future.

In your child's lesson book on the left hand side, have them make three boxes and a drawing in each. These drawings can be of themselves: past, present, and future or of any other concept you discuss. On the right hand side, have your child practice writing the words: PAST, PRESENT AND FUTURE

Movement, Body Awareness & Health

1. Time Travel Game

   Supplies Needed:
   Big Bag or Box
   Items from Past, Present & Future

   This is a fun game and can be used to simply practice this concept with items from your family story (such as old photos, heirlooms, etc.) or can be expanded to help your child learn past, present and possible future historical events and times. Think of your curriculum and how to weave this game into your current learning.

   Tell your children you will be playing a time travel game. Ask them to close their eyes and pick an item out from the time travel machine (or bag). When they open their eyes, have them first guess whether the item represents something in the past, present or future. Then ask them to talk about what it is and how it falls within the category. Before starting again, be sure to discuss with your child each item's relevance and you can take a few moments to read a bit of history or tell a story about each item.

   Continue until your bag is empty. Your child may wish to make their very own time travel machine and have you play next.

2. Sorting Recyclables Game

   Talk to your children about how people can save their used paper, cardboard, plastic, glass, and metal and recycle them into new things.

   Explain that in order to recycle at home or school, we must sort these things into bins before it is taken to a recycling plant.

At the plant, they turn these things into new things by melting them or mixing them with other material.

Supplies Needed:
Four Bins with a Photo Representing One of Each of the Following:
Paper, Plastic, Glass and Metal

Put all items in a pile and work together, allowing each child a turn, sorting the appropriate material into the correct bin. Talk about the importance of recycling and where the items will go after they leave your home.

Afternoon Lessons

1. Form Drawing/Art – Stars

   With sidewalk chalk draw a star outdoors. Label each point 1-5. Have your child walk from one point along the line to the next until they have formed a complete star.

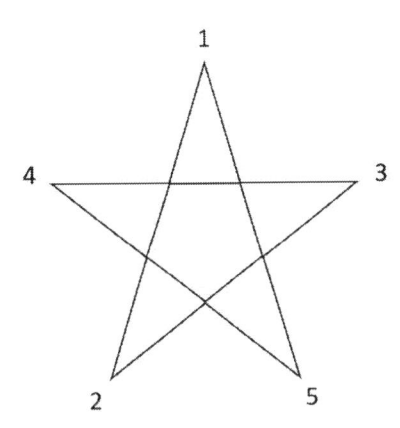

2. Standing tall your child can then expand both legs and arms to be a star themselves.

Here is a verse to share:

I stand erect between earth and sky
The center of the world am I

My right hand points to the cold north star
My left hand points to where the hot lands are

Behind my back is the rising sun
In front of me is where day is done

North, south, east, and west
Where I am is the best

3. In your child's lesson book, have them practice making all different sizes of stars. They can work from one point to the next just as they did outside (and as the image above). They can then color in all their stars with various colors.

4. Handwork: Hand Stitching/Embroidery

    Supplies Needed:
    Embroidery Needle
    Embroidery Floss
    White Scrap Fabric
    Embroidery Hoop (optional)
    Scissors

    Using our embroidery instructions, work with your child to make a letter P embroidery piece. You can do this with a simple running stitch, or you may choose to learn more complicated stitches together.

Friday Student Lessons – Week Sixteen
(Modeling/Housework – Green Day)

Language Arts

1. Today have your child continue to practice writing the letter P in their lesson book on unlined paper.

2. In your child's lesson book, have them practice writing the alphabet from A-P copying each letter a few times on each line.

3. Ask your child to tell YOU the story of *The Prince and The Pea*.

4. Today you can explore some words that have silent letters inside. Make a point to point them out to your child when you see them in your everyday activities and while reading together. Here are some examples to put on your blackboard and ask your child to circle the letter that remains silent:

Cu**p**board
Thum**b**
Ras**p**berry
Clim**b**
Knee
Li**gh**t

Mathematics

Learning About Time: Minutes

1. Review the hour hand lesson we learned earlier this week. Next, explain to your child that the large hand on a clock is the minute hand. Show your child an analog clock and which hand is the minute hand. Draw a few analog clocks without hands or minutes and have your child create both the hour hand and the minute hand to show various times you dictate (it helps to make the two hands in different colors). You can also use the template we have provided below.

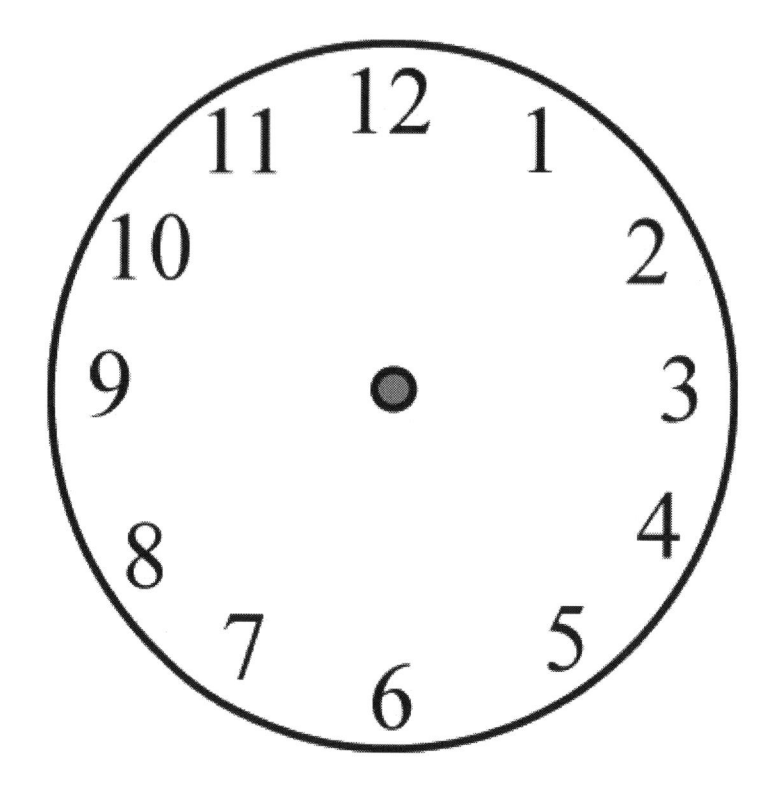

2. Show your child a digital clock. Have them identify the minute positions.

3. Use your lesson book to practice drawing the hours and minutes on a clock and different times.

4. Explain that an hour is made up of 60 minutes. Also explain that one minute is made up of 60 seconds. We will learn more about seconds next week. Begin introducing seconds by simply counting to 60 and watching a digital clock change from minute to minute.

Learning About Time: Telling Time Flip Clock

Here is a creative way to teach young children how to tell time and memorize the minute positions. This concept can be made even more beautifully with your own artwork or you can simply use our templates provided here. Simply cut the clocks and hands out carefully. On the clock with the hour numbers cut on the dotted lines so the hour numbers can be folded down. Using a brad, put the hour number clock on top and the red minute number clock on bottom. Be sure to also attach the clock hands on top. Use a bit of tape to secure the two clocks to the correct positions. Your child can then fold down the flaps to check which minute position it is when practicing.

First Grade Curriculum | WINTER | Little Acorn Learning

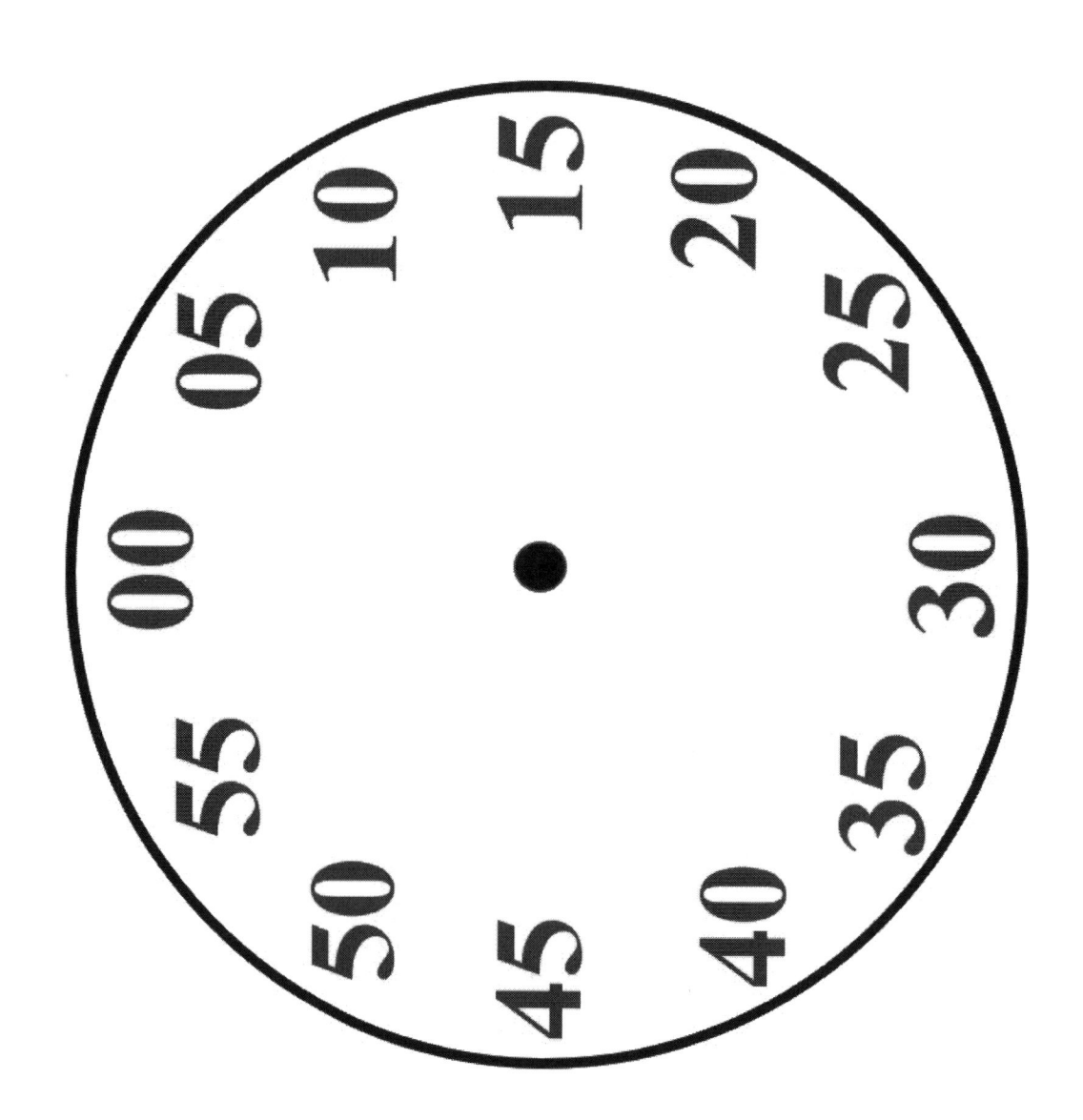

First Grade Curriculum | WINTER | Little Acorn Learning

Learning About Time: Calculating the Minutes

When your child is ready, they can next learn how to calculate the minutes on a clock. Start simply. Show your child that the minutes are counted in fives. Count along the clock by fives together. Next, using your Flip Clock, explain the minute positions. This lesson may take some time. Do not worry if you must work on this for a few weeks together. When ready, have them work on writing down the minutes on an analog clock after looking at examples. You can use a real clock, draw them on your blackboard or use this template below. Showing the minute hand the same color as the minute numbers in position helps with identification.

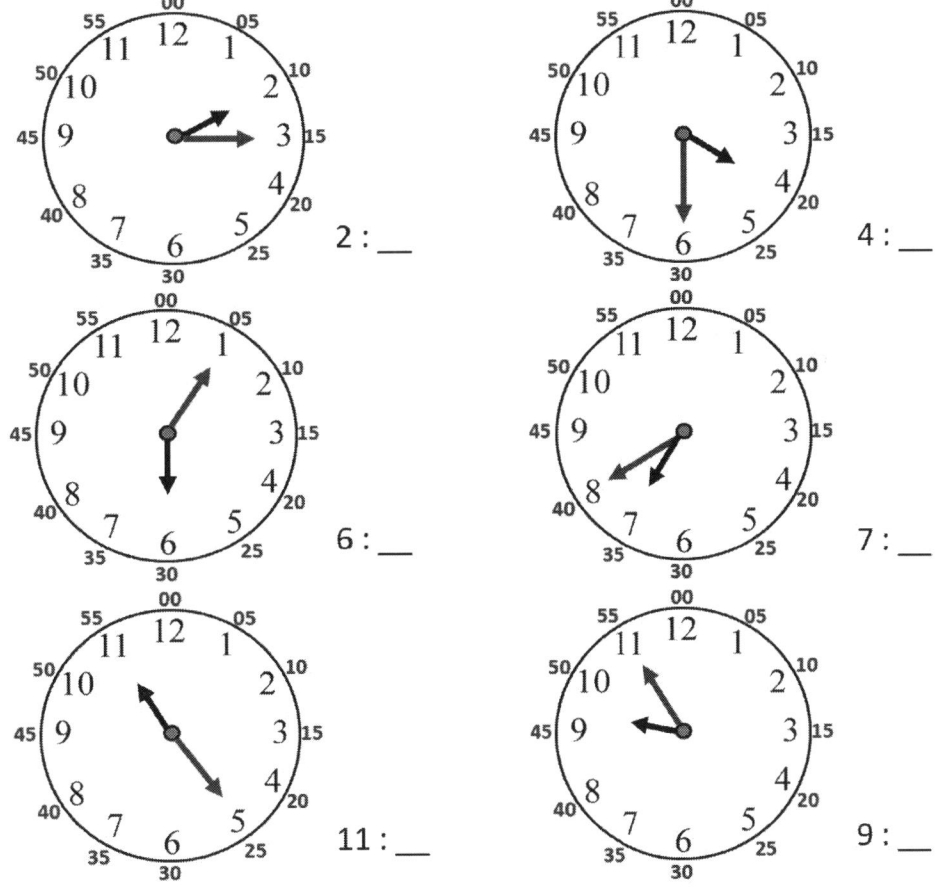

How many minutes after the hour is it?

2 : __

4 : __

6 : __

7 : __

11 : __

9 : __

First Grade Curriculum | WINTER | Little Acorn Learning

Outdoor Time/Nature Walk

Take your children outside each day regardless of the weather. Invest in good rain gear, snow gear and wool undergarments if your location requires it. Do your lessons outdoors whenever possible.

Science, Nature Study, Earth Discovery

Creating a Family Time Capsule

Supplies Needed:
Container or Box for Time Capsule
Items to Include in Capsule of Present Time

Time is such a mystery and to young children it can be amazing for them to imagine the world before and after the present moment. Showing your children photographs from long ago of your family or history is a wonderful way to open up a discussion about past, present and future.

This is a fun activity to do around the end of the year or upcoming new year, but it can be done anytime. You will need to set a special date to open your time capsule and it should be far away, so it really strikes you how things have changed. Maybe a homeschool graduation or a special birthday year?

Gather up items together that capture where you are in time. Some ideas:

- a current newspaper
- photographs from the last year or two
- a letter to each family member or to your future self
- descriptions of the latest technology (phones, Alexa, television, headphones, etc.)
- government information such as president, laws, governors of your state, etc.
- a description of what each member of your family is doing this year (work, homeschool, activities, etc.)
- photos of your pets, ages, and information
- prices of common store bought items or sales clippings
- most popular songs, movies, clothing, styles, trends of the year
- a description of what each one of you expects the world to be like when you open your capsule

Have the children help you fill up your container (capsule) and secure it tight. Think of a safe place to hide it away where it will be safe for years to come. Make a reminder somehow of when to open your capsule together.

Domestic Arts/Practical Life Skills

1. Light a Candle on Your Living Wreath

   If your family celebrates Advent and you are doing this lesson during that time of year, you can light the last candle on your living wreath. If you do not celebrate Advent, lighting a candle on your Living Wreath is still a beautiful way to welcome winter. Here is a simple verse to share when doing so:

   > Color – Purple
   > Theme – Peace
   >
   > *Peace it comes*
   > *We rise above*
   > *Now is time to spread our love*

   Allow the candle to burn as you enjoy your meal, and then snuff your candle out when you are done.

2. Holiday Clean Up

   Depending on when you are using this curriculum, it may be time to clean up after the holiday season. Have your children help you put the house back in order and clean up. Vacuum up pine needles, dispose of wrapping paper, wash, dry and put away silverware and china. Be sure to find homes for new toys and presents if applicable. Regardless of the time of year, doing a reorganization and clean up is always refreshing and your children are quite capable in helping.

Afternoon Lessons

Use the afternoon hours today to review areas from this week's afternoon lessons that you feel may need a bit more attention. Bring these into your weekend as you find time.

Week Seventeen, Winter
First Grade

Theme: Nocturnal & Diurnal Animals, Warmth

This Week's Lessons:

Language Arts:
The Wolf and The Quick Little Lamb Story
Letter Q

Mathematics:
Number 17
Counting from 70 - 80
Determining Relative Length & Height
Methods of Multiplication

Social Studies, Geography, Weather, Time:
Learning About Time: Half Hours & Seconds

Science, Nature Study, Earth Discovery:
Learning About Animals: Nocturnal & Diurnal
Learning About Animals: Echolocation, Hibernation & Migration

Teacher's Classroom Work:
Creating Warmth in Your Home
Make a Homeschool Felt Board

For the Caregiver:
Caregiver Meditation: Warmth
Caregiver Focus: Preserving Energy

Domestic Arts/Practical Life Skills:
Making Bear Print Snacks
Sewing Herbal Eye Pillows
Folding

Music:
Animal and Warmth Fingerplays & Songs
Beginning Recorder or Flute

Art/Handwork:
Handwork: Sewing, Herbal Eye Pillows
Art: Making Bear Tracks & Clay Caves
Embroidery, Letter Q
Alphabet Card Letter Q

Form Drawing:
Form Drawing/Art – Trees in a Row

Movement, Body Awareness & Health:
Yoga for Children: Butterfly & Child's Pose
Mitten Match Game
Evening Flashlight Tag

Supplies Needed for Week Seventeen

Cooking List:

<u>For Bear Print Snack:</u>
Pears Halves
Yogurt
Sliced Bananas
Cashews

Homeschooling List:

Blackboard
Chalk
White Cotton or Wool, Small Box, Gray or Brown Wool, Silk
Lesson Book
Stockmar Stick Crayons
Stockmar Block Crayons
Colored Pencils
Stockmar Beeswax Modeling Material
Embroidery Needle
Embroidery Floss
White Scrap Fabric
Embroidery Hoop (optional)
Heavy White Cardstock
Scissors
Piece of Plywood or Heavy Cardboard
Felt or Flannel Fabric large enough to cover board
Extra Felt, Velcro or Sandpaper
Contact Paper or Laminator
Glue
Staple Gun
Brown or Black Modeling Clay or Playdough
Dried Lavender or Chamomile Leaves
Flax Seed
Thread
Fabric
Sewing Needed or Sewing Machine
Plaster of Paris
Measuring Cup

First Grade Curriculum | WINTER | Little Acorn Learning

Water
Container to Mix Plaster
Spoon and Knife
Shallow Pan or Tub
Sand or Dirt
Sharp Pencil, Nail or Stick
Magnifying Glasses
Nature Notebooks/Journal
Field Book
Camera

Week Seventeen Book Recommendations

Visit your local library the weekend before to check out books based on your theme for the week. Older children can help you look up the books by author and title. When setting up your play space for the week ahead, mindfully display these books in baskets for the children to enjoy.

Once A Wolf: How Wildlife Biologists Fought to Bring Back the Gray Wolf ~ Stephen R. Swinburne and Jim Brandenburg
From Sheep to Sweater (Start to Finish) ~ by Robin Nelson
Charlie Needs a Cloak ~ Tomie dePaola
Red Berry Wool ~ Robyn Eversole
Warm as Wool ~ Scott Russell Sanders and Helen Cogancherry
Animals That Hibernate ~ Larry Dane Brimner
Do Not Disturb ~ Margery Facklam
The Mitten ~ Jan Brett
Animals in Winter ~ Henrietta Bancroft
Annie and the Wild Animals ~Jan Brett
Little Penguin's Tale ~Audrey Wood
Little Polar Bear Finds a Friend ~ Hans de Beer
What Do Animals Do in Winter? ~ Melvin Berger and Gilda Berger
Winter Rabbit ~ Patrick Yee
The Bear Snores On ~ Karma Wilson
The Big Snow ~ Berta and Elmer Hader
Footprints in the Snow ~ Cynthia Benjamin
Chipmunk At Hollow Tree Lane ~ Victoria Sherrow
Sleepy Bear ~ Lydia Dabcovich
Time to Sleep ~ Denise Fleming
Wake Me in Spring ~ James Preller
The Tasty Treat: The Nocturnals ~ Tracey Hecht
Out of Sight Till Tonight! All About Nocturnal Animals ~ Tish Rabe
Explore My World Nighttime ~ Jill Esbaum
Where Are the Night Animals? ~ Mary Ann Fraser
Owling: Enter the World of the Mysterious Birds of the Night: Mark Wilson
Keepers of the Night: Native American Stories and Nocturnal Activities for Children ~ Michael J. Caduto
Moonlight Animals – Elizabeth Golding
Anybody Home? ~ Marianne Berkes
Night Creepers ~ Linda Stanek & Shennen Bersani
Daytime Nighttime, All Through the Year ~ Diane Lang & Andrea Gabriel

First Grade Curriculum | WINTER | Little Acorn Learning

Week Seventeen Circle, Songs & Movement

The following songs and verses should be shared during circle time each day this week after you open your circle.

Five Wise Owls
(a fingerplay, begin with five fingers)

Five Wise Owls perched on a door.
One flapped his wings and then there were four.

Four wise owls sat down to tea.
One spilled his tea and then there were three.

Three wise owls hooted who, who, whoooo!
One lost his voice and then there were two.

Two wise owls could not find any fun.
"I am going to nap" he said, and then there was one.

One lonely owl saw the rising sun.
He flew off to his home and then there were none.

Baa, baa, black sheep, have you any wool?
Yes, sir, yes, sir, three bags full;
One for the master, one for the dame,

One for the little boy that lives in the lane.
Baa, baa, black sheep, have you any wool?
Yes, sir, yes, sir, three bags full

Mary's Lamb

Mary had a little lamb,
Its fleece was white as snow;
And everywhere that Mary went,
The lamb was sure to go.
He followed her to school one day,
That was against the rule;
It made the children laugh and play,
To see a lamb at school.

So the teacher turned him out,
But still he lingered near,
And waited patiently about,
Till Mary did appear.
Then he ran to her, and laid
His head upon her arm,
As if he said, "I'm not afraid,
You'll keep me from all harm."

"What makes the lamb love Mary so?"
The eager children cry.
"Oh, Mary loves the lamb, you know,"
The teacher did reply.

Racoon Racoon
(to the tune of Twinkle, Twinkle)

Raccoon, raccoon, climbing a tree,
Wearing a mask, you can't fool me.

Hiding there so I can't see
What you're doing in that tree.

Raccoon, raccoon, climbing a tree,
Wearing a mask, you can't fool me.

Who flies around in the dark of night?
Who glides on wings over silent night?
Who eats his dinner by late moonlight?
It's a little hoot owl with his owl eyesight!

Who who, who who, little hoot owl.
Who who, who who, little hoot owl.
Who who, who who, little hoot owl.
It's a little hoot owl with his owl eyesight!

The Frog's Goodbye

Goodbye, little children, I'm going away,
In my snug little home all winter to stay.
I seldom get up, once I'm tucked in my bed,
And as it grows colder, I cover my head.

I sleep very quietly all winter through,
And really enjoy it; there's nothing to do,
The flies are all gone, so there's nothing to eat,
And I take this time to enjoy a good sleep.

My bed is a nice little hole in the ground,
Where snug as a bug in the winter I'm found.
You might think long fasting would make me grow thin,
But no! I stay plump as when I go in.

And now, little children, goodbye, one and all,
Some warm day next spring I shall give you a call;
I'm quite sure to know when to get out of bed,
When I feel the warm sun shining down on my head.

Winter Fingerplay

Winter is cold
(hug yourself and shiver)

There is snow in the sky
(flutter fingers above your head)

The squirrel gathers nuts
(pretend to gather nuts)

And the wild geese fly
(flap arms)

The fluffy red fox
(cup hands over head to form ears)

Has his fur to keep warm
(stroke arms as if stroking fur)

The bear's in her cave
(form a cave shape with your arms)

Sleeping all through the storm
(fold hands under cheek and pretend to sleep)

Here is a Cave

Here is a cave.
(bend fingers to form cave)

Inside is a bear.
(put thumb inside fingers)
Now he comes out.
(thumb out)
To get some fresh air.

He stays out all summer
In sunshine and heat.

He hunts in the forest
For berries to eat.
(move thumb in circle)

When snow starts to fall
He hurries inside.

His warm little cave
(thumb in)
And there he will hide.

Snow covers the cave
Like a fluffy white rug.
(cover with other hand)

Inside the bear sleeps
All cozy and snug.

First Grade Curriculum | WINTER | Little Acorn Learning

Five Little Squirrels
(a fingerplay – begin with five fingers)

Five little squirrels with acorns to store.
One went to sleep and then there were four!

Four little squirrels hunting acorns in a tree.
One fell down, and now there are three!

Three little squirrels wondering what to do.
One got lost, and now there are two!

Two little squirrels tossing acorns for fun.
One got tired, and now there is one!

One little squirrel playing in the sun.
He ran away, now there are none.

Week Seventeen Blackboard Drawing

Drawing Ideas for This Week: Capital letter Q as shown in the shape of the sheepfold (a sheepfold can be circular with stones or fencing, add a line outward for the Q or simply put a capital letter Q on the door), wolf, sheep, little lamb hiding, full moon over meadow, day and nighttime animals, bear in cave, squirrel in snow, animal tracks, Roman numeral XVII, SEVENTEEN, 17

Week Seventeen Teacher's Classroom Work

1. Creating Warmth

    This week spend time making sure your home is a place of warmth. Some ideas and suggestions:

    - Each child can have his or her own space for napping or relaxing. Purchase wool blankets, sheepskin rugs, natural bedding, and other cozy materials to assist with this.

    - Wake early and start a fire in the fireplace or woodstove before the children wake up.

    - In the winter months, start a ritual of having warm decaffeinated tea with your morning snack (herbals are wonderful).

    - Give each child a pair of indoor shoes or slippers that they wear throughout the day.

    - Keep the children very warm and dressed in wool undergarments, warm hats, gloves, and scarves.

    - Keep an extra sweater or robe for each child handy on a special hook with their name or symbol.

    - If you knit or do handcrafts, pull out your warm yarns and fibers and display them in baskets for easy access.

2. Make lots of warm soups and breads together during the winter months. See our Winter Childcare Menu for ideas on our website www.littleacornlearning.com

3. Felt Board

    Supplies Needed:
    Piece of Plywood or Heavy Cardboard
    Felt or Flannel Fabric large enough to cover board
    Extra Felt, Velcro or Sandpaper
    Contact Paper or Laminator
    Glue
    Staple Gun

    Make a felt board for your learning area. This board can be used to tell stories, to learn letters and numbers and to add props during lessons. It can also be used to keep children busy indoors and in the car.

    Stretch fabric across board and staple to back on all sides pulling tightly. You can print out photos of all kinds, laminate them and glue sandpaper or Velcro to the back to use with your Felt Board.

4. Review any handwork before working on projects with your children

Week Seventeen Caregiver Meditation

This Week's Reflection: *Warmth*

"Perhaps I am a bear, or some hibernating animal underneath, for the instinct to be half asleep all winter is so strong in me." ~ *Anne Morrow Lindbergh*

Winter is a time of sleep, of hibernation, a time when many living creatures withdraw from the outside world and go deep within to rest and keep warm. How can we discover this deep rest and warmth in our busy lives?

Warmth is important both physically and emotionally for every human being. Young children need to be dressed and cared for in a way that warms their bodies and souls. And, you need to find time to warm yourself with the things you love and surround yourself with people you enjoy.

It is also important to find the time to go deep within and to slow down like our winter animal friends do. Become the caregiver of your own body and soul and tend to yourself during these cold and darker months. Spend time this week meditating on how you can create a warm environment for yourself, your family and those you invite into your home.

Week Seventeen Story

This week's story ties into our theme very well by incorporating both the sheep and the wolf. It is a favorite among the children who use our program! When talking to the children about these animals, explore the types of feelings they bring forth. The sheep: innocent, pure, and passive. The wolf: hunter, fierce, and aggressive. Do the children see these animals in the same way that you do?

If you would like to use props for this week's story, consider white cotton or wool rolled tightly to symbolize the sheep. You can keep some contained inside a small open box for the sheepfold. Have another gray or brown piece of material to use for the wolf. Small felted, stuffed or wooden animals would work just as well. The little lamb can crawl underneath and to the center of a silk when it goes into the thorn-bush. This story can be told in parts over the week if you have children that cannot sit for long.

The Wolf and The Quick Little Lamb

Part 1

Once there was a little lamb. He had soft white wool and pretty bright eyes, and he lived with his brothers and sisters and the old mama sheep on a big farm. All day long the lambs played in a field. But at night, when the sun began to go down behind the hill, the old farmer came, and locked them all up in a place called the quiet sheepfold, where they would be safe and warm until the morning.

Now the little lambs did not like this at all. They thought it was horrid to be locked up while the meadow was still warm and sunny, and they fretted and grumbled because they had to come in so early. But when the old mama sheep told them it would soon be quite dark outside, and that then a great wolf would come prowling around looking for little lambs to eat, they were glad to be safe inside, all but this naughty and quick little lamb who liked to have his own way. He wanted to see what the dark was like. He said he wasn't afraid of an old wolf; he didn't believe there was one, and if there was, it couldn't hurt him; he could run faster than any old wolf.

At last, one day, he crept behind a big bush and kept as still as a mouse until the mama sheep and his brothers and sisters were all locked up in the quiet sheepfold and the old farmer had gone away to his house. Then he scampered out. How nice it was to be out all alone by himself! He could not keep still a moment; he was so happy. He ran round and round the big meadow. He nibbled at the green grass and sweet clover, and by and by, when he was thirsty, trotted off to the brook and took a good long drink of the cool water. Then he scampered through the field again and rolled over and over in the soft long grass. The sun went lower and lower behind the hill, until at last he was quite gone, and the quick little lamb could not see him anymore. It grew darker and darker. Then the stars came out, one by one, and blinked at him in such a strange way that he began to think he would not like being alone in the night, after all.

Part 2

Then, up from behind the dark woods, came the big round moon. As it rose higher and higher in the sky, it seemed to be looking right at him. He tried to hide, but everywhere he went the moon was watching him, and seemed to be saying, " You naughty and quick little lamb! You naughty and quick little lamb!"

Big black shadows began to move over the fields. He had never seen anything like that in the daytime, and it frightened him. He was too frightened to play now, and he didn't even feel hungry anymore. The night wind swept through the field, and the dew came down and wet the grass and his pretty coat and his poor little feet. He was so cold, he shivered.

Just then, from out the dark woods came a dreadful sound. It was the howl of the old wolf. Oh, how frightened the little lamb was! How he ran! Through the cold, wet grass, over briers and stones, and up the rough, dark road, never stopping till, all out of breath, he reached the quiet sheepfold.

The door was shut. He pushed against it with all his might, and cried, "Oh, let me in! Please let me in! "

But the old farmer had locked it tight, and it would not open.

"Oh, let me in! " cried the quick little lamb, as he butted his poor little head against the door. "Let me in; the old wolf is coming! Oh, please let me in!"

And the mama sheep heard him, and you cannot think how sad and worried she felt to have her little lamb out there in the cold and dark, and the old wolf coming, too.

"Oh, my little lamb!" she called through the door, "how did you get out there?" And the little lamb said, "I stayed out to see the dark; but, oh, if you only will let me in, I'll never, never be naughty anymore."

And the poor mama sheep cried, "Oh, I cannot open the door!" And just then came that dreadful sound again, the howl of the old wolf, nearer and nearer. The quick little lamb heard it; how it frightened him! The old mama sheep heard it, too, and oh, how frightened she was for her little lamb!

"Oh, my child, my child!" she called through the door. "Run, run quick to the thorn-bush, and creep away under to the very middle, and stay there all night long, so the old wolf will not get you! Oh, run! Run quickly, my good and quick little lamb, my precious little lamb! "

And the little lamb ran as fast as he could to the thorn-bush, and pushed away under it, to the very middle, as the mama sheep had told him. The branches grew very close to the ground, and the big, ugly thorns stuck into him and tore his pretty coat and scratched him. But he did not care for that or for anything, if only the old wolf did not get him. And there he lay all in a heap, he was so frightened.

Part 3

Just then, up came the old wolf, snarling and growling. He went running and jumping round and round the bush, poking his nose in everywhere, trying to get the quick little lamb.

But the sharp thorns stuck into his nose and eyes, and hurt him so much, he was glad to jump back. Over and over again he tried, but every time the big, ugly thorns stuck into him and made him go howling back. And this made the old wolf so mad that he growled and snarled all the more.

The little lamb was so frightened. Oh, how he wished he were with his mama safe in the quiet sheepfold!

It was dreadful! But at last the long night was over, and down under the thorn-bush came little streaks of light that grew bigger and brighter every moment, and at last the old wolf crept away. He could hear him snarling and growling as he ran across the fields, but he was quickly lost to sight in the shadows of the dark woods.

The little lamb began to breathe easier now, but still he did not dare to crawl out from under the thorn bush just yet, for fear the old wolf might come back and catch him after all. So he kept very quiet and just waited for the sun to come up and make it all bright day, for then he knew the quiet sheepfold would open and his mama and all his brothers and sisters would surely come and look for him.

Then all the little birds began to twitter and chirp, and the morning air blew fresh and cool, rustling the leaves, and bringing the sweet odor of the clover from the meadows; and pretty soon the sun shone right under the bush, and then he heard his mama calling, "Oh, my sweet little lamb, are you there? " Oh, how glad he was to hear his dear mama's voice once more and know he was safe at last!

And when he crawled out with his pretty coat all dirty and torn, the good mama sheep just ran up and loved him and called him her "precious little lamb" over and over and over. And all his brothers and sisters crowded around him and smiled on him, they were so glad to find him safe and sound, and to know the old wolf did not get him.

Then the mama sheep took him down to the brook, and washed him and gave him some of the sweetest grass she could find for his breakfast, and let him stay in the warm sun, close by her side, all day because he had been so cold and frightened all night long. And after that he never wanted to have his own way anymore, but did whatever the mama sheep told him, and tried to be a good little lamb and stay safe and warm.

Monday Student Lessons – Week Seventeen

(Baking/Cooking – Purple Day)

Language Arts

1. Begin your lesson time by reading (or telling) part one of *The Wolf and The Quick Little Lamb* to your child. Let the children look at the sentences as you read as this visual will aid with their knowledge of letters, words and sentences. If possible, use simple props to accompany the story as we have suggested.

2. When your story is finished, unveil your blackboard drawing that you have prepared ahead of time as suggested at the beginning of this week's curriculum. If your child has his or her own small blackboard and chalk, have them take a few moments to create their own drawing.

3. Review what your child worked on last week in their lesson book. Have them practice writing the capital letter P a few times on their blackboard or an extra piece of paper. Be sure they have a good grasp of this letter before moving onto the next.

4. In your child's lesson book, have them create a similar image of the Quiet Sheepfold or the Quick Little Lamb from our story (or whatever depiction you used) with the letter Q revealed inside. On the righthand side, have your child practice writing the capital letter Q. Share this poem as you work to form the letter:
    Capital Q is like a quarter to spend.
    Make a line when you are at the end.

5. Letter Flashlight Learning

    Using letter cut outs and a flashlight, let your child play and spell words out on the wall. Hanging the letters by tape or thread across a hanger or dowel can help position the letters while you hold the flashlight.

Mathematics

1. In addition to the Roman numeral XVII, write down the number 17 and word SEVENTEEN in all capital letters for your child to see. Say each letter as you write: S, E, V, E, N, T, E, E, N, and the word out loud:

   S
   E
   V
   E
   N
   T
   E
   E
   N

   SEVENTEEN

   The little lamb thought he knew what was best

   S
   E
   V
   E
   N
   T
   E
   E
   N

   SEVENTEEN

   But mama was right, stay inside with the rest

2. Have the child draw images of the number SEVENTEEN. They may copy some of the items you made in your blackboard drawing for this week. Your child should then practice writing the number 17, Roman numeral XVII and the word SEVENTEEN in all capital letters on the opposite page of their book. If you

feel they need extra time with writing, let them continue to practice as needed. Here is a verse to share when forming the number 17:

Write the number one to start
Then seven comes to do its part

3. Now that your child is well versed in numbers 60-70 you can trust that they are able to move more quickly and practice their counting from 70-80. Count everything you can! If your child seems ready, you can expand your four processes math skills to include larger numbers up to 80 as well. Remember to go at your child's pace and pay close attention to how your child learns most effectively.

Domestic Arts/Practical Life Skills

Discuss with your child the characteristics of a bear. Ask your children if they think bears like to sleep in the winter or if they stay awake. Do bears sleep at night or during the day?

Pretend to crawl around like bears together and make a bear cave out of blankets. How would a mama or papa bear keep their babies warm at night and through the cold months?

This is a simple and healthy snack to make together that your children will enjoy. As always, be sure to tie mathematics in when you measure and cook with your child.

Bear Print Snack

Supplies Needed:
Pears Halves
Yogurt
Sliced Bananas
Cashews

On a dish, put one pear half. Spoon the yogurt over pear half. On top of the pear, place banana slices to represent each finger of the paw print. On top of the "finger" put a cashew for the claw.

Outdoor Time/Nature Walk

Take your children outside each day regardless of the weather. Invest in good rain gear, snow gear and wool undergarments if your location requires it. Do your lessons outdoors whenever possible.

Caregiver Focus

Preserving Energy

As we talk about creating warmth within us and in our surroundings, it is also important to consider how best to preserve energy as caregivers and models to our children. There are many ways to be a more energy efficient household. Here are some ideas:

- Turn lights and utilities off when you are not using them.
- When possible, consider handwashing and drying certain items.
- Consider putting up a clothing line to dry your clothing outdoors.
- Warm your home with a fireplace or woodstove.
- Bundle up a bit more so you aren't as inclined to turn up the heat.
- Consider installing energy efficient/smart thermostats.
- Insulate windows.
- Use less hot water.
- Set your washing machine to cold.
- Make sure your dishwasher is full when you run it to save energy.
- When replacing old appliances, choose the most energy efficient you can afford.
- When possible walk, bike or use mass transit.
- Plant shade trees to help keep your home and lawn cool.

Science, Nature Study, Earth Discovery

1. Learning About Animals: Nocturnal & Diurnal

    Today explain to the children that some animals are more active at night and are called nocturnal and others are more active during the day and are called diurnal.

Show your child photos or figures of animals that are nocturnal. Ask your child to think of some animals that they believe to be nocturnal. (owl, bat, mouse, fox, hedgehog, etc.)

What are some differences about these animals compared to animals we know are more active during the day?

How do nighttime animals see so well in the dark? (bigger eyes, better night vision, etc.)

Over time, certain animals adapted to function better in the night. Here are some ways how:

Sight

Many animals have larger eyes to see better with in the evening. Did you know an owl's eyeballs takes up 75% space of their skulls while human eyeballs only take up 5%?

Not only do some nocturnal animals have larger eyes but they also often have incredible eyesight so they can see things more clearly in the dark. However, because of this, they are sometimes colorblind.

Hearing

Nocturnal animals often have cupped ears which helps them hear the night's noises better. Their ears sometimes also can hear separately with each ear so they can know exactly where a sound is coming from.

Do you know what an echo is? An echo is when a sound bounces off an area and you can hear it back again. Did you know that the way bats "see" things is like an echo? It is called echolocation (what two words do you hear?). When an animal that has echolocation makes a very high-pitched sound, the sound then bounces off things and returns to the animal. Objects that are close come back differently than those that are far away. That is how the animal, like a bat, can then tell where something is and its shape!

Smell

Many nocturnal animals have a stronger sense of smell so that they can hunt for food very far away in the dark.

Let your child take a flashlight outside and see if they can observe or hear any nocturnal animals tonight.

2. Learning About Animals: Categorizing Nocturnal & Diurnal

Read books together about daytime and nighttime animals. What animals can you think of that fall into each category. Using the Felt Board you made from the Teacher's Classroom Work, print out, laminate and use Velcro to present examples of different animals to your child. You may also choose to use the photos we have provided below. Have your child group them into nocturnal or diurnal.

Nocturnal & Diurnal Animals

First Grade Curriculum | WINTER | Little Acorn Learning

Social Studies, Geography, Weather, Time

1. Learning About Time: Reviewing Hours

   Last week your child learned how to recognize the hours on both an analog and digital clock. Review this with your child pointing out the hour hand. You can use the template from last week to continue to review and work in your lesson book.

2. Learning About Time: Half Hours

   This week introduce the concept of the half hour to your child. Explain to them that a half hour is 30 minutes, exactly half of an hour, which is 60 minutes. The 30 minute point is at the 6. Using our minute templates from last week, practice half hours. Ask your child to show you on the template and in their lesson book various times.

Afternoon Lessons

Handwork: Sewing, Herbal Eye Pillows

Supplies Needed:
Dried Lavender or Chamomile Leaves
Flax Seed
Thread
Fabric
Sewing Needed or Sewing Machine

Cut out two 4x9 inch rectangles from your fabric. Putting right sides together sew around the edges, backstitching at each end to secure. Leave one of the small ends of the rectangle open. Turn the fabric right side out and fill the interior of the pillow with approximately 1 cup of flax seed and ½ cup of herbs. Fold the open seam inside and pin closed. Stitch the opening across to seal.

These pillows are wonderful when kept in the freezer. They can be placed on eyes or used as boo-boo packs in your home.

Tuesday Student Lessons – Week Seventeen
(Painting – Red Day)

Language Arts

1. Like yesterday, begin your lesson time by continuing to read (or tell) part two of *The Wolf and The Quick Little Lamb*. Provide your child with a piece of beeswax modeling material as you read. Let them hold this piece of beeswax as they listen, warming it with their hands so it softens.

2. Have your child form the softened beeswax material into the letter Q. Roll it into a long snake, form it just so and then put it back together again. Next, have them form it into the number 17.

3. Open your lesson book and review the work you did yesterday. Have your child trace the letter Q number 17 and word SEVENTEEN with their fingers.

4. Practice saying the sounds of the letter Q. Notice how our mouth forms to make the sound. Bringing awareness to the way our body forms sounds and words is very important. This process helps us to notice the use of air and our body muscles as we communicate.

5. Today we will work on a tongue twister to practice and memorize with your child to help learn the letter Q and its sound. Tongue twisters and rhymes are fun ways to learn and help with finding rhythm. As we have begun bringing awareness to syllables, pay careful attention with your child to be sure they get it correctly.

   To begin, say the following tongue twister to your child slowly **and tap one finger on the palm of your other hand to the syllables** to create a pattern for memory:

   Did you know the quiet queen quit?
   She quit, the queen, and she was quiet.

Mathematics

1. Using tangible items continue counting backwards with your children today. This week start from 30 to 1.

2. Write numbers 1- 40 on your blackboard. Using your finger point to 40 and count backward to the number one. Have your child do this with you.

3. In your child's lesson book, have them draw 50 items on the left side. This could be 50 little dots, trees, buttons, hearts or even simply sticks. Count them together first in order and then backward. Next, on the right side of your child's layout, have them write the number 50 and downward to the number 1. You can help them if they are struggling.

4. Continue these types of exercises over the next week or two aiming to be able to increase the amount of numbers your child can count backwards.

Outdoor Time/Nature Walk

Take your children outside each day regardless of the weather. Invest in good rain gear, snow gear and wool undergarments if your location requires it. Do your lessons outdoors whenever possible.

Social Studies, Geography, Weather, Time

1. Learning About Time: Reviewing Minutes

Last week your child learned how to read both hours and minutes on both an analog and digital clock. Take time to review the minutes this week with the templates we provided you last week. The minutes can take time to learn as it is confusing because we refer to them with different numbers than shown on the clock. For this reason, the Telling Time Flip Clock can come in very handy.

2. Learning About Time: Seconds

Within a minute, is 60 seconds. Have your child practice counting seconds from 1 to 60. In between each number they can say the word "Mississippi" like you may have done as a child! Show your child the second hand on the analog clock and how fast it moves in comparison to the others. Watch as the minute hand turns slowly after the second hand passes 60.

Afternoon Lessons

Art: Making Bear Tracks

Supplies Needed:
Plaster of Paris
Measuring cup for powder
Water and measuring cup
Container to mix in
Shallow Pan or Tub
Sand or Dirt
Sharp Pencil, Nail or Stick
Spoon and knife

Even if you do not live where you can find tracks left by bears, you can have fun making pretend bear tracks, using your own feet! The hind foot of a bear has a shape that is very similar to the shape of our feet, as you can see below:

A bear's foot: A human foot:

To make your "bear track" you will need to fill a shallow pan or small tub (big enough for you to put your foot in) with moist sand or dirt. With your bare foot, step into the sand, pressing down hard, to make a good, clear print. Using a nail, sharpened pencil, or other small, pointed stick, make "claw prints" above each of your toes.

Measure ½ cup water into the bowl. Slowly add 1 cup plaster, sifting it through your fingers. Stir until smooth. It should be like pancake batter. Carefully pour into track, filling all of it (claw marks, too). Wait until it is dry - probably 30-45 minutes. When it is hard, gently cut around it and lift it out. When you pour the plaster into the print, be sure to get some into the "claw prints." When your cast is hard and dry, lift it out carefully. Brush or rinse the sand off, and you will have your own "bear track".

Wednesday Student Lessons – Week Seventeen
(Coloring – Yellow Day)

Language Arts

1. Practice our tongue twister again. Keep working on this until you have it memorized together. Say the following tongue twister to your child slowly **and tap one finger on the palm of your other hand to the syllables** to create a pattern for memory:

    Did you know the quiet queen quit?
    She quit the queen and she was quiet.

2. In your child's lesson book have them make a drawing of the little lamb hiding from the wolf.

3. On the opposite page, your child is likely ready to write simple sentences (do not worry about punctuation at this time). Remember we are still writing in all capital letters. Provide your child with a simple sentence on the blackboard to copy such as:

    THE QUICK LAMB HID
    THE SHEEP WERE QUIET
    THE WOLF WAS BAD

4. Tonight, at bedtime, tell your child part three of the story of *The Wolf and The Quick Little Lamb*.

5. When out and about, ask your child to find things that begin with the letter Q. This can be done while shopping or when driving in the car. Throughout the week, ask your child to think of all the words they can that begin with the letter Q. How many can they come up with? Make a list.

Mathematics

Determining Relative Length: Shortest to Longest

Today work with your child to determine relative length of various items. Have them tell you which item is shortest to longest. This can be done with sticks, items in your home and other tangible items.

Outdoor Time/Nature Walk

Take your children outside each day regardless of the weather. Invest in good rain gear, snow gear and wool undergarments if your location requires it. Do your lessons outdoors whenever possible.

Science, Nature Study, Earth Discovery

Learning About Animals: Hibernation

1. Talk to your child about hibernation today. When the cold weather comes, some animals hide and rest or sleep through the winter. This is called Hibernation. Animals that do this have adapted to survive long cold stretches of time when food is not easy to find. The animal's body goes through an amazing change to help it survive the winter. Their heart rate slows down, their body temperature drops, and their breathing is slower. Depending on which animal, some do not wake up much at all…not even to eat, drink or go to the bathroom! Other animals stay in a lighter rest and do these things but less than usual.

2. Ask your child if they know of any animals that hibernate? (bats, woodchucks, squirrels, etc.) You can read books from our recommendation list prior to this lesson to help with this concept. This would be another nice time to use your Felt Board with the children. You can also have the children draw and color their own animals and laminate them for your board.

Hibernating Animals

3. Ask your child to think of some of the places that animals would go to sleep in the winter.

   A bear may go find a nice warm cave.
   A squirrel may go inside a tree trunk.
   The frogs dig holes in the ground to go into to keep warm.

Afternoon Lessons

1. Art: Clay Caves

   Supplies Needed:
   Brown or Black Modeling Clay or Playdough

   Have each child create a small cave with their modeling material. Your child may also like to make a small bear to fit inside. These creations can be placed on your seasonal table with the bear tucked inside until spring arrives, then he can 'appear' from his cave. If the children are enjoying this activity, have them create other winter animals out of clay for your table.

2. Music: Continue Practicing Flute or Recorder

Thursday Student Lessons – Week Seventeen
(Crafting/Games – Orange Day)

Language Arts

1. Continue to tell your child the story of *The Wolf and The Quick Little Lamb*.

2. Alphabet Cards

   Supplies Needed:
   Heavy White Cardstock
   Beeswax Stick Crayons
   Scissors

   Spend time cutting cards out of cardstock with your child. Using beeswax crayons, continue to finish drawing each letter we have learned so far and include the letter Q. Next to the letter, have your child draw an image that begins with it. Using scissors, round the corners of these cards and keep working on them throughout the year. You can use them in your lessons and for an upper case and lowercase match game later in the curriculum when we learn those as well.

3. Continue reading simple reader books together.

Mathematics

Determining Relative Height: Shortest to Tallest

Today work with your child to determine relative height of various items. Have them tell you which item are taller and shorter. Consider measuring each member of your family and making a growth chart in your home. Who is the tallest? Who is shortest?

Outdoor Time/Nature Walk

Take your children outside each day regardless of the weather. Invest in good rain gear, snow gear and wool undergarments if your location requires it. Do your lessons outdoors whenever possible.

Movement, Body Awareness & Health

1. Yoga for Children: Butterfly Pose & Child's Pose

   ### Butterfly Pose (*Badda Konasana*)

   This pose is a nice way to begin movement time and is a good stretch that opens the hips and leg muscles.

   - Begin in a seated floor position.

   - Bring the souls of your feet together to touch.

   - Clasp your feet with your hands and gently lean down and feel the stretch in your back and hips.

   - Holding feet, sit up again and flap your "wings" (legs) like a butterfly.

   - Repeat.

   ### Child's Pose (*Balsana*)

   Child's pose is a wonderful beginner's pose and helps to continue to stretch the legs, thighs and hips while also creating a safe state for rest. It is a good way to rest in between poses and calm your innermost being.

   - Begin on hands and knees. Breath slow and steady and start to shift your focus inward.

   - Spread your knees apart and keep your toes touching. Rest your bottom on your heels.

   - Take a deep breath in and when you exhale lean forward down to the ground, resting your chest and forehead on the ground.

   - Keep arms extended on the ground in front of your body above your head with palms facing down.

   - Breath in and out and rest.

- Stretch and extend your body in this position.

- You can also move your arms facing behind you laying on the ground with palms facing upward.

2. Mitten Match

   Gather a bunch of mittens making sure each has a match (a few gloves will do as well). Place all the mittens in a basket and mix them up. Have the children find the match to complete each pair. Point out the various colors, patterns, and shapes as they choose the next mitten to match. (this game can also be played with SOCKS during laundry time!)

3. Flashlight Tag

   Many adults have very fond memories of this old and well-loved game from their own childhood. In the evening, invite some friends over or play as a family. Give each child a flashlight and play tag style hide and seek and find each other in the dark.

Afternoon Lessons

1. Form Drawing/Art – Trees in a Row

   When you work on learning relative length and height this week, have your child place his or her sticks in a symmetrical pattern going from short to tallest and then back down again. Imagine this being a beautiful row of trees on a mountain or next to a river. Then, using sticks again, match this image in the "reflection" of the river underneath. This can also be a bridge or the gate to the quiet sheepfold. Use your imagination and explore with storytelling as you work together.

   Next, have your child practice making this form repetitively in their lesson book. Work on ensuring the short lines and middle lines are all the same height and that the spacing between all lines are the same.

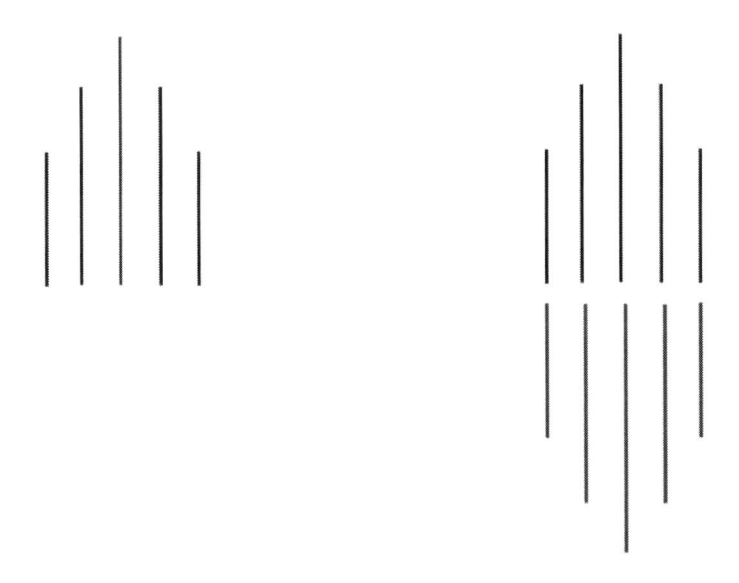

2. Handwork: Hand Stitching/Embroidery

   Supplies Needed:
   Embroidery Needle
   Embroidery Floss
   White Scrap Fabric
   Embroidery Hoop (optional)
   Scissors

   Using our embroidery instructions, work with your child to make a letter Q embroidery piece. You can do this with a simple running stitch, or you may choose to learn more complicated stitches together.

Friday Student Lessons – Week Seventeen
(Modeling/Housework – Green Day)

Language Arts

1. Today have your child continue to practice writing the letter Q in their lesson book on unlined paper.

2. In your child's lesson book, have them practice writing the alphabet from A-Q copying each letter a few times on each line.

3. Ask your child to tell YOU the story of *The Wolf and The Quick Little Lamb*.

Mathematics

Methods of Multiplication

Today let's dig a little bit deeper into the various methods of multiplication. On your blackboard or a separate piece of paper, make five columns labeled as follows:

Factors
Repetitive Addition
Groups
Array
Product

Working together fill in each column. Continue these together, allowing your child to work more independently as they gain confidence. If your child has mastered multiplication up to 10, try expanding to higher double-digit numbers using these methods. Can you fill in the answers on our example below? This can also be done in your child's lesson book.

Factors	Repetitive Addition	Groups	Array	Product
3 x 2	3 + 3	(•••)(•••)	:::	6
4 x 2	4 + 4	(::)(::)	::::	
5 x 3				15
6 x 3	6 + 6 + 6			
7 x 4	7 + 7 + 7 + 7		::::::::	
8 x 4				
9 x 5				

Outdoor Time/Nature Walk

Take your children outside each day regardless of the weather. Invest in good rain gear, snow gear and wool undergarments if your location requires it. Do your lessons outdoors whenever possible.

Science, Nature Study, Earth Discovery

1. Learning About Animals: Wildlife Tracking

   Supplies Needed:
   Magnifying Glasses
   Nature Notebooks/Journal
   Field Book
   Camera

   During your outside time today, go hunting for signs of the nighttime frolics of wildlife. Can you find little animal tracks? Big tracks? What types of animals do you think created them? Can you tell from the prints whether the animal hops or walks? Bringing magnifying glasses will encourage your little detectives to really search for clues!

Let children journal about their findings. You may even choose to take photos of the tracks you find to keep in your notebooks. Make drawings of each print. Which animal do you think it came from? Go to your library or online to research further.

2. Learning About Animals: Migration

Talk to your child about how some animals move long or short distances to find food, mates, shelter, warmth or safety. This is called migration.

Some types of animals that migrate are:

Monarch Butterflies

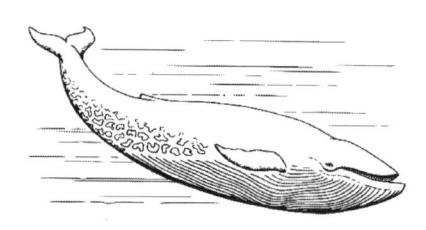

Whales

Birds (some fly south in the winter)

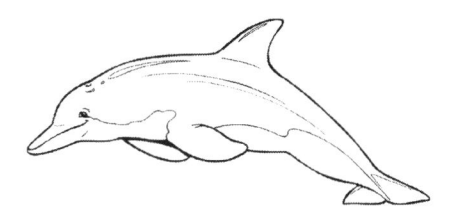

Dolphins

Red Bats

Salmon

Frogs

Different migrating animals go different distances for different reasons.

Ask your child if they think a frog would go very far? (they go to the pond or lake where they hatched to lay eggs)

How about dolphins? (depending on where they live, they migrate far distances to warmer water)

Domestic Arts/Practical Life Skills

Folding

Teach your child simple folding skills with easy to fold items. You can do this when it is time to clean up the blankets from your bear cave, when folding napkins or even towels.

Afternoon Lessons

Use the afternoon hours today to review areas from this week's afternoon lessons that you feel may need a bit more attention. Bring these into your weekend as you find time.

Week Eighteen, Winter
First Grade

Theme: Kings & Queens, Peace in Our Homes

This Week's Lessons:

Language Arts:
Rapunzel Story
Letter R
Heteronyms

Mathematics:
Number 18
EIGHTEEN
Counting from 80-90
Determining Relative Weight: Heaviest to Lightest
Playing Cards
Math with Blocks

Social Studies, Geography, Weather, Time:
Learning About Time: A.M. & P.M.
Being a Good Citizen

Science, Nature Study, Earth Discovery:
Nature's Peace Wreath
Sink or Float
Learning About Mater: Liquid, Gases & Solids

Teacher's Classroom Work:
Prepare for Relative Weight Lesson
Familiarize Yourself with Card Games & Math Blocks Lesson

For the Caregiver:
Caregiver Meditation: Peace in Our Homes
Caregiver Focus: Finding Peace with Patience

Domestic Arts/Practical Life Skills:
King & Queen's Cake
Bed Making

Music:
Kings & Queens, Peace Fingerplays & Songs
Beginning Recorder or Flute

Art/Handwork:
Handwork: Knitting & Braiding, Braided Rapunzel Scarf
Art: Watercolor Painting with Three Colors
Felting, Old Sweaters & Crown Making
Embroidery, Letter R
Alphabet Card Letter R

Form Drawing:
Form Drawing/Art – Braided Lines

Movement, Body Awareness & Health:
Ball Games: Bouncing, Catching & Throwing

Supplies Needed for Week Eighteen

Cooking List:

<u>For King & Queens Cake:</u>
Eggs
Sifted Flour
Sugar
Cup of Sour Cream
Vanilla Flavoring
Lemon Favoring
Round Cake Tin
Dried Bean
Cake Rack
Cream Cheese
Butter
Honey
Lemon Juice

Homeschooling List:

Blackboard
Chalk
Three Silks to Braid
Lesson Book
Stockmar Stick Crayons
Stockmar Block Crayons
Colored Pencils
Stockmar Beeswax Modeling Material
Knitting Needles
Super Bulky Single Ply 100% Wool Yarn
Embroidery Needle
Embroidery Floss
White Scrap Fabric
Embroidery Hoop (optional)
Heavy White Cardstock
Scissors
Round Wire Wreath Frame
Flexible Wire
Wire Cutter

Hot Glue Gun
Twigs, Sticks and Nature Items
Watercolor Paint in Yellow, Blue and Red
Water
Watercolor Paper
Paintbrush
Painting Board
Yellow Yarn
2 Yellow Hair Ties
Old Wool Sweaters or Blankets of Various Colors
Washing Machine
Dryer
Detergent
Various Items to Sink or Float
Large Bowl of Water
Deck of Cards
Large Bouncing Ball
Small Bouncing Ball
Blocks

Week Eighteen Book Recommendations

Visit your local library the weekend before to check out books based on your theme for the week. Older children can help you look up the books by author and title. When setting up your play space for the week ahead, mindfully display these books in baskets for the children to enjoy.

I am Peace: A Book of Mindfulness ~ Susan Verde and Peter H. Reynolds
Wangari's Trees of Peace: A True Story from Africa ~ Jeanette Winter
Can You Say Peace? ~ Karen Katz
The Peace Book ~ Todd Parr
Peace Week in Miss Fox's Class ~ Eileen Spinelli
Peace, Love, Action!: Everyday Acts of Goodness from A to Z ~ Tanya Zabinski
Peace ~ Wendy Anderson Halperin
A Little Peace ~ Barbara Kerley
Find Your Happy, A Kids Self Love Book ~ Patricia May and Snezana Grncaroska
Peace, Bugs, and Understanding: An Adventure in Harmony ~ Gail Silver
I Am Human: A Book of Empathy ~ Susan Verde
Peaceful Pieces: Poems and Quilts About Peace ~ Anna Grossnickle Hines
Peace Crane ~ Sheila Hamanaka
The Peace Tree from Hiroshima: The Little Bonsai with a Big Story ~ Sandra Moore and Kazumi Wilds
Kings & Queens of England and Scotland ~ Pamela Egan
Three Wise Queens: A Story of the Nativity Gifts ~ James Allen
Why Kings and Queens Don't Wear Crowns ! Princess Martha Louise
Three Wise Men: A Christmas Story ~ Loek Koopmans
If the Three Kings Didn't Have their Camels ~ Gilberto Mariscal
King Mouse ~ Cary Fagan
King Matt the First ~ Janusz Korczak
The Snow Queen ~ Hans Christian Andersen
The Queen is Coming to Tea ~ Linda Ravin Lodding
King Bidgood's in the Bathtub ~ Audrey Wood
The King Who Rained ~ Fred Gwynne
Illustrated Tales of King Arthur ~ Sarah Courtauld

First Grade Curriculum | WINTER | Little Acorn Learning

Week Eighteen Circle, Songs & Movement

The following songs and verses should be shared during circle time each day this week after you open your circle.

Three Wise Kings

Three Kings
The good, the beautiful, the true
Step forth amidst the night so blue

Three Kings
The wise, the strong, the light
Seek out the star of magic bright

Five Queens Fingerplay

There were five queens on a quest
(hold up five fingers)

To see who was the very best
(wiggle fingers)

The first queen went to take a test
(touch thumb)

The second queen said, I'll go out west
(touch index finger)

First Grade Curriculum | WINTER | Little Acorn Learning

The third queen climbed Mount Everest
(touch middle finger)

The fourth queen made a beautiful vest
(touch ring finger)

The fifth queen said, I'll just take a rest
(touch little finger)

Come To The Castle
(Sing with the tune Down by the Station)

Come to the castle early in the morning,
See the lords and ladies all in a row.
See the prince and princess leaving in the carriage.
People throw confetti as they go.

Come to the castle early in the evening.
See the king and queen sitting on their thrones.
See the knights in armor coming in from battle.
See the captured dragons rattling their bones.

Here is the Prince with the feathered cap.
(pretend to take off caps and bow)

Here are his boots that go tap, tap.
(march around)

Here is the Princess with a crown.
(touch 'crown' with both hands)

Here is her lovely velvet gown.
(hold out imaginary skirt and curtsy)

Here is the castle tall and wide.
(lift arms for tall and wide)

Here they can play safely inside!
(wraps arms around self and hug self)

Can you wash your father's shirt?
Can you wash it clean?
Can you wash your father's shirt?
And bleach it on the green?

Yes, I can wash my father's shirt,
And I can wash it clean.
I can wash my father's shirt,
And send it to the Queen.

Pussycat, pussycat,
Where have you been?

I've been to London
To visit the Queen.

Pussycat, pussycat,
What did you there?

I frightened a little mouse
Under the chair.

Sing a song of sixpence,
A pocket full of rye;
Four and twenty blackbirds
Baked in a pie!

When the pie was opened
The birds began to sing:
Wasn't that a dainty dish to set before the king?

The king was in his counting house,
Counting out his money;
The queen was in the parlor,
Eating bread and honey.

The maid was in the garden,
Hanging out the clothes;
When down came a blackbird,
And pecked off her nose!

As it fell upon the ground
Twas spied by Jenny Wren,
Who took a stick of sealing wax
And stuck in on again.

As they saw the nose stuck on
The maids cried out "Hurray!"
Till someone said, "But it is stuck
The topsy turvy way!"

They took her to the king,
Who just replied "What stuff!"
Tis better far put on that way,
So nice for taking snuff!"

They bought a pound of lundy foot
And threw it in her face.
She sneezed "Achoo!" which twisted it
Into its proper place.

Week Eighteen Blackboard Drawing

Drawing Ideas for This Week: Capital letter R as shown in Rapunzel's long hair out of the tower window, crown, King, Queen, Peace Symbol, Roman numeral XVIII, EIGHTEEN, 18

Week Eighteen Teacher's Classroom Work

1. Prepare for Relative Weight Lesson

   Be sure to have the scales you need on hand for the relative weight lesson this week. Also, consider what items your child can use for the activity.

2. Familiarize Yourself with Card Games

   This week we will teach the children the rank of each of the 52 cards in a deck. Be sure to familiarize yourself with the two games included in the lesson and practice before presenting it to the children.

3. Prepare for Math Blocks Lesson

   Make sure you have blocks for the math lesson this week. If you are choosing to present certain equations and answers on the blocks, prepare this ahead of time.

4. Review any handwork before working on projects with your children

Week Eighteen Caregiver Meditation

This Week's Reflection: Peace in Our Homes

"Everybody today seems to be in such a terrible rush, anxious for greater developments and greater riches and so on, so that children have very little time for their parents. Parents have very little time for each other, and in the home begins the disruption of peace of the world." ~ Mother Teresa

Peace begins in the home. This is precisely why your job is so very important in the healing of our planet. If we teach our children love, acceptance, beauty, kindness and truth, they take it with them when they go out into the world as adults. Focus on your words, your actions and your environment. Slow down the pace. Make your home a place of peace and love throughout the year.

Week Eighteen Story

This is a very popular fairy tale and works well while we learn about the letter R with the children this week. A nice way to share this story is to braid three pretty silks together as you read. Alternatively, you might wish to braid yarn, rope, or string.

Rapunzel
~ The Brothers Grimm

There were once a man and a woman who had long in vain wished for a child. At length the woman hoped that God was about to grant her desire. These people had a little window at the back of their house from which a splendid garden could be seen, which was full of the most beautiful flowers and herbs. It was, however, surrounded by a high wall, and no one dared to go into it because it belonged to an enchantress, who had great power and was dreaded by all the world.

One day the woman was standing by this window and looking down into the garden, when she saw a bed which was planted with the most beautiful rampion - Rapunzel, and it looked so fresh and green that she longed for it, and had the greatest desire to eat some. This desire increased every day, and as she knew that she could not get any of it, she quite pined away, and began to look pale and miserable.

Then her husband was alarmed, and asked, "What ails you, dear wife?"

"Ah," she replied, "if I can't eat some of the rampion, which is in the garden behind our house, I shall die."

The man, who loved her, thought, sooner than let your wife die, bring her some of the rampion yourself, let it cost what it will. At twilight, he clambered down over the wall into the garden of the enchantress, hastily clutched a handful of rampion, and took it to his wife. She at once made herself a salad of it and ate it greedily. It tasted so good to her - so very good, that the next day she longed for it three times as much as before. If he was to have any rest, her husband must once more descend into the garden. In the gloom of evening, therefore, he let himself down again. But when he had clambered down the wall, he was terribly afraid, for he saw the enchantress standing before him.

"How can you dare," said she with angry look, "descend into my garden and steal my rampion like a thief? You shall suffer for it."

First Grade Curriculum | WINTER | Little Acorn Learning

"Ah," answered he, "let mercy take the place of justice, I only made up my mind to do it out of necessity. My wife saw your rampion from the window and felt such a longing for it that she would have died if she had not got some to eat."

Then the enchantress allowed her anger to be softened, and said to him, "If the case be as you say, I will allow you to take away with you as much rampion as you will, only I make one condition, you must give me the child which your wife will bring into the world. It shall be well treated, and I will care for it like a mother."

The man in his terror consented to everything, and when the woman was brought to bed, the enchantress appeared at once, gave the child the name of Rapunzel, and took it away with her.

Rapunzel grew into the most beautiful child under the sun. When she was twelve years old, the enchantress shut her into a tower, which lay in a forest, and had neither stairs nor door, but quite at the top was a little window. When the enchantress wanted to go in, she placed herself beneath it and cried,

> "Rapunzel, Rapunzel,
> Let down your hair!"

Rapunzel had magnificent long hair, fine as spun gold, and when she heard the voice of the enchantress she unfastened her braided tresses, wound them round one of the hooks of the window above, and then the hair fell twenty ells down, and the enchantress climbed up by it.

After a year or two, it came to pass that the king's son rode through the forest and passed by the tower. Then he heard a song, which was so charming that he stood still and listened. This was Rapunzel, who in her solitude passed her time in letting her sweet voice resound. The king's son wanted to climb up to her, and looked for the door of the tower, but none was to be found. He rode home, but the singing had so deeply touched his heart, that every day he went out into the forest and listened to it. Once when he was thus standing behind a tree, he saw that an enchantress came there, and he heard how she cried,

> "Rapunzel, Rapunzel,
> Let down your hair!"

Then Rapunzel let down the braids of her hair, and the enchantress climbed up to her. "If that is the ladder by which one mounts, I too will try my fortune," said he, and the next day when it began to grow dark, he went to the tower and cried,

"Rapunzel, Rapunzel,
Let down your hair!"

Immediately the hair fell down and the king's son climbed up. At first Rapunzel was terribly frightened when a man, such as her eyes had never yet beheld, came to her. But the king's son began to talk to her quite like a friend and told her that his heart had been so stirred that it had let him have no rest, and he had been forced to see her. Then Rapunzel lost her fear, and when he asked her if she would take him for her husband, and she saw that he was young and handsome, she thought, he will love me more than old dame Gothel does. And she said yes and laid her hand in his.

She said, "I will willingly go away with you, but I do not know how to get down. Bring with you a skein of silk every time that you come, and I will weave a ladder with it, and when that is ready I will descend, and you will take me on your horse."

They agreed that until that time he should come to her every evening, for the old woman came by day.

The enchantress remarked nothing of this, until once Rapunzel said to her, "Tell me, Dame Gothel, how it happens that you are so much heavier for me to draw up than the young king's son - he is with me in a moment."

"Ah! You wicked child," cried the enchantress. "What do I hear you say. I thought I had separated you from all the world, and yet you have deceived me."

In her anger she clutched Rapunzel's beautiful tresses, wrapped them twice round her left hand, seized a pair of scissors with the right, and snip, snap, they were cut off, and the lovely braids lay on the ground. And she was so pitiless that she took poor Rapunzel into a desert where she had to live in great grief and misery.

On the same day that she cast out Rapunzel, however, the enchantress fastened the braids of hair, which she had cut off, to the hook of the window, and when the king's son came and cried,

"Rapunzel, Rapunzel,
Let down your hair!"

she let the hair down. The king's son ascended, but instead of finding his dearest Rapunzel, he found the enchantress, who gazed at him with wicked and venomous looks.

"Aha," she cried mockingly, "you would fetch your dearest, but the beautiful bird sits no longer singing in the nest. The cat has got it and will scratch out your eyes as well. Rapunzel is lost to you. You will never see her again."

The king's son was beside himself with pain, and in his despair, he leapt down from the tower. He escaped with his life, but the thorns into which he fell pierced his eyes. Then he wandered quite blind about the forest, ate nothing but roots and berries, and did naught but lament and weep over the loss of his dearest wife.

Thus, he roamed about in misery for some years, and at length came to the desert where Rapunzel, with the twins to which she had given birth, a boy and a girl, lived in wretchedness. He heard a voice, and it seemed so familiar to him that he went towards it, and when he approached, Rapunzel knew him and fell on his neck and wept. Two of her tears wetted his eyes and they grew clear again, and he could see with them as before. He led her to his kingdom where he was joyfully received, and they lived for a long time afterwards, happy and contented.

Monday Student Lessons – Week Eighteen

(Baking/Cooking – Purple Day)

Language Arts

1. Begin your lesson time by reading (or telling) the story of *Rapunzel* to your child. Let the children look at the sentences as you read as this visual will aid with their knowledge of letters, words and sentences. If possible, use simple props to accompany the story as we have suggested.

2. When your story is finished, unveil your blackboard drawing that you have prepared ahead of time as suggested at the beginning of this week's curriculum. If your child has his or her own small blackboard and chalk, have them take a few moments to create their own drawing.

3. Review what your child worked on last week in their lesson book. Have them practice writing the capital letter Q a few times on their blackboard or an extra piece of paper. Be sure they have a good grasp of this letter before moving onto the next.

4. In your child's lesson book, have them create a similar image of Rapunzel's long hair from our story (or whatever depiction you used) with the letter R revealed inside. On the righthand side, have your child practice writing the capital letter R. Share this poem as you work to form the letter:

> *Straight line down*
> *Then a curve at the top*
> *Add a ramp and*
> *then you stop*

Mathematics

1. In addition to the Roman numeral XVIII, write down the number 18 and word EIGHTEEN in all capital letters for your child to see. Say each letter as you write: E, I, G, H , T, E, E, N, and the word out loud:

E
I
G
H
T
E
E
N

EIGHTEEN

Rapunzel, Rapunzel let down her long hair

E
I
G
H
T
E
E
N

EIGHTEEN

The dame tricked the Prince and she wasn't there

2. Have the child draw images of the number EIGHTEEN. They may copy some of the items you made in your blackboard drawing for this week. Your child should then practice writing the number 18, Roman numeral XVIII and the word EIGHTEEN in all capital letters on the opposite page of their book. If you feel they need extra time with writing, let them continue to practice as needed. Here is a verse to share when forming the number 18:

> *Make a one just like you know*
> *Then an 8 and off we go!*

3. Now that your child is well versed in numbers 70-80 you can trust that they are able to move more quickly and practice their counting from 80-90. Count everything you can! If your child seems ready, you can expand your four processes math skills to include larger numbers up to 90 as well. Remember to go at your child's pace and pay close attention to how your child learns most effectively.

Domestic Arts/Practical Life Skills

<u>King & Queen's Cake</u>

King's Cake (or Twelfth Night Cake) is a pastry traditionally consumed near the Epiphany in January. Regardless of when you are doing this week's lesson, this is a very fun recipe to make with your child with a little surprise inside!

Recipes for this famous cake abound, ranging from the typical medieval vagueness (taek ye a measure of flour, and a measure of almonds, mix them together with enough eggs, etc...) to the simple French Galette Des Rois (Three Kings Cake) in which there is a dried bean hidden in the almond paste filling that is simply sealed between two layers of puff pastry.

Traditionally the cake was presented crowned with a gold paper cut-out crown and a dried bean or pea was baked in the cake. Whoever was lucky enough to find the legume in his or her piece would be crowned king or queen for the day.

Supplies Needed:
2 Eggs
1 ½ Cup of Sifted Flour
Cup of Sugar or a Half a Cup of Honey
Cup of Sour Cream
Teaspoon of Vanilla Flavoring
1/2 Teaspoon of Lemon Flavoring
Round Cake Tin (8" x 3")
Dried Bean
Cake Rack

Cream cheese icing:
Mix one package of cream cheese with 1/2 stick butter, some honey and lemon juice.

Beat the eggs and sugar until light and fluffy.
Add the cream and beat, then add the natural flavorings.
Lightly fold in the sifted flour.
Spoon the batter into the well-buttered tin.
Make sure you add the bean.
Bake for 40-60 minutes (check often) at 350 degrees.

Outdoor Time/Nature Walk

Take your children outside each day regardless of the weather. Invest in good rain gear, snow gear and wool undergarments if your location requires it. Do your lessons outdoors whenever possible.

Caregiver Focus

Finding Peace with Patience

A very important step in creating a more peaceful home for yourself and for your family is by working to cultivate more patience. Working hard to be patient with yourself, your children, and your expectations of how things should go can change the entire climate of your household.

When trying to become more patient, begin by reminding yourself to simply slow down. Remind yourself that it is better to enjoy the process and the moment with your child than it is to rush through an activity or lesson, all while yelling (or crying) through the experience. Your child will learn so much more when they are at ease and you will feel better as a parent and teacher when you are as well.

This week work hard to 'practice the pause' when things feel frantic and your patience is thin. Remind yourself that it is ok to stop, to breathe and just to simply do nothing while you regroup. Set realistic expectations for yourself and your child and try your best to let go when things do not go as planned.

Science, Nature Study, Earth Discovery

Nature's Peace Wreath

Supplies Needed:
Round Wire Wreath Frame
Flexible Wire
Wire Cutter
Hot Glue Gun
Twigs, Sticks and Nature Items

Today go for a hike or a nature walk with your children. Gather all different sticks and twigs. Be sure to gather some with natural curves. You can also include long grasses, flowers, leaves and any other interesting nature items to add to your Peace Wreath.

At home, use the wire to create the peace symbol shape in the center of the wreath. Use more than one string of wire for each of the three peace sign lines so that you can weave items in and out if desired.

Using a hot glue gun, begin adhering all your twigs and sticks around the circular wreath frame and also through the three peace sign lines in the center. Weave any grasses, flowers and other items that you can as well.

Hang this beautiful piece in your home as a reminder that we are the ones who can help bring peace into our homes and hearts.

Social Studies, Geography, Weather, Time

Learning About Time: A.M. & P.M.

Explain to your child that there are 24 hours in one day. Show your child an analog clock and point out how the hour numbers only go up to 12, not 24.

In order to tell time, each day is divided into two halves. You can create a visual of this by splitting 24 items (blocks, marbles, etc.) in half.

From midnight until noon is called A.M.

From noon until midnight is called P.M.

A.M. stands for *ante meridiem* which mean before midday. P.M. stands for *post meridiem* which stands for after midday. Your child does not need to know this yet, but it is good for you to know in case the question arises.

Provide your child with a few scenarios and have them decide if this is during the A.M. or P.M. time. It may be nice to use your blackboard and draw a few of these activities for your child to copy in their lesson book and include A.M. or P.M. under each option. Here are some ideas:

Breakfast
Dinner
Sunset
Starting School
Campfire
Stargazing
Sunrise

During the week and as you move ahead, remember to continue looking at clocks with your child and pointing out all you have learned and what time of day it is.

Afternoon Lessons

Handwork: Braided Rapunzel Scarf

Supplies Needed:
Yarn
Knitting Needles
Yellow Yarn
2 Yellow Hair Ties

Cast on approximately 150 stitches. The cast on really depends on how long you want your scarf to be and what type of yarn you use. Be sure the length is how long you wish your scarf to be. Continue in garter stitch for about 5 rows. Cast off.

Make two more. Attach all three pieces together at the top using a yellow hair tie. Braid the three pieces together to the end and secure again with another yellow hair tie.

Tuesday Student Lessons – Week Eighteen
(Painting – Red Day)

Language Arts

1. Like yesterday, begin your lesson time by continuing to read (or tell) the story of *Rapunzel*. Provide your child with a piece of beeswax modeling material as you read. Let them hold this piece of beeswax as they listen, warming it with their hands so it softens.

2. Have your child form the softened beeswax material into the letter R. Roll it into a long snake, form it just so and then put it back together again. Next, have them form it into the number 18.

3. Open your lesson book and review the work you did yesterday. Have your child trace the letter R number 18 and word EIGHTEEN with their fingers.

4. Practice saying the sounds of the letter R. Notice how our mouth forms to make the sound. Bringing awareness to the way our body forms sounds and words is very important. This process helps us to notice the use of air and our body muscles as we communicate.

5. Today we will work on a tongue twister to practice and memorize with your child to help learn the letter R and its sound. Tongue twisters and rhymes are fun ways to learn and help with finding rhythm. As we have begun bringing awareness to syllables, pay careful attention with your child to be sure they get it correctly.

   To begin, say the following tongue twister to your child slowly **and tap one finger on the palm of your other hand to the syllables** to create a pattern for memory:

   Ray Rag ran across a rough road.
   Across a rough road Ray Rag ran.
   Where is the rough road Ray Rag ran across?

Mathematics

1. Using tangible items continue counting backwards with your children today. This week, start from 40 to 1.

2. Write numbers 1-50 on your blackboard. Using your finger point to 50 and count backward to the number one. Have your child do this with you.

3. In your child's lesson book, have them draw 60 items on the left side. This could be 60 little dots, trees, buttons, hearts or even simply sticks. Count them together first in order and then backward. Next, on the right side of your child's layout, have them write the number 60 and downward to the number 1. You can help them if they are struggling.

4. Continue these types of exercises over the next week or two aiming to be able to count from 1-100 and backward from 100-1.

Outdoor Time/Nature Walk

Take your children outside each day regardless of the weather. Invest in good rain gear, snow gear and wool undergarments if your location requires it. Do your lessons outdoors whenever possible.

Social Studies, Geography, Weather, Time

Being a Good Citizen

A citizen is a person who lives in a certain town or area. Explain to your child that they are a citizen of where you live, as is each member of the family.

Talk about how it is important to be a good citizen. Explain how there are rules that have been created for citizens to follow as well.

There are many ways to be a good citizen. Discuss with your child a few of these (help people in need, respect community workers and the law, clean up the neighborhood, volunteer, vote, etc.)

Next write out a few sentences on your blackboard. Have your child read them with you and circle the ones that they feel explains what a good citizen would say. Here are some examples:

I DO NOT LITTER
I DO NOT LISTEN TO RULES
I HELP PEOPLE WHO NEED IT
I VOLUNTEER AT THE LIBRARY
I DO NOT RESPECT OTHER PEOPLE'S PROPERTY
I DO NOT TELL THE TRUTH
I BREAK LAWS
I WORK HARD IN SCHOOL
I TRY MY BEST
I AM A GOOD FRIEND

In your child's lesson book, have them draw a picture of themselves being a good citizen on the left hand side. On the right, have them copy a few of the sentences they feel make a good citizen.

Afternoon Lessons

Art: Watercolor Painting

Supplies Needed:
Watercolor Paint in Yellow, Blue and Red
Water
Watercolor Paper
Sponge
Paintbrush
Painting Board

Set up your workspace to do watercolor painting with the children with the three primary colors. Wet the watercolor paper with a damp sponge before beginning. It is wise to place a piece of wood, canvas or a cutting board under each child's paper to keep it from curling and bleeding through. Be sure to set up an area for yourself!

Here is a nice verse to share while painting:

Carefully, quietly everyone hush
Bring paper, paints, water and brush.
Then call the colors to come and play
And listen, listen to what they say.

Wednesday Student Lessons – Week Eighteen
(Coloring – Yellow Day)

Language Arts

1. Practice our tongue twister again. Keep working on this until you have it memorized together. Say the following tongue twister to your child slowly **and tap one finger on the palm of your other hand to the syllables** to create a pattern for memory:

   Ray Rag ran across a rough road.
   Across a rough road Ray Rag ran.
   Where is the rough road Ray Rag ran across?

2. In your child's lesson book have them make a drawing of the story of *Rapunzel*.

3. On the opposite page, your child is likely ready to write simple sentences (do not worry about punctuation at this time). Remember we are still writing in all capital letters. Provide your child with a simple sentence on the blackboard to copy such as:

RAPUNZEL HAD LONG HAIR
THE PRINCE CLIMBED UP
THE DAME WAS THERE

4. Tonight, at bedtime tell part three to your child of the story of *Rapunzel*.

5. When out and about, ask your child to find things that begin with the letter R. This can be done while shopping or when driving in the car. Throughout the week, ask your child to think of all the words they can that begin with the letter R. How many can they come up with? Make a list.

Mathematics

Determining Relative Weight: Heaviest to Lightest

This week work with your child to determine relative weight of various items. Begin with simple items around the home. Have your child hold the item and then compare it with another. Have your child tell you which item is heavier and which is lighter. If you have a scale, you can place the items on the scale to see if you are correct.

In your child's lesson book, have them draw a few of these items next to one another writing underneath HEAVIER and LIGHTER.

Outdoor Time/Nature Walk

Take your children outside each day regardless of the weather. Invest in good rain gear, snow gear and wool undergarments if your location requires it. Do your lessons outdoors whenever possible.

Science, Nature Study, Earth Discovery

Sink or Float

Density is what determines whether an item sinks or floats in a liquid, but this is a difficult and unnecessary concept to teach children at this age. Instead, today explore the very simple concept of sink or float.

Supplies Needed:
Various Items to Sink or Float
Large Bowl of Water

Have your child experiment with various items. Can they guess which items will sink and which will float? Are there things you can use to make something that is heavy float? Experiment with little toy boats, aluminum foil, other containers, etc.

Afternoon Lessons

1. Music: Continue Practicing Flute or Recorder

2. Handwork: Felting Old Sweaters

   Supplies Needed:
   Old Wool Sweaters or Blankets of Various Colors
   Washing Machine
   Dryer
   Detergent

Find and collect various old sweaters and blankets from flea markets and consignment shops. Wash items on hot in washing machine with a small amount of detergent. Rinse them in cold water. To felt even more, place into the dryer for a half of a cycle.

Cut felted material into squares and organize by color. Light whites and tans can be hand-dyed in the springtime using plant materials. This newly made wool felt can be used in your classroom for crafting various toys and items.

In particular, you can make them into crowns sometime this week to celebrate our theme. Keep them handy for Three Kings Day either this year or next. Simply cut the felt to shape and use elastic to attach in the back. Experiment with some of your embroidery and hand sewing skills.

Thursday Student Lessons – Week Eighteen
(Crafting/Games – Orange Day)

Language Arts

1. Continue to tell your child the story of *Rapunzel*.

2. Alphabet Cards

    Supplies Needed:
    Heavy White Cardstock
    Beeswax Stick Crayons
    Scissors

    Spend time cutting cards out of cardstock with your child. Using beeswax crayons, continue to finish drawing each letter we have learned so far and include the letter R. Next to the letter, have your child draw an image that begins with it. Using scissors, round the corners of these cards and keep working on them throughout the year. You can use them in your lessons and for an upper case and lowercase match game later in the curriculum when we learn those as well.

3. Continue reading simple reader books together.

4. Practice saying the sound of R. Notice how our mouth forms to make the sound. Bringing awareness to the way our body forms sounds and words is very important. This process helps us to notice the use of air and our body muscles as we communicate.

5. Print out or share the following photos and practice saying them together with your child. Your child may be ready to copy these words into their lesson book.

RING

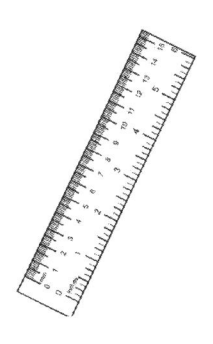

RULER
(also, the king is the 'ruler' of the castle)

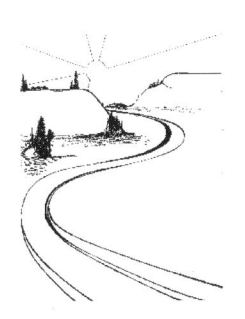

ROAD

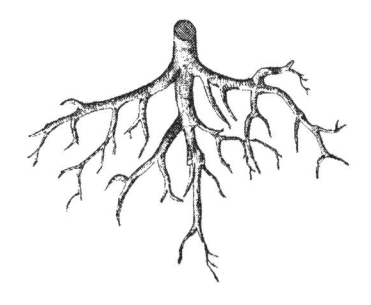

ROOT

First Grade Curriculum | WINTER | Little Acorn Learning

Mathematics

Playing Cards

Supplies Needed:
Deck of Cards

Playing cards is such a wonderful way to spend time with children and helps with learning math skills. How fitting for Kings & Queens week too!

1. Begin by teaching your child the rank of cards in a standard 52 card deck. Cards rank as follows from high to low:

    Ace
    King
    Queen
    Jack
    10
    9
    8
    7
    6
    5
    4
    3
    2

    You may also wish to teach your child about the four suits that the cards are categorized into: clubs, diamonds, hearts and spades. There is no rank among the suits.

    The number cards all stand for the exact number they represent. The Ace can be 1 or 11 and the King, Queen and Jack are equal to 10.

    You can experiment with addition and subtraction with the value of the cards. There are also fun games you can play with your child at this age. Here are two:

2. Go Fish

    For two players, deal each player 7 cards. For more than 2 players, deal each player 5 cards. Players can look at their cards.

    Place the remaining cards in a pile face down on the table.

    The idea of the game is to gather four of a kind and discard until you have no more cards. For example, if you see you have a 3 in your hand, you can ask your opponent if they have any 3s. Your opponent must give you all of their 3s and cannot lie. When you have four of them, you place them on the table in a discard pile. If your opponent does not have the card you need, they say, "Go Fish" and you choose from the pile of remaining cards on the table. Then the next person goes again. Players take turns going back and forth. The suit does not matter when making four of a kind.

    The first person to have no cards wins or when the remaining card pile has been gone through.

3. War

    Deal out all the cards. If there are two players, each player should have 26 cards. In this game, players do not look at their cards. Just place them in a pile face down in front of you. The object of the game is to win all the cards.

    Each player flips over the first card of their pile for everyone to see. Whichever person has the highest card, takes both cards and adds them to the bottom of their pile. Then they flip again.

    If there is a tie and the cards are both equal, there is a war. The players keep those cards on the table and flip next to it. Whoever has the highest this time, takes all four cards. If those were also equal, the war continues.

    Whoever has all the cards in the end wins the game.

Outdoor Time/Nature Walk

    Take your children outside each day regardless of the weather. Invest in good rain gear, snow gear and wool undergarments if your location requires it. Do your lessons outdoors whenever possible.

Movement, Body Awareness & Health

Ball Games

Supplies Needed:
Large Bouncing Ball
Small Bouncing Ball

Provide your child with a large bouncing ball. Have them practice bouncing and catching the ball in front of them with two hands. Next, have them practice bouncing a ball with both hands repetitively (not catching). Finally, have them practice bouncing the ball with alternating hands in front of them. Try all these activities with the smaller ball as well.

Have your child practice throwing the larger ball to you. Throw the ball back and forth adding more space in between the two of you each time. Do this as well with the smaller ball.

Your child can then practice throwing the larger ball into the air and catching it themselves. After some time, have them try to do this without moving their feet or location. With the smaller ball, do the same and also experiment throwing the ball from one hand to the next.

Afternoon Lessons

1. Form Drawing/Art – Braided Lines

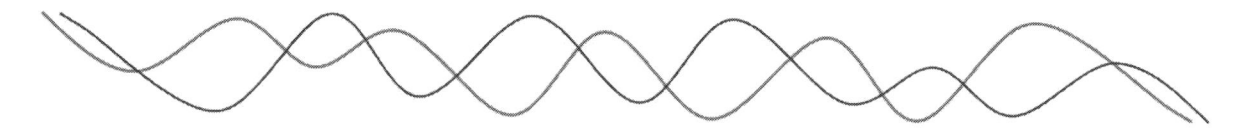

Let your child experiment with making waving lines that overlap and seem to weave or braid into one another. They can start with two lines and expand to three or four. Using a different color for each line is helpful.

Throughout the week, practice braiding with your child. You can braid hair, ribbon, embroidery floss, yarn, rope, grasses, and many other things.

2. Handwork: Hand Stitching/Embroidery

Supplies Needed:
Embroidery Needle
Embroidery Floss
White Scrap Fabric
Embroidery Hoop (optional)
Scissors

Using our embroidery instructions, work with your child to make a letter R embroidery piece. You can do this with a simple running stitch, or you may choose to learn more complicated stitches together.

Friday Student Lessons – Week Eighteen
(Modeling/Housework – Green Day)

Language Arts

1. Today have your child continue to practice writing the letter R in their lesson book on unlined paper.

2. In your child's lesson book, have them practice writing the alphabet from A-R copying each letter a few times on each line.

3. Ask your child to tell YOU the story of *Rapunzel*.

4. Today talk about words that are spelled the same but have different meanings. These types of words are called heteronyms (you do not have to share this definition with your child yet).

   Some examples of these types of words are:

   Ruler
   Bow
   Close
   Read
   Dove
   Tear
   Wind

   Take out a dictionary together and look up the meanings of the words above. Did you guess the correct meanings? Keep an eye out for more words that are spelled the same but have different meanings as you work together throughout the year.

Mathematics

Math with Blocks

Blocks are a wonderful and fun way to teach math skills. They are also an amazing way to build a huge castle for Kings & Queens week! Here are some ideas:

1. How Tall Am I?

    Have your child try to match their height or the height of another person or thing with blocks. How many blocks did it take to match the height? If you wish, you can take out a measuring tape and see how many inches it ended up being.

2. Weight of Blocks

    If you have a balance scale, it is always fun for children to try to balance the weight on both sides with different sized blocks. If you do not, have your child guesstimate how many blocks it would take to match another group of blocks and use a regular scale to check the weight of both groups.

3. Patterns

    Provide your child with patterns on a piece of paper that they can fit the blocks into. Have them work to continue the pattern using various blocks on the entire sheet of paper. Next, have your child create their own patterns with the blocks.

4. Four Processes

    Blocks can be grouped, added, subtracted, multiplied and divided as your child practices their four process skills. Additionally, you can tape math equations onto longer blocks and tape the answer onto smaller blocks. Mix up the blocks and have your child work to match the correct answer with the equation.

Outdoor Time/Nature Walk

Take your children outside each day regardless of the weather. Invest in good rain gear, snow gear and wool undergarments if your location requires it. Do your lessons outdoors whenever possible.

Science, Nature Study, Earth Discovery

Learning About Matter: Liquids, Gases & Solids

Anything that takes up space is called matter. Matter is made of three forms: solid, liquids and gas.

Ask your child if they can guess a few things that fall under each of the three categories. Some ideas:

Solid: Ice
Liquid: Water
Gas: Water Vapor

Here are a few fun ideas to experiment with this idea:

- If there is snow where you live, let your child capture a cup of it. Then have them guess where the water level will be when the snow melts after bringing it indoors for a while.

- Take two glasses. Fill one with hot water and the other with cold water. Drop an ice cube in each glass and start a timer. See which one melts the fastest.

- Fill a container with water and mark where the water level is. Leave space for expansion and put a lid on top. Freeze the container and when you take it out, have your child check to see where the ice level is now. When water gets extremely cold, it freezes and turns into ice. Water takes up more space when it is frozen.

Domestic Arts/Practical Life Skills

Bed Making

Practice making the beds with your children. Take off the sheets for washing, put on new sheets together. Show your child how a fitted sheet is created differently to fit on the mattress. Work together to tuck and fold over the regular sheet, put on pillowcases and add a warm blanket or quilt. Your child is old enough to make their bed very simply each day as part of their daily routine if you so choose.

Afternoon Lessons

Use the afternoon hours today to review areas from this week's afternoon lessons that you feel may need a bit more attention. Bring these into your weekend as you find time.

Week Nineteen, Winter
First Grade

Theme: Snow & Ice, Forgiveness

This Week's Lessons:

Language Arts:
North Wind and Little Jack Frost Story
Letter S
Learning Vowels
Long and Short Vowel Sounds
Learning Consonants

Mathematics:
Number 19
Counting from 80-90
Snowflake Pattern Match
Domino Math

Social Studies, Geography, Weather, Time:
Learning About Goods & Services

Science, Nature Study, Earth Discovery:
Learning About Ice & Snow

Teacher's Classroom Work:
Make Ahead Meals
Ice Skating Field Trip
Prepare for Snowflake Study
Learn or Practice Circular Knitting
Learn or Practice Joining Knitting in the Round

For the Caregiver:
Caregiver Meditation: Forgiveness
Caregiver Focus: Forgiving Others and Ourselves

Domestic Arts/Practical Life Skills:
Pancake Snowmen
Winter Chores

Music:
Snow & Ice Fingerplays & Songs
Beginning Recorder or Flute

Art/Handwork:
Handwork: Cutting, Six Pointed Paper Snowflakes
Art: Snow Lanterns
Handwork: Beginner Knitting, Circular Knitting
Handwork: Beginner Knitting, Easy 'In the Round' Ribbed Hat
Embroidery, Letter S
Alphabet Card Letter S

Form Drawing:
Form Drawing/Art – Snowflake Drawings

Movement, Body Awareness & Health:
Vowel Gestures/Eurythmy
Vowel Yoga
Freeze Dance
Indoor Ice Skating

Supplies Needed for Week Nineteen

Cooking List:

For Pancake Snowmen:
4-6 Eggs
1 Teaspoon Vanilla
½ Teaspoon Cinnamon
Pinch of Sea Salt
Butter or Coconut Oil for Cooking
Banana Slices

Homeschooling List:

Blackboard
Chalk
White Silk, Blue Silk, Paper Snowflakes
Lesson Book
Stockmar Stick Crayons
Stockmar Block Crayons
Colored Pencils
Stockmar Beeswax Modeling Material
Embroidery Needle
Embroidery Floss
White Scrap Fabric
Embroidery Hoop (optional)
Heavy White Cardstock
Various Types of Paper
Scissors
Snowballs
Candle or Small Battery-Operated Light
Long Stemmed Lighter or Very Long Match Sticks
Colored Cardstock or Old Watercolor Paintings
Glue
Ruler
Circular Needles Size 6 mm (10 US)
Bulky Yarn
Stitch Marker
Aluminum Pie Dish or Shallow Plastic Tupperware Dish
Outdoor Materials such as Pine, Twigs, Leaves, Berries, etc.

Wax Paper
Magnifying Glasses
Black Cloth
Snowflakes

Week Nineteen Book Recommendations

Visit your local library the weekend before to check out books based on your theme for the week. Older children can help you look up the books by author and title. When setting up your play space for the week ahead, mindfully display these books in baskets for the children to enjoy.

Ice Palace ~ Deborah Blumenthal and Ted Rand
Ivy's Icicle: Book Three--Forgiving Others ~ Gary Bower
The Icicle Forest ~ Gail Herman and Laura Maestro
Out on the Ice in the Middle of the Bay ~ by Peter Cumming
Skating with Bears ~ Andrew Breakspeare
Hans Brinker ~ Bruce Coville
The Tale of Jack Frost ~ David Melling
Show Each Other Forgiveness ~ Melody Carlson and Susan Reagan
Red Blue & Yellow Yarn: A Tale of Forgiveness ~ Miriam Kosman and Valeri Gorbachev
Under the Lemon Moon ~ Edith Hope Fine
Snowflakes for all Seasons ~ Cindy Higham
Snowflake Bentley ~ Jacqueline Briggs Martin and Mary Azarian
Millions of Snowflakes ~ Mary McKenna Siddals and Elizabeth Sayles
Ken Libbrecht's Field Guide to Snowflakes ~ Ken Libbrecht
No Two Snowflakes ~ Sheree Fitch and Janet Wilson
The Friendly Snowflake ~ M. Scott Peck
Winter's First Snowflake ~ Cheri L. Hallwood
Toby and the Snowflakes ~ Julie Halpern, Matthew Cordell, and Matthew Cordell
Sophie: The One-of-a-Kind Snowflake ~ Mary Kilc
Nanook ~ Larry Hulsey
Whale Snow ~ Debby Dahl Edwardson
The Lonely Polar Bear ~ Khoa Le
Winston of Churchill ~ Jean Davies Okimoto
Arctic White ~ Danna Smith
Winter Dance ~ Marion Dane Bauer
Hello World! Artic Animals ~ Jill McDonald
The Snowy Nap ~ Jan Brett
Magic Treehouse: Polar Bears Past Bedtime ~ Mary Pope Osborne
Trouble with Trolls ~ Jan Brett
Moominland Midwinter ~ Tove Jansson

Week Nineteen Circle, Songs & Movement

The following songs and verses should be shared during circle time each day this week after you open your circle.

Ten Little Icicles

One little, two little, three little icicles,
Four little, five little, six little icicles,
Seven little, eight little, nine little icicles,
Ten little icicles hanging from the roof.

Icicle Fingerplay

I'm a frozen icicle hanging in the sun.
(pretend to hang over while standing)

First, I start to melt, then I start to run.
(drop body lower like melting)

Drip, drip, drip, drip.
(go lower and lower)

Melting can be fun!!
(sink or fall to the floor)

The Icicle

Drip, drip
The rain trickles off the roof.
The cold winter air breezes in.
The water slowly turns into ice.
The rain keeps dripping down the icicle and freezing.
The triangle of water is frozen.
In the morning we break it off and eat it.

The Little Artist

Oh, there is a little artist
Who paints in the cold night hours
Pictures for wee, wee children,
Of wondrous trees and flowers.

Pictures of snow-capped mountains
Touching the snow-white sky;
Pictures of distant oceans,
Where pygmy ships sail by;

Pictures of rushing rivers,
By fairy bridges spanned;
Bits of beautiful landscapes,
Copied from elfin land.

The moon is the lamp he paints by,
His canvas the windowpane,
His brush is a frozen snowflake;
Jack Frost is the artist's name.

Snowman Poem

There was a chubby snowman
And he had a carrot nose
(put fist to nose like carrot)

Along came a bunny
(two fingers up for ears)
And what do you suppose
(hands on hips)

The hungry little bunny
(rub tummy)
Was looking for his lunch
(hand to forehead, looking)

He grabbed that snowman's carrot nose
NIBBLE! NIBBLE! CRUNCH!!
(pretend to eat carrot)

Dance Like Snowflakes
(to the tune of Frère Jacques)

Dance like snowflakes
Dance like snowflakes
In the air
In the air

Whirling, twirling snowflakes
Whirling, twirling snowflakes
Here and there
Here and there

Snowflakes

Little fairy people
Dancing in the sky.

Dressed in soft white raiment
As they downward fly,

Play with little children;
Kiss their cheeks so red;

Keep the flowers cozy
In their earthy bed;

Robe the world in beauty
In a single night,

Covering trees and houses
Till they sparkle bright.

When their work is over
They will find the way

Back to their cloud palace,
Till another day.

Two Little Snowflakes

Way up high in the winter sky,
Two little snowflakes caught my eye.
Down to the ground they fell without a sound.
And before very long,
It was snowing all around.

Help One Another

"Help one another," the snowflakes said,
As they cuddled down in their fleecy bed.
"One of us here would not be felt,
One of us here would quickly melt;
But I'll help you, and you help me,
And then what a splendid drift there'll be."

"Help one another," the maple spray
Said to its fellow leaves one day;
"The sun would wither me here alone,
Long enough ere the day is gone;
But I'll help you, and you help me,
And then what a splendid shade there'll be."

"Help one another," the dewdrop cried,
Seeing another drop close to its side;
"The warm south wind would dry me away,
And I should be gone ere noon to-day;
But I'll help you, and you help me,
And we'll make a brook and run to the sea."

"Help one another," a grain of sand
Said to another grain close at hand;
"The wind may carry me over the sea,
And then, oh, what will become of me?
But come, my brother, give me your hand,
We'll build a mountain and then we'll stand."

And so, the snowflakes grew to drifts;
The grains of sand to a mountain;
The leaves became a summer shade;
The dewdrops fed a fountain.

Week Nineteen Blackboard Drawing

Drawing Ideas for This Week: Capital letter S as shown in a snowman or in a drift of snow from our story, icicles, frozen water, children skating, igloo, snowflakes, snowballs, Roman numeral XIX, NINETEEN, 19

Week Nineteen Teacher's Classroom Work

1. Make Ahead Meals

   This week set aside one or two full days to cook in bulk and freeze. Once a month cooking saves you both time and money. Choose some of your favorite meals and spend time with your children making large quantities to freeze. There are many recipes that can be frozen for breakfast, lunch, dinner, and snacks. Our seasonal childcare menus are full of freezable meals that the children will love helping you prepare and eat! Visit our website to see the menus: www.littleacornlearning.com

2. This week take your children ice skating! See if there is a local pond or lake that is safe for skating or drive to your nearest indoor ice rink. Many places have lessons for beginners and children. The sport is an excellent way to practice balance for adults and children alike.

3. Freeze a black cloth if you are wishing to use it to help with your Snowflake Study this week.

4. Review any handwork before working on projects with your children.

Week Nineteen Caregiver Meditation

This Week's Reflection: Forgiveness

"Forgiveness is the giving, and so the receiving, of life." ~ *George MacDonald*

Accepting what has occurred in the past as well as what is occurring in the present, is, in itself, an act of forgiveness. When we forgive the moments in our lives, we accept them for what they are without trying to change them. In return, we open ourselves up to receiving life with all its lessons, beauty and sorrows. We accept that every event in our life has a purpose.

Spend time this week contemplating issues that are causing pain in your life. Allow yourself to use this meditation time to forgive the events and accept them for what they are. Allow yourself to break free of resistance and the desire to make it right or change it. This type of surrender and radical acceptance will in turn give you the peace you desire.

Week Nineteen Story

For this little tale, use a white silk to symbolize the North Wind and a blue silk for Jack Frost. During the first few paragraphs, have your silks travel around the air of the room until they land near a window. As they paint Willie's window, you could tape a few small paper snowflakes of your own to yours. If your window has a bit of frost or dew on it, outline a few trees and vines with your fingertips. Use your imagination and take up your silks again and travel to the 'brooklet' and 'little pond' following the North Wind and Little Jack Frost's journey.

North Wind and Little Jack Frost

One winter night, Old North Wind and Little Jack Frost had a talk which I happened to overhear.

North Wind called Jack Frost to see a snowdrift which he had blown into a fence corner, and, with his gray wing, swept into curves as pretty as one ever sees anywhere except in a little child's face. Jack Frost looked and laughed, saying, "I can make things quite as pretty, but I must work in the water."

North Wind wrapped his cloak of clouds about him and went to see Jack Frost work in a stream of water not far away.

As they flew, with clouds and snow before them, Jack Frost peeped in a window, and saw a little boy sleeping. "Let's do something for Willie Winkle," whispered Jack Frost.

"Agreed!" shouted North Wind. To work they went, North Wind puffing little starry gems of snow against the windowpane outside, while Jack Frost fastened them on, and, at the same time, drew pictures of trees and vines on the inside, which were so pretty that North Wind fairly shook the house, trying to get in to see them. Jack Frost, fearing all the noise of North Wind would waken Willie Winkle, hurriedly tasted the water in Willie's silver cup, which turned the water to ice, and crept out at the keyhole.

When North Wind and Jack Frost reached the brooklet, they were talking about the children they had seen that night; and the little brook stopped to listen, for she had missed the visits from the children for many a day. And, as she listened, every drop, ripple, and dimple of the brooklet turned to crystal, and stood still there, waiting until spring for the children.

When North Wind and Jack Frost passed a tiny pond, old North Wind fairly held his breath a moment with delight; then he, being the older, said, "Let's work together this winter."

"Agreed!" laughed Jack Frost, from the turret of an ice palace which he was finishing.

"Will you ripple the top of this water while I freeze it?"

"That I will," answered old North Wind.

"It will spoil the skating for the big boys, but we'll work for the little folks tonight."

So North Wind blew across the water till it wrinkled and waved like a broad field of wheat under the wing of South Wind in summer. Jack Frost followed close upon the breath of North Wind, kissed the ripples and wrinkles, and there they stood.

The waters were all curled and frozen over little caves, shining grottos, and glittering palaces of ice.

As North Wind and Jack Frost were going home next morning, they saw Willie Winkle looking at the pretty pictures on his window.

"Let us speak to him," said North Wind. But at his voice the window rattled and shook so noisily that Willie Winkle ran away to sit by the warm fire.

After breakfast Willie Winkle went again to the window, and, seeing the beautiful drifts, and wreaths, and banks, and puffs of snow in corners, on gateposts, and in treetops, he begged to go outside.

He was no sooner in the yard than Jack Frost came creeping, and North Wind came shouting; and one pinched his ears; the other blew off his hat. And such a wrestling match as Willie Winkle had with them made even his mamma laugh.

When he went in the house, his cheeks were as red as roses, and his fingers as purple as Jack Frost could make them with his kisses and pinches.

Monday Student Lessons – Week Nineteen

(Baking/Cooking – Purple Day)

Language Arts

1. Begin your lesson time by reading (or telling) the story of *North Wind and Little Jack Frost* to your child. Let the children look at the sentences as you read as this visual will aid with their knowledge of letters, words and sentences. If possible, use simple props to accompany the story as we have suggested.

2. When your story is finished, unveil your blackboard drawing that you have prepared ahead of time as suggested at the beginning of this week's curriculum. If your child has his or her own small blackboard and chalk, have them take a few moments to create their own drawing.

3. Review what your child worked on last week in their lesson book. Have them practice writing the capital letter R a few times on their blackboard or an extra piece of paper. Be sure they have a good grasp of this letter before moving onto the next.

4. In your child's lesson book, have them create a similar image of a snowman or snowdrift (or whatever depiction you used) with the letter S revealed inside. On the righthand side, have your child practice writing the capital letter S. Share this poem as you work to form the letter:

   Two curves make up the letter S
   Start at the top and curve to the left
   Then curve again around to the right
   And tuck it under below real tight

5. Learning Vowels

   Today talk to your children about a special group of letters that we call "vowels". We have already learned most of these letters. They are: A, E, I, O and U.

Vowels are very special letters that make a sound that flows more freely through the mouth as we say them. The sounds come without much obstruction and without our tongues having to touch certain areas of our mouth. Vowels vibrate the vocal cords more than the sounds of other letters. As we've been learning already, vowels also have a long and a short sound.

All the other letters in the alphabet are called consonants. When vowels join consonants, they create the words and syllables we have been practicing.

1. Practice saying the short and long sound of each vowel with your child. Notice how your mouth forms to make the sounds. Bringing awareness to the way our body forms sounds and words is very important. This process helps us to notice the use of air and our body muscles as we communicate.

2. Next, practice saying the sounds of various consonants that we've learned. Can your child notice the difference of how the sounds moves through their mouth?

3. On your blackboard, draw a fairy with each of the vowels included in their dress. As you create your drawing, keep in mind the following qualities of each letter:

Fairy A – This fairy is one of AWE and openness – she holds her arms out and downward as she takes in all the beautiful sounds, sights and feelings that surround her.

Fairy E – This fairy is more reserved – she holds her arms crossed in front of her to protect herself and stay safe. She absorbs what surrounds her and keeps it all tucked inside until it is needed.

Fairy I – This fairy keeps one arm upward and one down as he likes to stay connected to both what is above and below. He is one that helps lead when it is time to bring the sounds down to the consonants below to make words.

Fairy O – This fairy wants to include everyone and everything he sees and feels in one place. He joins his hands in front of him like a circle and enjoys singing and dancing in the round.

Fairy U – This fairy, holds her arms upward and rounded and she is calling down the sounds, colors and feelings that rise above everything below.

4. Read this sweet story to your children about The Vowel Fairies and then have your child draw each of the fairies in their lesson book on the left side and on the right side, have them practice writing each of the letters. You may also wish to tell this story while watercolor painting which would be quite beautiful.

The Vowel Fairies
by Eileen Foley

Way up high beyond rainbows and sunrays, there is a magical place where sound and music paint the air with beautiful colors.

All the music, sounds, feelings and colors from down below come to this place to float in a haze above the clouds. And, this is where the Vowel Fairies play.

There are five of these very special fairies. Each one of these fairies has two sounds: a short sound and a long sound. And the fairies love to climb up and slide down the vibrations of all the sounds they make and the sounds and feelings that float up to them from down below.

One day, as the fairies were playing, a new feeling floated above to them from far, far below and far away in the Land of Consonants. It was a call for help to the fairies from the elves that lived there.

These elves that lived below also enjoyed playing, dancing and sliding on sounds and feelings but each of these elves only had one sound each. And, while it was fun playing by themselves, they wanted to join hands and play together but each time they did, it made a horrible noise and it did not sound good at all. They needed something new. They needed the magic sounds of the Vowel Fairies to join them.

The Vowel Fairies were happy to help. These fairies had the most beautiful and unique sounds and they came out flowing like air without any effort. As said before, each Vowel Fairy has two sounds and they loved to practice them and sing them all day long. But, just like the elves in the Land of Consonants, they could only play on their own. When they held hands to play together, their sounds no longer sounded beautiful. They wondered if it would be the same way if they joined the elves.

Fairy A was so excited and was ready to jump right in. She opened her arms wide and downward and closed her eyes. She heard the call of the elves and felt their feelings pour inside of her which made her even more anxious to go.

Fairy E wanted to wait and be cautious. She was worried it was a trick or that it may not be safe to fly down to the Land of the Consonants. While the other fairies were all fluttering about, she stood very still and held her arms across her chest. She closed her eyes and let her body feel and hear everything around her. Inside her a light started to shine. It was warm and loving and good, and she knew that this was something important that the Vowel Fairies should do. She kept that light and all she took in deep inside of her to take it with her on their journey down below.

Fairy I really wanted to help. He just gets very homesick. He was wishing he could hold onto where they live and reach down to the Land of the Consonants at the same time. He puts one hand up and one hand down and realizes that this is the answer. If he holds the sounds of the Vowel Fairies with one hand and reaches to hold the sounds of the Elves with the other, they may be able to work together to create new sounds together. He tells the others that he will go but he will keep reaching toward both places to help join the sounds of all.

Fairy O has been dreaming about this day all his life. He loves playing near the other fairies but has been so lonely and always wanted to hold hands and dance together and join one another. He tells them all to form a circle so they can slowly fly downward in circle and song toward the Land of the Consonants.

Fairy U decides to gather as many of the sounds, colors and feelings she can bring down with them. She holds her arms up rounded and they all come and fill up the space above her.

As the fairies start to descend downward, the elves feel a new feeling come upon them. It is a feeling of hope and of unity. They look above and see the most beautiful sight of five colorful fairies in a circle coming toward them, being followed by sounds and colors they have never seen or heard before.

On land, the Vowel Fairies ask the elves to line up certain ways in different rows. Then each Vowel Fairy finds his or her place and they hold hands with those in their line.

As soon as they joined together, each line made the most amazing sound. These sounds were made up of syllables and they had never heard them before. Just then, certain feelings came into each line and gave them meanings. When joined together, they formed a word! The fairies and elves played all day long making new words together and now they could not only sing notes, but they could sing and talk with words together as well!

They loved this new way of being so much that they decided to never leave one another. To this day, the Vowel Fairies and the Elves of the Land of Consonants join together over and over again to share, laugh and play.

Mathematics

1. In addition to the Roman numeral XIX, write down the number 19 and word NINETEEN in all capital letters for your child to see. Say each letter as you write: N, I, N, E, T, E, E, N, and the word out loud:

N
I
N
E
T
E
E
N

NINETEEN

Jack Frost went from stream to stream,

N
I
N
E
T
E
E
N

NINETEEN

North Wind helped, they were a team.

2. Have the child draw images of the number NINETEEN. They may copy some of the items you made in your blackboard drawing for this week. Your child should then practice writing the number 19, Roman numeral XIX and the word NINETEEN in all capital letters on the opposite page of their book. If you feel they need extra time with writing, let them continue to practice as needed. Here is a verse to share when forming the number 19:

   Draw a one, it's first in line
   Then it's time to make a nine

3. Now that your child is well versed in numbers 70-80 you can trust that they are able to move more quickly and practice their counting from 80-90. Count everything you can! If your child seems ready, you can expand your four processes math skills to include larger numbers up to 90 as well. Remember to go at your child's pace and pay close attention to how your child learns most effectively.

Domestic Arts/Practical Life Skills

Pancake Snowmen

As always, let the children help you as you cook. They should be able to do much of the measuring and follow recipes with you. Make a point to emphasize the mathematical lessons in cooking.

Supplies Needed:
4-6 Eggs
1 Teaspoon Vanilla
½ Teaspoon Cinnamon
Pinch of Sea Salt
Butter or Coconut Oil for Cooking
Banana Slices

Beat eggs and mix with sea salt, vanilla, and cinnamon. Fry in small dollops (about 1 tablespoon full) in butter or coconut oil. Turn carefully. Place three pancakes on top of each other to make a 'snowman'. Add banana slices for eyes and a nose.

Outdoor Time/Nature Walk

Take your children outside each day regardless of the weather. Invest in good rain gear, snow gear and wool undergarments if your location requires it. Do your lessons outdoors whenever possible.

Caregiver Focus

Forgiving Others and Ourselves

This week we talk about forgiveness. There are many areas in our lives where we may have trouble with this. We may have people who have hurt us in the past or present who have not apologized or taken responsibility for how they hurt us.

If we make others responsible for how and when we heal in this way, they hurt us twice. We must work to practice detachment from the other person's actions and focus on how best to heal ourselves. If we are unable to forgive, we need to dig deep within ourselves and think of times when we have also made mistakes. Acknowledge the pain you feel and then choose to let it go. Close your eyes and imagine it floating away and fresh new space opening inside of you for something beautiful and new.

We may also have done things in our lives that we are having trouble forgiving ourselves for. There is not one person on this earth who has not made mistakes. Sometimes it takes many mistakes to learn a lesson. We are also very hard on ourselves. We are human. Allow yourself the freedom to live and learn and grow. Imagine yourself as a small child who has made a mistake looking up at yourself now. Feel love and empathy for that small you. Hold him or her. Tell this little person how wonderful they are and how worthy of love they are. Let your inner child smile and feel free and run off into the world to begin again.

Movement, Body Awareness & Health

Vowel Gestures/Eurythmy

Just like our fairies, have your child act out each vowel in gesture as described below. Have children start off with both feet planted on the ground standing straight. If they want to challenge themselves while doing each gesture, they can lift one foot up and balance it on the other leg in tree pose. As they do each vowel, have them take a deep breath in and when they exhale, practice the sounds of the letter (similar to OM while doing yoga):

Letter A – Hold arms down and outward like the letter A shape. Breathe in and out and take in all the beautiful sounds, sights and feelings that surround you.

Letter E – Hold your arms crossed in front of your chest. Close your eyes. Breathe in and out and go deep within yourself.

Letter I – Hold your right arm up to the sky and your left arm straight to the ground. Pull toward both directions, staying connected to both what is above and below.

Letter O – Joins your hands in front of you, fingers intertwined, like a circle and breathe deep in and out.

Letter U – Hold your arms upward rounded like the letter U toward the sky. Breathe deep in, calling down the positive sounds, colors and feelings that rise above everything below. Exhale fully outward, letting anything go that you no longer need.

Afternoon Lessons

1. Music: Continue Practicing Flute or Recorder

2. Handwork: Cutting, Six-Pointed Paper Snowflakes

    Making paper snowflakes is so much fun at any age. Experiment with different types of paper. You can use white paper, tissue paper of all colors or patterned designs. Your child may also like to decorate their snowflakes after they are made. Hang these in a window or in your homeschool area to welcome winter!

Supplies Needed:
Various Types of Paper
Scissors

Cut your paper into a square with four equal sides.

Fold the square into a triangle from one corner to the one across.

Again, fold this triangle in half by matching two corners and making a smaller triangle.

Next fold both sides of this small triangle to the center into thirds.

With the point facing down, cut the top of the folded paper and an angle.

Cut all different shapes from the sides. If you want a hole in the center of your snowflake, clip off the point.

Tuesday Student Lessons – Week Nineteen
(Painting – Red Day)

Language Arts

1. Like yesterday, begin your lesson time by continuing to read (or tell) *North Wind and Little Jack Frost.* Provide your child with a piece of beeswax modeling material as you read. Let them hold this piece of beeswax as they listen, warming it with their hands so it softens.

2. Have your child form the softened beeswax material into the letter S. Roll it into a long snake, form it just so and then put it back together again. Next, have them form it into the number 19.

3. Open your lesson book and review the work you did yesterday. Have your child trace the letter S number 19 and word NINETEEN with their fingers.

4. Practice saying the sounds of the letter S. Notice how our mouth forms to make the sound. Bringing awareness to the way our body forms sounds and words is very important. This process helps us to notice the use of air and our body muscles as we communicate.

5. Today we will work on a tongue twister to practice and memorize with your child to help learn the letter S and its sound. Tongue twisters and rhymes are fun ways to learn and help with finding rhythm. As we have begun bringing awareness to syllables, pay careful attention with your child to be sure they get it correctly.

   To begin, say the following tongue twister to your child slowly **and tap one finger on the palm of your other hand to the syllables** to create a pattern for memory:

   Sippity sup, sippity sup,
   Bread and milk from a china cup.
   Bread and milk from a bright silver spoon
   Made of a piece of the bright silver moon.
   Sippity sup, sippity sup,
   Sippity, sippity sup.

Mathematics

1. Using tangible items continue counting backwards with your children today. This week start from 40 to 1.

2. Write numbers 1-50 on your blackboard. Using your finger, point to 100 and count backward to the number one. Have your child do this with you.

3. In your child's lesson book, have them draw 60 items on the left side. This could be 60 little dots, trees, buttons, hearts or even simply sticks. Count them together first in order and then backward. Next, on the right side of your child's layout, have them write the number 60 and downward to the number 1. You can help them if they are struggling.

4. Continue these types of exercises over the next week or two aiming to be able to increase the amount of numbers your child can count backwards.

Outdoor Time/Nature Walk

Take your children outside each day regardless of the weather. Invest in good rain gear, snow gear and wool undergarments if your location requires it. Do your lessons outdoors whenever possible.

Social Studies, Geography, Weather, Time

Learning About Goods and Services

Everything we purchase is either a good or a service. Goods can either be used, touched or consumed. A service is work that can be done for others.

1. Think about the types of goods that can be purchased in your community. Next, think about where you can get these goods. On the top of your blackboard write GOODS. Underneath make two columns. On one side write the type of item and on the other write where you could get that item. For example:

Books	Library/Bookstore
Milk	Grocery Store/Farm Stand
Paint	Art Store

In your child's lesson book, have them choose one of these items and locations to draw on the left side. On the right, have them write the word for the item as well as the word for the location they can find it.

Next, think about the types of services that can be sought out in your community. Who can provide this service? On the top of your blackboard write SERVICES. Underneath make two columns. On one side write the type of service and on the other side write who can provide it. For example:

Haircut	Hair Stylist
Check Up	Doctor
Transportation	Bus Driver/Cab Driver

Afternoon Lessons

Art: Snow Lanterns

If you have snow where you live, this is a very fun activity for children. You can also make an igloo together!

Snow Lanterns

Supplies Needed:
Snowballs (if climate permits)
Candle on Plate or Other Small Light Source Such as Battery-Operated Light
Long Stemmed Lighter or Very Long Match Sticks

Form snowballs and make one layer of a small circle on ground. Continue to build up like an igloo and about halfway up place candle or light inside. If you are using a battery operated light source, you can light it now. If you are using a candle, continue to build up your lantern wall and use a very long lighter or matches to light before completing. Be very careful doing this activity with young children. This is a perfect way to welcome in the light of the New Year.

Wednesday Student Lessons – Week Nineteen
(Coloring – Yellow Day)

Language Arts

1. Practice our tongue twister again. Keep working on this until you have it memorized together. Say the following tongue twister to your child slowly **and tap one finger on the palm of your other hand to the syllables** to create a pattern for memory:

   Sippity sup, sippity sup,
   Bread and milk from a china cup.
   Bread and milk from a bright silver spoon
   Made of a piece of the bright silver moon.
   Sippity sup, sippity sup,
   Sippity, sippity sup.

2. In your child's lesson book have them make a drawing of the story of *North Wind and Little Jack Frost*.

3. On the opposite page, your child is likely ready to write simple sentences (do not worry about punctuation at this time). Remember we are still writing in all capital letters. Provide your child with a simple sentence on the blackboard to copy such as:

   NORTH WIND BLEW THE SNOW
   JACK FROST PAINTS WITH ICE
   THIS IS A SNOWMAN
   I LIKE SNOW

4. Tonight, at bedtime tell your child of the story of *North Wind and Little Jack Frost*.

5. When out and about, ask your child to find things that begin with the letter S. This can be done while shopping or when driving in the car. Throughout the week, ask your child to think of all the words they can that begin with the letter S. How many can they come up with? Make a list.

Mathematics

Snowflake Pattern Match

They say no two snowflakes are alike but in this case that's not true! Have the children help you create a snowflake matching game out of old watercolor paintings and hand cut paper snowflakes. The game can be used face up or turned over as a pattern memory game. To add in some more mathematical practice, write an equation and an answer on each match.

Supplies Needed:
Colored Cardstock or Old Watercolor Paintings
White Paper for Snowflakes
Glue
Pencil
Ruler

The first thing you will need to do is figure out how many cards you are able to make out of your watercolor paintings and what size you want them to be. Use a pencil and a ruler to make marks on your paper so you know where to cut. This is a good opportunity for children to continue to practice measuring, cutting and handling scissors properly.

After you have the correct number of cards planned out, work with the children to cut out paper snowflakes that will fit on your cards. To get two of the same snowflakes, simply use two sheets of your white paper folded together before you cut. Here is a sweet verse to share as you work:

Snowflake, snowflake,
(flutter snowflakes or one hand)
Little snowflake,
Falling from the sky
(move snowflake down)

Snowflake, snowflake,
(flutter snowflakes or one hand)
Little snowflake,
Falling on my nose.
(point to nose or bring snowflake to touch it)

Snowflake, snowflake,
(flutter snowflakes or one hand)
Little snowflake,
Falling on my head.
(point to head or touch snowflake)

Snowflake, snowflake
(flutter snowflakes or one hand)
Little snowflake,
Falling on my toes.
(touch hands or snowflake to toes)

Next, have the children use glue to adhere the snowflakes to each card and let dry. These cards can also be laminated for added durability before playing.

Outdoor Time/Nature Walk

Take your children outside each day regardless of the weather. Invest in good rain gear, snow gear and wool undergarments if your location requires it. Do your lessons outdoors whenever possible.

Science, Nature Study, Earth Discovery

1. Learning About Ice: Icicles, Ice Shelters

    If your climate allows, take the children outside to look for icicles. How many can you find? Observe the difference in length and shape of each one. Under supervision, allow the children to hold an icicle. How does it feel? The children can sketch the icicles and write about their discoveries in a journal or in their lesson books. This would be a good time to go to the library and do some further research on ice, snow and home and shelters made of ice or snow.

    Here are some questions to ask your child to inspire free discussion:

    How does ice feel? (cold, wet)
    What must happen for water to turn into ice? (it must get freezing cold)
    What types of things can turn into ice? (water, ponds, lakes, food in the freezer)

    What must happen for ice to melt back into water? (it must get warmer)
    If you put ice cubes in the sun, would they melt?

If you put water in the freezer, would it get frozen?
How do you suppose an icicle forms? (water that is running or dripping freezes)
Do you know that some people build homes and shelters out of ice? Do you know what they are called? (igloos)

2. Learning About Ice: Frozen Suncatchers

Supplies Needed:
Aluminum Pie Dish or Shallow Plastic Tupperware Dish
Yarn/String
Outdoor Materials (pine, twigs, leaves, berries, birdseed, etc.)

For this activity, it is even easier to hang your suncatcher if you use a pan that has a hole in the center such as an Angel Food Cake or Bundt Cake Pan. If you do not have these, a flat pie dish will work. Just place your string or yarn with a loop on top down through as much of the water as possible so it freezes well.

Fill each dish approximately half full with water. Allow children to drop items into their pan. Place string or yarn leaving a loop on top for hanging. Put each dish in the freezer or leave outside overnight. When frozen, pull suncatcher out of dish and hang outdoors (can be kept in freezer after observation if you live in a warm climate). Watch the sun shine through your suncatcher and talk about what will need to happen for it to melt.

Afternoon Lessons

1. Handwork: Beginner Knitting, Knitting in the Round

Supplies Needed:
Circular Needles Size 6 mm (10 US)
Bulky Yarn
Stitch Marker

Up until this point, your child has been knitting back and forth the traditional way. There are also many projects you can learn that allow for you to knit in the round. This is also called circular knitting.

Circular knitting produces a tube without a seam and is worked in a spiral. A stitch marker is used on each row to place where you begin. This method of knitting can be done with four or five double pointed needles or on a pair of circular needles. For this lesson, we recommend using circulars and learning later how to work with numerous needles.

Circular knitting needles are joined together with a flexible cable. Knitting in the round is perfect for things like hats, socks and mittens as it creates a tube-like opening.

When you are knitting in the round, there is no wrong side. You will always be knitting on the same side facing you. You will never turn your work as we do in regular knitting as you are always knitting on the same side. As you knit in a circle, you will be spiraling up – just like you could spiral up and around a mountain to the top.

When choosing a pair of circular needles for your project, be sure the length of the needles is less than the circumference of your project. For example, if you are making a 16" hat, be sure to use needles that are less than 16" so your project does not stretch to reach around.

You will need to learn how to join in the round. We will provide written instructions here, but it is also helpful to look online or work with an experienced knitter before teaching your child. There are wonderful videos online you can watch to practice.

There are a few ways to join in the round. This option works up nicely and is our favorite:

Move the first stitch you casted on to your left needle by sliding it over the circular cable as if you are about to start knitting. Instead of knitting into it, slip it from your left needle to the right needle.

Next, lift the stitch next to it on your right needle over it and onto your left needle in its place.

Pull tight and start knitting into the stitches that are on your left needle.

2. Handwork: Beginner Knitting, Easy 'In the Round' Ribbed Hat

Cast on 90 stitches

Place a marker, then join in the round – before doing this, be absolutely sure your stiches are not twisted. Look carefully making sure all loops are facing the same direction on your needles before joining the row together.

K2, P2 to marker

Continue K2, P2 around, making ribbed pattern until hat measures approximately 9". Be careful not to get off pattern. The knits should go into knits and the purls should go into purls, all the way around.

To close up the hat:

K2, P2 together to marker
K2, P1 to marker
K2 together, P1 to marker
K1, P1 to marker

Continue K2 together all the way around until there are only two stitches left on the needle.

Finish off, pull yarn through last stitch and weave into hat.

Thursday Student Lessons – Week Nineteen
(Crafting/Games – Orange Day)

Language Arts

1. Continue to tell your child the story of *North Wind and Little Jack Frost.*

2. Alphabet Cards

    Supplies Needed:
    Heavy White Cardstock
    Beeswax Stick Crayons
    Scissor

    Spend time cutting cards out of cardstock with your child. Using beeswax crayons, continue to finish drawing each letter we have learned so far and include the letter S. Next to the letter, have your child draw an image that begins with it. Using scissors, round the corners of these cards and keep working on them throughout the year. You can use them in your lessons and for an upper case and lowercase match game later in the curriculum when we learn those as well.

3. Continue reading simple reader books together.

4. Practice saying the sound of S. Notice how our mouth forms to make the sound. Bringing awareness to the way our body forms sounds and words is very important. This process helps us to notice the use of air and our body muscles as we communicate.

5. Print out or share the following photos and practice saying them together with your child. Your child may be ready to copy these words into their lesson book.

SNOWMAN

SWAN

SOAP

SPOON

SUN

Mathematics

Domino Math

Below we have provided you cut out dominoes that you can use for these activities. For more durability, glue them onto cardstock. They can also be laminated. Alternatively, you can use a regular set of 28 dominoes if you have them on hand.

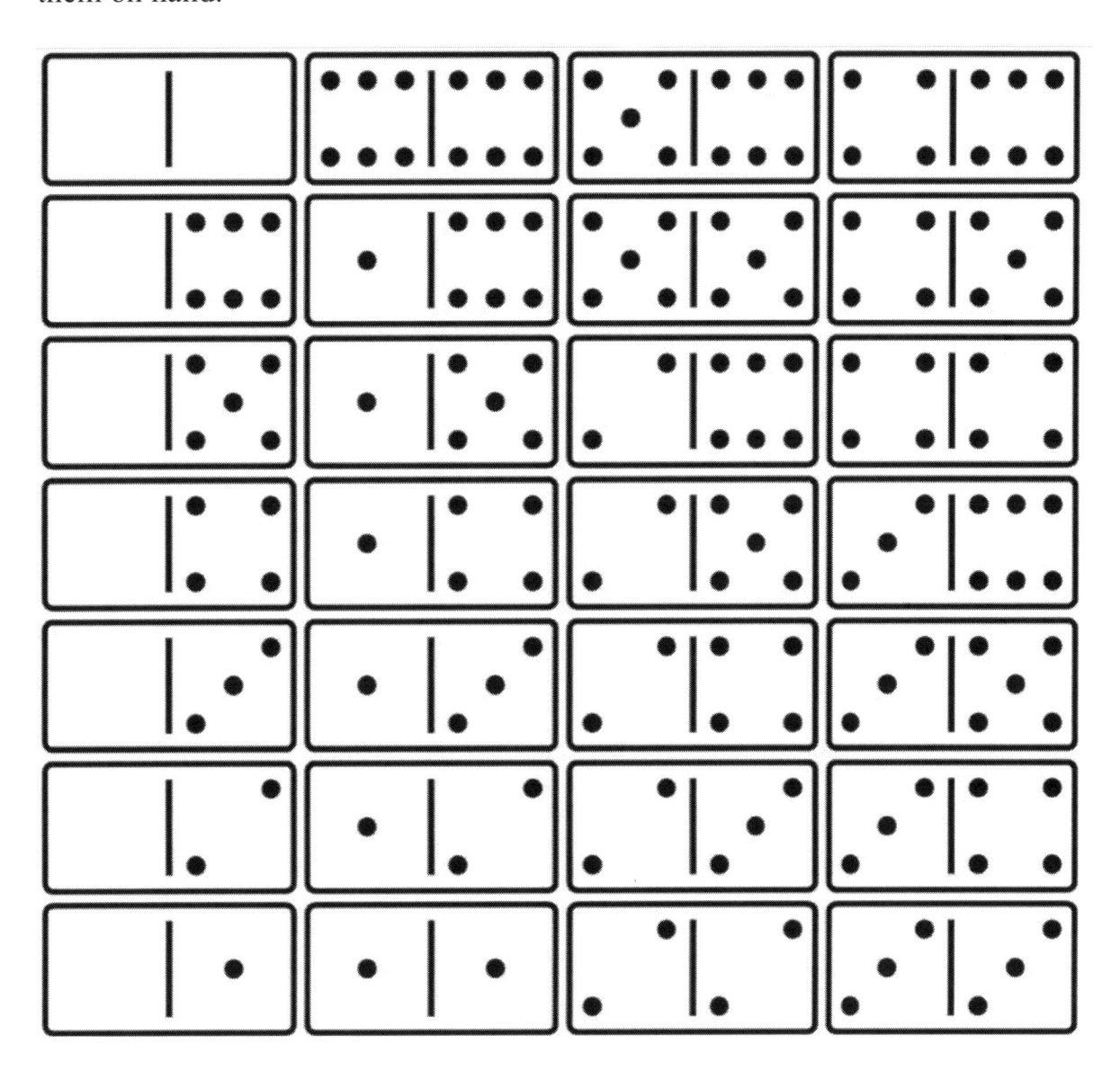

1. Domino War

   As with the card game, this should be played with two players. Each player should have a pad of paper and pencil as well.

   Place all your dominoes face down on the table. Both players choose a domino at the same time and shares the sum of their domino (i.e. 3 dots + 3 dots = 6). The player with the highest sum, keeps both dominos. If the sum is the same, they each keep their own domino.

   When all 28 dominos have been played, the player with the most dominoes is the winner.

2. Race to 100

   Again, keep paper and pencil next to each player with all dominoes face down on the table. The goal is for each player to try to get to 100 first. Practicing with either addition or multiplication, players pull a domino at the same time and share the sum or the product. On paper, write down the total and keep playing. The first player to reach 100 wins.

3. Countdown to Zero

   To practice subtraction, each player begins with 100 points. Then using either multiplication or addition, each player subtracts their answers from the running total until they reach zero. The first player to reach zero wins.

Outdoor Time/Nature Walk

Take your children outside each day regardless of the weather. Invest in good rain gear, snow gear and wool undergarments if your location requires it. Do your lessons outdoors whenever possible.

Movement, Body Awareness & Health

<u>Ice and Snow Movement Games</u>

1. Ask your children if they think when something is frozen it is moving or standing still.

   Have them show you how they stand very still just like ice. Next, ask them to show you how they can move like running water.

2. Freeze Dance

   Play a game of freeze dance with your children. This is a great way to get exercise indoors during the cold winter months.

   To begin, you will need some form of music. This can be done with a musical instrument that you play (bells, drums, guitar, etc.), singing a song, or with recorded music.

   Explain to the children that they should DANCE while the music is playing but as soon as the music stops, everyone must freeze and stand still.

   You can then have those who did not freeze sit out one turn or you can just continue and play over again.

3. Indoor Ice Skating

   Supplies Needed:
   Sheet of Wax Paper for Each Foot
   Carpet

   Have each child place a piece of wax paper under their shoes and "ice skate" on the carpet. Allocate an area to be your "skating rink".

Afternoon Lessons

1. Form Drawing/Art – Snowflake Drawings

   Let your child experiment with putting straight lines together to make "snowflake" forms. First start with six pointed snowflakes. Then, have your child use more lines to experience how adding more lines creates more fullness in the forms.

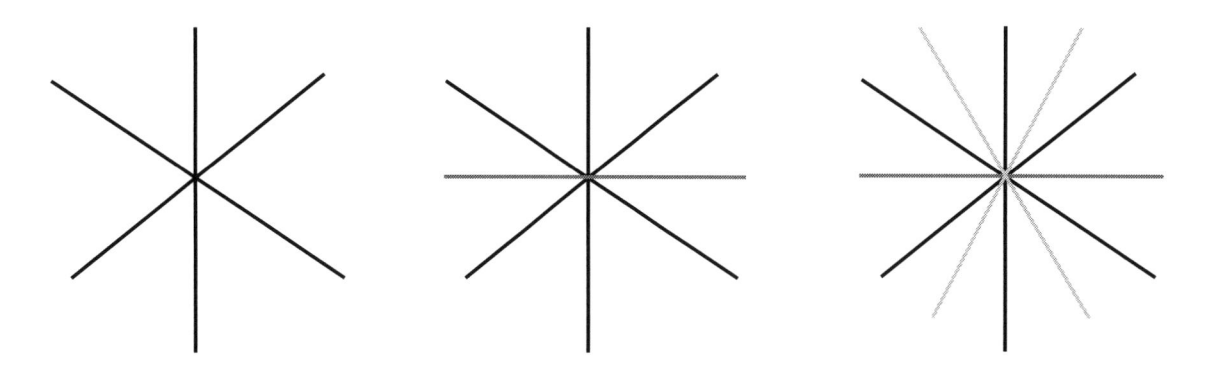

2. Handwork: Hand Stitching/Embroidery

   Supplies Needed:
   Embroidery Needle
   Embroidery Floss
   White Scrap Fabric
   Embroidery Hoop (optional)
   Scissors

   Using our embroidery instructions, work with your child to make a letter S embroidery piece. You can do this with a simple running stitch, or you may choose to learn more complicated stitches together.

Friday Student Lessons – Week Nineteen
(Modeling/Housework – Green Day)

Language Arts

1. Today have your child continue to practice writing the letter S in their lesson book on unlined paper.

2. In your child's lesson book, have them practice writing the alphabet from A-S copying each letter a few times on each line.

3. Ask your child to tell YOU the story of *North Wind and Little Jack Frost*.

4. Continue sharing the Vowel Fairy story with your children. Mix up a bag of letters (scrabble tiles work great!) and have your child pull out the letters A, E, I O and U. Work together to make as many words using the vowels together.

Mathematics

1. Domino Math: Even and Odd Sort

    For this game, the players choose their domino and either add or multiply the dots to get their answer. Then each player should decide whether their answer is even or odd and sorted into a pile for each.

2. Old Fashioned Dominoes

    Now that you've had fun with math using your dominoes, play a game the old-fashioned way!

    How to play:

    Turn all dominoes face down on table (this is called the "boneyard")

    Each player draws one domino to determine who goes first. The one with the highest number will begin the game. Each player then draws seven dominoes.

    The first player goes by putting one domino down face up on the table. The next player must match a domino at the end of that one. For example, if the first domino ends with three dots, the next domino must have three also and be placed next to it.

If a player does not have a domino that works, they may choose from the boneyard until they do. The object of the game is to play all your dominos and be left empty handed. If this doesn't happen and there is no winner when the boneyard is dry (empty), then the game is over and nobody wins.

Outdoor Time/Nature Walk

Take your children outside each day regardless of the weather. Invest in good rain gear, snow gear and wool undergarments if your location requires it. Do your lessons outdoors whenever possible.

Science, Nature Study, Earth Discovery

Snowflake Study

Supplies Needed:
Magnifying Glasses
Black Cloth
Snowflakes (you may need to save this activity for a day that cooperates!)

Each and every snowflake is different from the other, but each snowflake is made up of exactly SIX ice needles. If the weather allows, spend time outdoors with your child using a magnifying glass to study these beautiful flakes more closely.

Snowflakes can be hard to study as they melt very quickly. To assist you, freeze a black cloth prior to this experiment. When the first snow appears, lay your cloth outside and allow snowflakes to land on the fabric. Before they melt, have each child look through their magnifying glass to see the different sizes and shapes of each snowflake.

If you do not have snowflakes where you live (or even if you do!), you can spend time instead examining ice from your freezer.

Domestic Arts/Practical Life Skills

Winter Chores

Today have your children help you do work that is important to keep your home functioning well in the winter. Some ideas:

Shovel walkways and driveways
Put salt down on ice
Cover outdoor furniture
Protect the garden from colder weather
Stock and organize the pantry
Can foods
Organize warmer clothing

Afternoon Lessons

Use the afternoon hours today to review areas from this week's afternoon lessons that you feel may need a bit more attention. Bring these into your weekend as you find time.

Week Twenty, Winter
First Grade

Theme: Different Cultures, Religions, & Traditions, Tolerance

This Week's Lessons:

Language Arts:
Little Tom Thumb Story
Letter T

Mathematics:
Number 20
Counting to Ten in Spanish
Math Marbles

Social Studies, Geography, Weather, Time:
Learning About Different Cultures, Religions, Traditions, Languages & Climates

Science, Nature Study, Earth Discovery:
Make Your Own Hurricane
Slime Making: Liquid to Solid

Teacher's Classroom Work:
Plan a Visit to a Religious Place of Worship
Seek Out Individuals for Native Speaking and Different Countries Interview

For the Caregiver:
Caregiver Meditation: Tolerance
Caregiver Focus: Practicing Tolerance in Everyday Living

Domestic Arts/Practical Life Skills:
Multicultural Apple Lesson
Cooking Around the World Recipes
Practicing Manners

Music:
Cultural and Tolerance Fingerplays & Songs
Beginning Recorder or Flute

Art/Handwork:
Art: String Around the World
Handwork: Beginner Knitting, Practice Circular Knitting
Handwork: Beginner Knitting, Continue Easy 'In the Round' Ribbed Hat
Embroidery, Letter T
Alphabet Card Letter T

Form Drawing:
Form Drawing/Art – Galloping Line

Movement, Body Awareness & Health:
Movement Games from Ireland, Brazil & Columbia
Galloping Like Horses
Game of Marbles

Supplies Needed for Week Twenty

Cooking List:

Apples of All Shapes & Colors
Avocado
Garlic
Small Bunch Cilantro
Three Onions
Tomato
Lime
Salt
Pepper
4 Cups Cut Cucumbers
4 Cups Cut Tomatoes
1 Large Bell Pepper (Any Color)
3 Tablespoons Cilantro
3 Tablespoons Mint
1 Cup Feta
½ Cup Pitted Kalamata Olives
Lemon Juice
Extra Virgin Olive Oil

Homeschooling List:

Blackboard
Chalk
Bowl & Silk
Lesson Book
Stockmar Stick Crayons
Stockmar Block Crayons
Colored Pencils
Stockmar Beeswax Modeling Material
Knitting Needles
Super Bulky Single Ply 100% Wool Yarn
Embroidery Needle
Embroidery Floss
White Scrap Fabric
Embroidery Hoop (optional)
Heavy White Cardstock

Blue and Green Cotton String or Yarn
Balloon
Glue
2 Empty Soda Bottles
¼ Cup of Sand
Funnel
3 Paperclips
3 Peanuts
Water
Duct Tape
Marbles
Sidewalk Chalk or String
White Glue
Food Coloring
Borax

Week Twenty Book Recommendations

Visit your local library the weekend before to check out books based on your theme for the week. Older children can help you look up the books by author and title. When setting up your play space for the week ahead, mindfully display these books in baskets for the children to enjoy.

Strictly No Elephants ~ Lisa Mantchev
Whoever You Are ~ Mem Fox
All the Colors of the Earth ~ Sheila Hamanaka
There's a Skunk in My Bunk: Helping Children Learn Tolerance
black is brown is tan ~ Arnold Adoff
Hey, Little Ant ~ Phillip M. Hoose & Hannah Hoose
Miss Twiggley's Tree ~ Dorothea Warren Fox
Lost and Found Cat: The True Story of Kunkush's Incredible Journey ~ Doug Kuntz
Whoever You Are ~ Mem Fox
People ~ Peter Spier
Konnichiwa & Hello ~ Tammy Robertson
This Is How We Do It: One Day in the Lives of Seven Kids from around the World ~ Matt Lamothe
One Big Heart: A Celebration of Being More Alike Than Different ~ Linsey Davis
It's Ok to be Different: A Children's Picture Book About Diversity and Kindness ~ Sharon Purtill
The Big Umbrella ~ Amy June Bates
What If We Were All The Same! ~ C.M. Harris
Happy in Our Skin ~ Fran Manushkin
Many: The Diversity of Life on Earth ~ Nicola Davies
I Am Enough ~ Grace Byers
Rainbow Village: A Story to Help Children Celebrate Diversity ~ Emmi Smid
How Pete met Lizard: Happy Friends Diversity Stories ~ Patricia Furstenberg
My Religion, Your Religion ~ Lisa Bullard
Same, Same But Different ~ Jenny Sue Kostecki-Shaw
Celebrating Different Beliefs ~ Steffi Cavell-Clarke
The Kids Book of World Religions ~ Jennifer Glossop
Different Like Me ~ Xochitl Dixon
The Smeds and the Smoos ~ Julia Donaldson
A Picture Book of Martin Luther King, Jr. ~ David A. Adler

Week Twenty Circle, Songs & Movement

The following songs and verses should be shared during circle time each day this week after you open your circle.

I am different from my head to my toes
(point to self then to head and toes)

I am different from my eyes to my nose
(point to self then eyes and nose)

I come from a place that is far and wide
(point to self then spread arms wide open)

A place where we are all the same inside
(hug self)

I have ten little fingers and ten little toes,

Two little arms and one little nose,

One little mouth and two little ears,

Two little eyes for smiles and tears,

One little head and two little feet,

One little chin, that's me complete.

I have ten fingers and they all belong to me
(hold hands up)
I can make them do things
Would you like to see?

I can shut them up tight
(form fist)
Or open them wide
(hold fingers out)
I can put them together
Or make them all hide
(close both fists)

I can make them jump high
(put hands over head)
I can make them go low
(put hands down)
I can fold them quietly and hold them just so
(put hands in lap)

Two tiny toads jumping around
(hold up two fingers while turning around)

Two turtles crawling on the ground
(squat down while holding up two fingers)

They all tiptoed without making a sound.
(tiptoe & hold up two fingers on each hand)

And they turned their heads round and round
(pretend to turn head round and round)

Grateful
(sung to Twinkle, Twinkle, Little Star)

Grateful for the sun so bright,
Grateful for the moon at night,
Grateful for my family,
For different friends who play with me,
Grateful for everything I see,
Grateful for you and me

Week Twenty Blackboard Drawing

Drawing Ideas for This Week: Capital letter T as shown in the shape of Tom Thumb tied to a thistle or in the shape of a mushroom he is lying under, different flags, religious symbols, globe, different children holding hands, Letter T, words beginning with T, Roman numeral XX, TWENTY, 20

Week Twenty Teacher's Classroom Work

1. Plan visit to place of worship other than your own for this week's lesson.

2. Review and practice circular knitting.

3. Review and practice joining knitting in the round.

4. Seek out individuals for native speaking and different countries interview.

Week Twenty Caregiver Meditation

This Week's Reflection: Tolerance

"One day our descendants will think it incredible that we paid so much attention to things like the amount of melanin in our skin or the shape of our eyes or our gender instead of the unique identities of each of us as complex human beings."
~ Franklin Thomas

There is much beauty to be found in our differences. Spend time contemplating the individuals that have come in and out of your life. Think about their difference in appearance, beliefs, approach, and dreams.

Consider how each difference has enriched your life in some way. Or, consider how their differences have challenged you to become a better person, to grow, to forgive, or to move on.

Our children also need for us to practice tolerance. They are their own person, with their own feelings and ways of being. We can only guide them in this life to the best of our ability. The rest is up to them and they will truly blossom when we let them develop in their own way and at their own pace.

Week Twenty Story

There is no better way to make this story come to life and represent Tom Thumb then by using your thumb while telling the tale! As we focus on diversity and differences this week, the story of Little Tom Thumb demonstrates the strength in this little child's ability to do many things and be loved regardless of his size. You can use a bowl nearby for when Tom falls into the pudding. When the king is surprised by Tom Thumb coming out of the fish, have your thumb pop out from under a silk or tabletop. Use your imagination and create excitement as you share with your child.

Little Tom Thumb

Long ago, in a small cottage in the woods, there lived an honest man and his wife. They had all they could ask for and loved each other very much but they were sad because they could not have children.

One night the husband and wife sat crying. They wished so badly to have a child that the wife said, "I would be happy to have a son, even if he was no larger than my thumb."

It just so happened that the Queen of the Fairies was passing by the cottage and heard this cry coming from inside. As she looked into the window and saw the couple wishing for a child, she decided to grant their wish.

Shortly after the wife was surprised to have the good fortune of having a child. When the child was born, he only grew as tall as his mother's thumb. The mother was so happy to have her son that she did not mind his size at all and gave him the name of Tom Thumb.

The Queen of the Fairies was happy to see this and quickly summoned several fairies to clothe the child:

"An oak leaf hat he had for his crown,
His shirt it was by spiders spun;
With doublet wove of thistle's down,
His trousers up with points were done.
His stockings, of apple rind, they tie
With eye-lash plucked from his mother's eye,

His shoes were made of a mouse's skin,
Nicely tanned, with the hair within."

Tom never was any bigger than his mother's thumb, which was not a large thumb either; but, as he grew older, he became very cunning and sly. His mother loved her son very much and never disciplined his bad behavior which did not help him learn good manners.

One day, Tom's mother was making a batter pudding. Although he was told never to go near the pudding, Tom wanted to see how she mixed it and he climbed on the edge of the bowl. Before he knew it, his foot happened to slip, he fell over head and ears into the batter, and his mother not observing him, stirred him into the pudding, and popped him into the pot to boil!

The hot water made Tom kick and struggle; and his mother, seeing the pudding jump up and down in such a furious manner, thought it was bewitched. She threw the pudding out the window and a poor woman coming by just at that exact moment quickly grabbed the pudding bowl and walked on.

As soon as Tom could get the batter out of his mouth, he began to cry aloud; which so frightened the poor woman, that she flung the pudding over the hedge, and ran away from it as fast as she could run.

The pudding was broken to pieces by the fall and Tom was released. He walked home to his mother who gave him a kiss and put him to bed.

Another time, Tom Thumb's mother took him with her when she went to milk the cow; and it being a very windy day, she tied him with a needleful of thread to a thistle, that he might not be blown away. The cow liking Tom's oak leaf hat took him and the thistle up at one mouthful. While cow chewed the thistle, Tom, terrified at her great teeth, which seemed ready to crush him to pieces, roared, "Mother, Mother!" as loud as he could bawl. "Where are you, Tommy, my dear Tommy?" said the mother. "Here, mother, here in the red cow's mouth." The mother began to cry and wring her hands. The cow was surprised at such odd noises in her throat coming from Tom's yelling and opened her mouth and let him drop out. His mother clapped him into her apron and ran home with him.

Again, Tom fell into trouble. Tom's father made him a whip of a barley straw to drive the cattle with and one day in the field Tom slipped into a deep furrow. A raven flying over, picked him up with a grain of corn, and flew with him to the top of a giant's castle, by the seaside, where he left him; and the hungry old giant, came and swallowed Tom like a pill, clothes and all! Luckily, the hungry old giant did not like the way Tom felt in his stomach and so he spit him up into the sea.

Even more trouble met Tom Thumb at that time! No sooner did he fall into the sea when a great fish swallowed him whole. Inside the fish lived Tom wondering how he would ever get out.

The fish was soon after caught and sent as a present to King Arthur. When it was cut open, inside was little Tom Thumb singing with joy to be free. Everybody was delighted with little Tom Thumb. The king made him his dwarf; he was the favorite of the whole court; and, by his merry pranks, often amused the queen and the knights of the Round Table.

The king, when he rode on horseback, frequently took Tom in his hand; and, if a shower of rain came on, he used to creep into the king's waist-coat pocket, and sleep till the rain was over. The king also, sometimes questioned Tom concerning his parents; and when Tom informed his majesty they were very poor people, the king led him into his treasury, and told him he should pay his parents a visit, and take with him as much money as he could carry. Tom procured a little purse, and putting a threepenny piece into it, with much labor and difficulty got it upon his back; and, after travelling two days and nights, arrived at his father's house.

His parents were glad to see him, especially when he had brought such an amazing sum of money with him. They placed him in a walnut shell by the fireside and fed him well.

It rained and rained, and Tom could not travel back to the king so his mother took him in her hand, and with one puff blew him into King Arthur's court; where Tom entertained the king, queen, and nobility for many a day. Tom Thumb soon got very weary and ill, as he was always asked to perform and entertain, and it was too much for his little body.

"His shirt was made of butterflies' wings;
His boots were made of chicken skins;
His coat and breeches were made with pride;
A tailor's needle hung by his side;
A mouse for a horse he used to ride."

Upon news of Tom Thumb's illness, the Queen of the Fairies came in a chariot drawn by flying mice. She placed Tom by her side and drove through the air without stopping till they arrived at her palace. There she and the other fairies took good care of him for many years and restored him to health and commanded a fair wind and blew Tom back to the court of king. But, by this time, there was a new king and King Arthur was no longer in command.
When Tom arrived at the court, the king asked who this little creature was. Tom Thumb replied:

"My name is Tom Thumb,
From the Fairies I come;
When King Arthur shone,
This court was my home.
In me he delighted,
By him I was knighted,
Did you never hear of
Sir Thomas Thumb?"

The king was so charmed with this address, that he ordered a little chair to be made, in order that Tom might sit on his table, and also a palace of gold a span high, with a door an inch wide, for little Tom to live in. He also gave him a coach drawn by six small mice.

And there Tom lived for the rest of his days.

Monday Student Lessons – Week Twenty

(Baking/Cooking – Purple Day)

Language Arts

1. Begin your lesson time by reading (or telling) the story of *Little Tom Thumb* to your child. Let the children look at the sentences as you read as this visual will aid with their knowledge of letters, words, and sentences. If possible, use simple props to accompany the story as we have suggested.

2. When your story is finished, unveil your blackboard drawing that you have prepared ahead of time as suggested at the beginning of this week's curriculum. If your child has his or her own small blackboard and chalk, have them take a few moments to create their own drawing.

3. Review what your child worked on last week in their lesson book. Have them practice writing the capital letter S a few times on their blackboard or an extra piece of paper. Be sure they have a good grasp of this letter before moving onto the next.

4. In your child's lesson book, have them create a similar image of the thistle or a mushroom near Tom Thumb (or whatever depiction you used) with the letter T revealed inside. On the righthand side, have your child practice writing the capital letter T. Share this poem as you work to form the letter:

Make a line just like a tree
Cross on top for letter T

Here is a movement verse as your child learns the letter T:

Ten toes way down low
(point to toes)
Arms out just like so!
(hold both arms straight out)
Head high in the shade
(hold head up high)
Letter T, I have made!

5. Practicing Vowels

   Spend time reviewing the vowels we learned last week. Say both the short and long sounds of each letter with your child. Do the vowel gestures from last week's movement lesson for each letter. Reread the story of The Vowel Fairies and make a point to bring your child's awareness to vowels when reading and writing.

Mathematics

1. In addition to the Roman numeral XX, write down the number 20 and word TWENTY in all capital letters for your child to see. Say each letter as you write.

2. Have the child draw images of the number TWENTY. They may copy some of the items you made in your blackboard drawing for this week. Your child should then practice writing the number 20, Roman numeral XX, and the word TWENTY in all capital letters on the opposite page of their book. If you feel they need extra time with writing, let them continue to practice as needed. Here is a verse to share when forming the number 20:

   The number two, and then you see;
   A zero next to make twenty

3. Now that your child is well versed in numbers 80-90 you can trust that they are able to move more quickly and practice their counting from 90-100. Count everything you can! If your child seems ready, you can expand your four processes math skills to include larger numbers up to 100 as well. Remember to go at your child's pace and pay close attention to how your child learns most effectively.

Domestic Arts/Practical Life Skills

1. Multicultural Apples

   Supplies Needed:
   Apples of All Shapes and Colors

   Show your child all the apples lined up in a row.
   What can they find that is different about each one?

Do the apples all have the same color skin?
Are they the same shape and size?

Talk about how on the outside the apples can look very different, just like people.

Next, cut the apples in half with your child.
What does your child see inside?
What looks the same or similar?
Do the apples all have seeds?
Do they all have juice?
Does the inside of the apple look almost the same even though the outside is different?

Explain again, that just like people, apples may look different on the outside but are mostly the same inside.

Enjoy your apples for a healthy snack!

2. Cooking Around the World

   Spend time today and this week making easy recipes from around the world. Here are a few to get you started:

   <u>Guacamole Dip from Mexico</u>

   Supplies Needed:
   1 Avocado
   1 Clove Garlic, Minced
   1 Small Bunch Fresh Cilantro, Chopped
   1 Small Onion, Chopped
   1 Tomato, Diced
   1 Lime
   Salt and Pepper

   Scoop out avocado flesh and put into bowl. Mash and add garlic, onion, tomato, and cilantro. Squeeze lime, salt, and pepper to taste. Mix well. Serve with corn chips.

Lebanese Cucumber and Tomato Salad

Supplies Needed:
4 Cups Peeled Cucumbers, Cut
4 Cups Tomatoes, Cut
1 Large Bell Pepper (Any Color), Cut
3 Tablespoons Cilantro, Chopped
3 Tablespoons Mint, Chopped
2 Onions, Cut in Slices
1 Cup Feta Cheese, Crumbled or Cut
½ Cup Pitted Kalamata Olives
3 Tablespoons Fresh Lemon Juice
3 Tablespoons Extra Virgin Olive Oil
Salt
Pepper

Place all vegetables in bowl and place in refrigerator to keep cold. When ready to eat, sprinkle olives, feta, herbs, and onion over the salad. In separate container mix oil, lemon juice, salt, and pepper. Pour dressing on when ready to eat.

Outdoor Time/Nature Walk

Take your children outside each day regardless of the weather. Invest in good rain gear, snow gear and wool undergarments if your location requires it. Do your lessons outdoors whenever possible.

Caregiver Focus

Practicing Tolerance in Everyday Living

When you find yourself judging or criticizing others this week, practice the pause and examine the situation.

Are you comparing yourself to another? Do you feel your positions and beliefs are correct and theirs are wrong? Are you frustrated that they cannot see things in the same way as you do or do not understand the world the same way that you do?

Remind yourself that each and every one of us is filled with the same light, and we are all entitled to experience life and this journey in our own way, and in our own time.

Imagine holding that person safely in your consciousness surrounding them with loving light and allowing them to be who they wish to be, while letting go of the need to change them.

Afternoon Lessons

1. Music: Continue Practicing Flute or Recorder

2. Handwork/Art: String Around the World Craft

    Supplies Needed:
    Blue and Green Cotton String or Yarn
    Balloon
    Glue

    Blow up a balloon. Dip string in glue in a dish to coat it. Using your fingers, remove excess dripping glue. Wrap the yarn around the balloon, crisscrossing strands until there are only small gaps. Cut the string. Tie your balloon on a clothing hanger and hang it to dry for a day or two. Pop the balloon and you will have a beautiful reminder of the world you live in to hang in your homeschool area.

Tuesday Student Lessons – Week Twenty

(Painting – Red Day)

Language Arts

1. Like yesterday, begin your lesson time by continuing to read (or tell) *Little Tom Thumb*. Provide your child with a piece of beeswax modeling material as you read. Let them hold this piece of beeswax as they listen, warming it with their hands so it softens.

2. Have your child form the softened beeswax material into the letter T. Roll it into a long snake, form it just so and then put it back together again. Next, have them form it into the number 20.

3. Open your lesson book and review the work you did yesterday. Have your child trace the letter T number 20 and word TWENTY with their fingers.

4. Practice saying the sounds of the letter T. Notice how our mouth forms to make the sound. Bringing awareness to the way our body forms sounds and words is very important. This process helps us to notice the use of air and our body muscles as we communicate.

5. Today we will work on a tongue twister to practice and memorize with your child to help learn the letter T and its sound. Tongue twisters and rhymes are fun ways to learn and help with finding rhythm. As we have begun bringing awareness to syllables, pay careful attention with your child to be sure they get it correctly.

   To begin, say the following tongue twister to your child slowly **and tap one finger on the palm of your other hand to the syllables** to create a pattern for memory:

   Try this tongue twister
   to train your tongue
   to twist and turn,
   to learn the letter "T"

Mathematics

1. Using tangible items continue counting backwards with your children today. This week start from 50 to 1.

2. Write numbers 1-60 on your blackboard. Using your finger point to 60 and count backward to the number one. Have your child do this with you.

3. In your child's lesson book, have them draw 70 items on the left side. This could be 70 little dots, trees, buttons, hearts or even simply sticks. Count them together first in order and then backward. Next, on the right side of your child's layout, have them write the number 70 and downward to the number 1. You can help them if they are struggling.

4. Continue these types of exercises over the next week or two aiming to be able to increase the amount of numbers your child can count backwards.

Outdoor Time/Nature Walk

Take your children outside each day regardless of the weather. Invest in good rain gear, snow gear and wool undergarments if your location requires it. Do your lessons outdoors whenever possible.

Social Studies, Geography, Weather, Time

Learning About Different Cultures: Around the World

Take a trip around the world with your child. Pick a few places to "visit" and go to the library, look online, and do some research together.

Make your child their very own passport and each time you explore a new place, fill it out with a stamp and information about the place you are learning about.

We have provided some lesson questions and an example passport below.

We are going on a trip to _____!

Do some research and make sure you are prepared.

What season is it right now?

_____

What is the temperature?

_____

Will you be likely to find snow, ice, rain or sunshine this time of year?

_____

How long would it take you to get to this place by airplane, car, bus or train?

_____

_____

_____

You have to pack for your trip! What items should you include in your suitcase?

_____

_____

_____

MY PASSPORT

back cover | front cover

THIS PASSPORT BELONGS TO:

Name: _____

Country of Origin: _____

Date of Birth: _____

Place of Birth: _____

inside left cover | inside right cover

First Grade Curriculum | WINTER | Little Acorn Learning

inside left page

COUNTRY VISITED

Name of Country:

_____

Books Read, Facts & Lessons Learned:

_____

_____

_____

inside right page

inside left page

COUNTRY VISITED

Name of Country:

_____

Books Read, Facts & Lessons Learned:

_____

_____

_____

inside right page

Afternoon Lessons

Music: Continue Practicing Flute or Recorder

Wednesday Student Lessons – Week Twenty
(Coloring – Yellow Day)

Language Arts

1. Practice our tongue twister again. Keep working on this until you have it memorized together. Say the following tongue twister to your child slowly **and tap one finger on the palm of your other hand to the syllables** to create a pattern for memory:

    Try this tongue twister
    to train your tongue
    to twist and turn,
    to learn the letter "T"

2. In your child's lesson book have them make a drawing of the story of *Little Tom Thumb*.

3. On the opposite page, your child is likely ready to write simple sentences (do not worry about punctuation at this time). Remember we are still writing in all capital letters. Provide your child with a simple sentence on the blackboard to copy such as:

    TOM THUMB IS SMALL
    THE KING LIKES TOM
    TOM FELL IN

4. Tonight, at bedtime tell your child of the story of *Little Tom Thumb*.

5. When out and about, ask your child to find things that begin with the letter T. This can be done while shopping or when driving in the car. Throughout the week, ask your child to think of all the words they can that begin with the letter T. How many can they come up with? Make a list.

Mathematics

Counting to Ten in Spanish

This week we are learning about different cultures and traditions. Using the key below, practice counting to ten in Spanish with your child out loud.

Write each number on your blackboard and share the Spanish word for it with your child. If you feel your child is ready, let them copy each in their lesson book.

0   1   2   3
cero   uno   dos   tres

4   5   6   7
cuatro   cinco   sies   siete

8   9   10
ocho   nueve   diez

Outdoor Time/Nature Walk

Take your children outside each day regardless of the weather. Invest in good rain gear, snow gear and wool undergarments if your location requires it. Do your lessons outdoors whenever possible.

Social Studies, Geography, Weather, Time

1. If any family members or friends speak another language, spend time sharing different words and sentences with your child. Consider visiting a native speaker of a language you wish to learn more about.

2. Find a few people from another country or location that you and your child can interview. Find their country together on the map and then work together to put together some questions for your interviews. Some ideas:

What kinds of foods did you eat in your country?

What language do the people in your country speak?

What is the biggest difference between your country and here?

Are there any laws or rules that are different there from where we live?

What are the seasons and weather like in your country?

3. Focusing on a few countries you've already discussed with your child, research climate and weather in those areas. Are hurricanes common? Does this place ever get snow? How cold does it get? How hot? Your child can add this information in their lesson book with drawings and spelling words you come up with.

Science, Nature Study, Earth Discovery

Make Your Own Hurricane

Supplies Needed:
2 Empty Soda Bottles
¼ Cup of Sand
Funnel
3 Paperclips
3 Peanuts
Water
Duct Tape

Fill your first bottle with one paperclip, all three peanuts and ¼ cup of sand. Place the funnel in the mouth of the bottle and pour water inside until is it ¾ full.

Turn the other soda bottle upside down and hold it over the first bottle so the mouths are touching. Using the duct tape, secure both bottles at the mouths and a few inches above and below making sure they cannot leak.

Quickly lift, turn the bottles over and set on the table so the water filled bottle is on top. The water will drain into the bottle below and air should begin to bubble up as it drains. You should notice that the air and water compete to push through the opening.

Turn the bottles over again and shake keeping them vertical. The water should now form a "hurricane" as it drains into the other bottle.

Afternoon Lessons

Handwork: Beginner Knitting, Review and Practice Knitting in the Round

Continue to work on your circular knitting and making the *Easy 'In the Round' Ribbed Hat* this week.

Thursday Student Lessons – Week Twenty
(Crafting/Games – Orange Day)

Language Arts

1. Continue to tell your child the story of *Little Tom Thumb*.

2. Alphabet Cards

    Supplies Needed:
    Heavy White Cardstock
    Beeswax Stick Crayons
    Scissors

    Spend time cutting cards out of cardstock with your child. Using beeswax crayons, continue to finish drawing each letter we have learned so far and include the letter T. Next to the letter, have your child draw an image that begins with it. Using scissors, round the corners of these cards and keep working on them throughout the year. You can use them in your lessons and for an upper case and lowercase match game later in the curriculum when we learn those as well.

3. Continue reading simple reader books together.

4. Practice saying the sound of T. Notice how our mouth forms to make the sound. Bringing awareness to the way our body forms sounds and words is very important. This process helps us to notice the use of air and our body muscles as we communicate.

5. Print out or share the following photos and practice saying them together with your child. Your child may be ready to copy these words into their lesson book.

THUMB

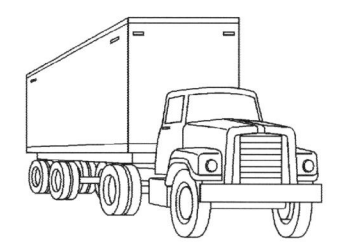

TRUCK

THISTLE

TOE

TWIG

Mathematics

Continue to practice counting to ten in Spanish with your child. Here is a little song that you can sing both in English and then in Spanish:

1 little, 2 little, 3 little fingers
4 little, 5 little, 6 little fingers
7 little, 8 little, 9 little fingers
10 little fingers in a row!

Two hands, ten little fingers,
Two hands, ten little fingers,
Two hands, ten little fingers,
Come and sing with me!

Uno, dos, tres deditos,
Cuatro, cinco, seis deditos,
Siete, ocho, nueve deditos
Y uno mas son diez.

Dos manitos, diez deditos,
Dos manitos, diez deditos,
Dos manitos, diez deditos,
Cuntalos conmigo!

Outdoor Time/Nature Walk

Take your children outside each day regardless of the weather. Invest in good rain gear, snow gear and wool undergarments if your location requires it. Do your lessons outdoors whenever possible.

Social Studies, Geography, Weather, Time

Teaching Tolerance

A wonderful way to help teach children religious tolerance is by visiting a place of worship that is not of your own faith. Share your feelings about the differences you see after the service. Teach your children to respect people from all walks of life and about how important it is to have the freedom to believe in what you choose. Try to point out some common aspects of your beliefs and of those of the congregation you visit.

Movement, Body Awareness & Health

Around the World Movement Games

Here are three fun movement games from different countries to play with your child this week:

Shadows – Ireland

This is a game of tag, but you must stand on the person's shadow in order to catch them. Once you do, they are the person who chases the shadows. You can run to a place that is shaded for base but can only stay there when you count to ten.

Luta de Galo – Brazil

Begin with two players. Each player has a handkerchief or piece of cloth tucked into their waistband or pocket. Each player must also cross their right arm across their chest, so they do not use it.

Hopping on one leg, each player must try to grab the handkerchief from the other player using their left hand only. They are out if they put down their other leg or use their other hand. If you have a group of people, you can all play and the last one to have their handkerchief at the end is the winner.

Oba – Columbia

Throwing the ball to a wall, the player must sing a song and do a different movement before catching it again. The player can throw with one arm and turn around, throw with two arms and jump, stand on one leg, etc.

You may like to call out movements for your child as they play.

Afternoon Lessons

1. Form Drawing/Art – Galloping Lines

    Talk about Little Tom Thumb and how the king loved him so much and would take him in his hand when he rode horseback.

    How does a horse gallop? Using your feet and movements, "gallop" around the house just like the king did on his horse in our story.

    Next, in your child's lesson book have them practice making galloping lines as demonstrated below. Here is a verse you can share as you practice:

    Oh, bring me a galloping horse to ride,
    A crown on my head, my sword by my side,
    For it is off the to castle we will go.
    Galloping, galloping, high and low.

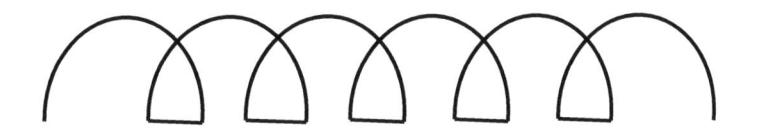

2. Handwork: Hand Stitching/Embroidery

   Supplies Needed:
   Embroidery Needle
   Embroidery Floss
   White Scrap Fabric
   Embroidery Hoop (optional)
   Scissors

   Using our embroidery instructions, work with your child to make a letter T embroidery piece. You can do this with a simple running stitch, or you may choose to learn more complicated stitches together.

Friday Student Lessons – Week Twenty
(Modeling/Housework – Green Day)

Language Arts

1. Today have your child continue to practice writing the letter T in their lesson book on unlined paper.

2. In your child's lesson book, have them practice writing the alphabet from A-T copying each letter a few times on each line.

3. Ask your child to tell YOU the story of *Little Tom Thumb*.

4. In your child's lesson book, have them work with you to think of as many words as they can write that include the letters A, E, I, O and U.

Mathematics

1. Review Four Processes

   Continue to work with your child on addition, subtraction, multiplication, and division work. Try to work toward being able to solve problems up to 100. If there are areas that your child needs to strengthen, go back through the curriculum, and review some lessons.

2. Game of Marbles

   Supplies Needed:
   Marbles
   Sidewalk Chalk or String

   Using your chalk, have your child draw an approximately 3 foot sized circle as evenly as possible. If you are playing indoors, you can make this circle out of string or tape on the floor.

   One marble will be the shooter or 'taw'. This marble is usually larger and heavier than the others.

   Place 10-15 marbles in the center of your circle, evenly spaced but more toward the center.

The game of marbles can be played "for fair" or "for keeps". If you are playing against someone "for fair", you keep the marbles you started out with when the game is over. If you are playing "for keeps", the other player gets your marbles that he or she wins throughout the game.

Decide who will go first. The player then kneels outside of the circle and shoots their taw marble from the ground. They are trying to knock as many marbles out of the circle as they can. To shoot, tuck all your fingers into your palm except your pointer. Wrap your pointer around the marble and when you are ready, flick the marble with your thumb.

Pick up any marbles you knocked out of the circle. Leave your taw inside the circle for your next turn. The other player now goes.

When it is your turn again, you will shoot from wherever your taw landed. If you can shoot your opponent's taw out of the circle, you automatically win! Otherwise, continue to gather up any marbles you got out of the circle and take turns.

The winner has the most marbles in the end when there are no more left in the circle.

*To make this game a math game, assign a number to each colored marble. When you gather your marbles after each turn, write down each number and add them together.

Outdoor Time/Nature Walk

Take your children outside each day regardless of the weather. Invest in good rain gear, snow gear and wool undergarments if your location requires it. Do your lessons outdoors whenever possible.

Science, Nature Study, Earth Discovery

Slime Making

Supplies Needed:
White Glue
Food Coloring
Borax

This is a favorite among children this age. It is a fun way for children to explore how something turns from a liquid to a solid. Borax should not be ingested so please use care when your child is working with it.

In a container, mix one tablespoon of glue and one tablespoon of water. Add one or two drops of food coloring if you want colored slime.

In another bowl, mix 4 tablespoons of water with 1 ½ teaspoons of Borax. Slowly, transfer this mixture one tablespoon at a time into the glue mixture. This will slowly begin to turn into a gel-like substance.

Children can then roll and manipulate the slime in their hands until it becomes more firm.

Social Studies, Geography, Weather, Time

Learning About Different Traditions and Customs

Review some of the places you and your child have "visited" this week. Dig a little deeper and discover if the place has a special flag or symbol. How do the people dress? What language do they speak? What do they like to eat?

We have provided some questions and templates below to help you with this lesson:

Do you remember your trip to _____?

Do some more research and get to know this place better.

Does this place have a special flag? If so, how does it look?

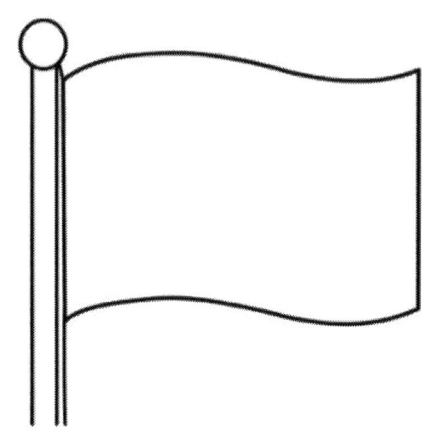

Does this place have a special symbol or flower? Draw it here:

What types of foods do the people enjoy?

_____

_____

What languages do they speak?

_____

_____

How do the people dress there? Show examples and make your own paper dolls:

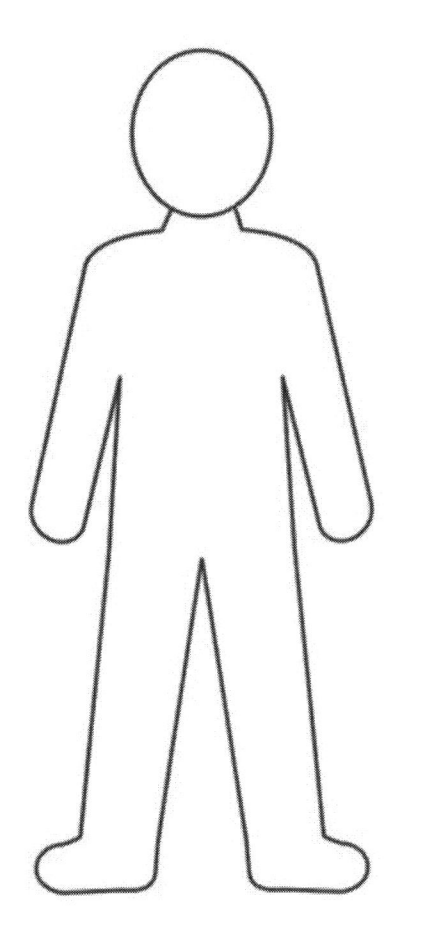

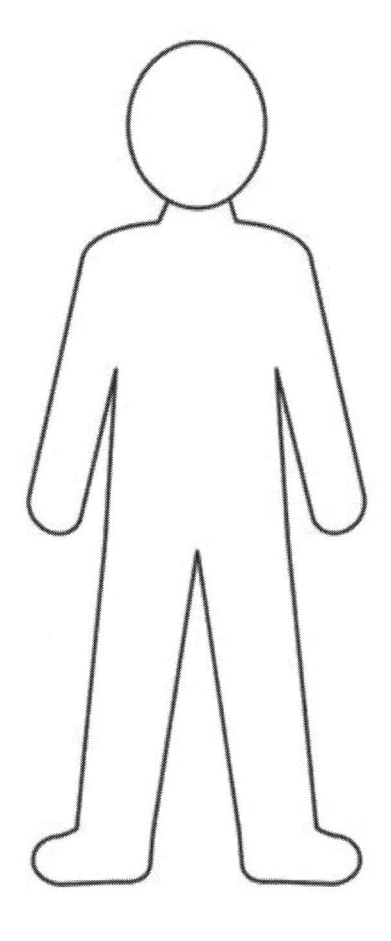

Domestic Arts/Practical Life Skills

Practicing Manners

Spend time today talking about manners with your child. Does your child remember in the story of Tom Thumb that he was not always using his best manners?

When is it the appropriate time to use please, thank you and excuse me? Present them with some hypothetical situations and ask them how they could use their manners in the best way in those circumstances.

What are some other ways to practice good manners?

Afternoon Lessons

Use the afternoon hours today to review areas from this week's afternoon lessons that you feel may need a bit more attention. Bring these into your weekend as you find time.

Week Twenty One, Winter
First Grade

Theme: Music & Sounds, Listening

This Week's Lessons:

Language Arts:

The Story of Echo
Letter U
Introduction to Poetry and Rhyming

Mathematics:
Number 21
Counting Music
Learning Sign Language Numbers
Musical Uno

Social Studies, Geography, Weather, Time:
Learning Sign Language, The Alphabet & Numbers
Learning About Music: Cultural, Religious & Geographical

Science, Nature Study, Earth Discovery:
Learning About Sound, The Sense of Hearing
Listening Walk
Name That Sound Game

Teacher's Classroom Work:
Soft Music at Rest Time
Plan Trip to Live Music Event
Practice Knitting, Changing Colors

For the Caregiver:
Caregiver Meditation: Listening
Caregiver Focus: Listening to Live Music

Domestic Arts/Practical Life Skills:
Simple Canning – Homemade Grape Jelly
Musical Pie Pans
Being a Good Listener

Music:
Music and Sounds Fingerplays & Songs
Beginning Recorder or Flute
Musical Pie Pans
Musical Uno
Homemade Musical Instruments

Art/Handwork:
Art/Fine Motor Skills: Cutting & Folding, Umbrellas
Handwork: Beginner Knitting, Learning to Change Colors
Art: Painting to Music
Embroidery, Letter U
Alphabet Card Letter U

Form Drawing:
Form Drawing/Art – Review, Straight and Curved Lines

Movement, Body Awareness & Health:
Cooperative Musical Chairs
Hide & Seek the Sound Game

Supplies Needed for Week Twenty One

Cooking List:

<u>For Simple Canning, Homemade Grape Jelly:</u>
3 1/2lbs Grapes
1/2 Cup Water
7 Cups Sugar
1 Package Liquid Pectin
Saucepan with Lid
Cheesecloth
Glass Jars with Metal Lids
Large Pot
Metal Kitchen Tongs

Homeschooling List:

Blackboard
Chalk
Paper Towel Roll
Lesson Book
Stockmar Stick Crayons
Stockmar Block Crayons
Colored Pencils
Stockmar Beeswax Modeling Material
Knitting Needles
Super Bulky Single Ply 100% Wool Yarn
Crochet Hook
Embroidery Needle
Embroidery Floss
White Scrap Fabric
Embroidery Hoop (optional)
Scissors
Heavy White Cardstock
Plastic Eggs
Small Pebbles, Beans or Marbles
Aluminum Pie Pans
Dried Beans, Rice or Beads
Tape or Stapler
Popsicle Sticks/Dowels

Glue
White Paper
Paints
Paint Brushes
Smocks
Water
Cloths/Paper Towels
Musical Instruments or Recorded Music to Play
Dried Corn still on the Cob
Plastic Container or Bottle with Lid or Top
Chair for Each Child
Symbol Drawn on Card for Each Child on Chair
Musical Instruments or Recorded Music to Play
Small Embroidery Hoops
Large Jingle Bells
Zip Ties
Two Flat Blocks or Pieces of Wood
Two Wooden Knobs
Sandpaper
Hot Glue
Bulky Yarn of Various Colors
Colored Number Cards or Uno Cards
Coins
Whistle or Bell
Cups or Containers with Lids
Pencil or Pen
Books
Paper or Foil
Ball
Timer
Other Items to Make Sounds

Week Twenty One Book Recommendations

Visit your local library the weekend before to check out books based on your theme for the week. Older children can help you look up the books by author and title. When setting up your play space for the week ahead, mindfully display these books in baskets for the children to enjoy.

Little Beaver and the Echo ~ Amy MacDonald
Listen, Listen! ~ Phillis Gershator
Little Rat Makes Music ~ Monika Bang-Campbell
My Family Plays Music ~ Judy Cox
The Amazing Adventures of Andy Owl :A Children's Guide to Understanding Music ~ D. Z. Russell
How Music Came to the World: An Ancient Mexican Myth ~ Hal & Carol Ober
Animal Music ~ Harriet Ziefert
A Sound Like Someone Trying Not to Make a Sound ~ John Irving
Musical Life of Gustav Mole ~ Kathryn Meyrick
The Music Box: The Story of Cristofori ~ Suzanne Guy & Donna Lacy
Charlie Parker Played Be Bop ~ Raschka
The Listening Walk ~ Paul Showers
Too Much Noise ~ Ann McGovern
Marsh Music ~ Marianne Berkes
The First Music ~ Dylan Pritchett
Listening to My Body ~ Gabi Garcia
Why Should I Listen? ~ Claire Llewellyn
Listen, Buddy ~ Helen Lester
Listen to the Birds ~ Ana Gerhard
Never Play Music Right Next to the Zoo ~ John Lithgow
Winter Song: A Day In The Life Of A Kid ~ Anetta Kotowicz
Zin! Zin! Zin! A Violin ~ Llyod Moss
The Man With the Violin ~ Kathy Stinson
Gus & Me: The Story of My Grandad and My First Guitar ~ Keith Richards
Library Lion ~ Michelle Knudsen
The Noisy Paint Box ~ Barb Rosenstock
Hearing ~ Maria Rius
The Sense of Hearing ~ Elain Landau
Fairy Earmuffs ~ Emily Martha Sorensen
Signing for Kids ~ Mickey Flodin
We Can Sign! ~ Tara Adams

Week Twenty One Circle, Songs & Movement

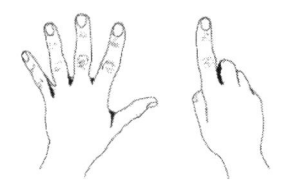

The following songs and verses should be shared during circle time each day this week after you open your circle.

Little Boy Blue

Little Boy Blue, come blow your horn
The sheep are in the meadow; the cows are in the corn
But where is the little boy who looks after the sheep?
He's under the haystack fast asleep

Cock-A-Doodle-Do

Cock-a-doodle-do!
My dame has lost her shoe,
My master's lost his fiddlestick
And knows not what to do.

Cock-a-doodle-do!
What is my dame to do?
Till master finds his fiddlestick,
She'll dance without her shoe.

Cock-a-doodle-doo!
My dame has lost her shoe,
And master's found his fiddlestick;
Sing doodle-doodle-doo!

Cock-a-doodle-doo!
My dame will dance with you,
While master fiddles his fiddlestick,
For dame and doodle-doo.

Cock-a-doodle-doo!
Dame has lost her shoe;
Gone to bed and scratched her head,
And can't tell what to do.

The Hokey Pokey

You put your right foot in,
You put your right foot out;
You put your right foot in,
And you shake it all about.
You do the Hokey Pokey,
And you turn yourself around.
That's what it's all about!

You put your left foot in,
You put your left foot out;
You put your left foot in,
And you shake it all about.
You do the Hokey Pokey,
And you turn yourself around.
That's what it's all about!

You put your right hand in,
You put your right hand out;
You put your right hand in,
And you shake it all about
You do the Hokey Pokey,
And you turn yourself around.
That's what it's all about!

<u>My Ears</u>
(*sing to tune of The Bear Went Over the Mountain*)

My ears are made for hearing.
My ears are made for hearing.
My ears are made for hearing.
So I can hear my world.

Continue with other senses:
eyes, seeing
mouth, tasting
hands, touching
nose, smelling

Open your hands,
Then clap, clap, clap
(clap hands 3x)

Now, you lay them in your lap.
(place hands on legs)

Two little eyes looking straight ahead.
(point to eyes)

Two little ears, hearing what is said.
(point to ears)

Week Twenty One Blackboard Drawing

Drawing Ideas for This Week: Capital letter U as shown in the shape of the Unkind Nymph or in her echo, musical instruments, musical notes, Letter U, words beginning with U, Roman numeral XXI, TWENTY ONE, 21

Week Twenty One Teacher's Classroom Work

1. Children often have difficulty transitioning at rest time after a full day of play and activities. Start a new tradition of playing soft music for them as they lay down. A wonderful instrument to begin with is a lap harp. These small harps can be purchased online and used to add gentle background sounds while the children fall asleep. You may instead choose to sing lullabies to your child or play soft recorded music.

2. Prepare various noises ahead of time to present to the children during the science experiment this week.

3. Schedule a trip this week to a local musical, concert, band performance or church choir.

4. Review any handwork before working on projects with your children.

Week Twenty One Caregiver Meditation

This Week's Reflection: Listening

There is a voice inside of you
That whispers all day long,
"I feel that this is right for me,
I know that this is wrong"

No teacher, preacher, parent, friend, or wise man can decide
What's right for you, just listen to
the voice that speaks inside.

~ Shel Silverstein

Stop, look and listen. What is going on around you? What do you hear? What is the voice inside of you speaking right now at this moment?

What is working for you right now? What is not? What does your body need? What does your soul need? What can you use more of in your life? What do you have too much of?

The universe is always speaking to you. Everything is a sign. Are you listening?

Week Twenty One Story

As we learn about sound and music, it is so fun to imagine what (or who!) is behind the noises we hear around us. This tale about the unkind nymph named Echo comes from ancient Greek mythology. Echo, the mischievous wood-nymph, ends up lonely after her unkind pranks upset those around her. Maybe she should listen to how others feel more often? You can take a simple paper towel roll to speak through while doing the voice of Echo in the story. This will give your voice a hollow sound and mimic that of an echo.

The Story of Echo

Among the trees of the forest, and where the cool streams run, beautiful wood-nymphs used to have their homes. They loved to play in the flickering sunlight and under the dancing leaves, and people sometimes caught sight of the gleam of their white feet as they dipped them in the rushing waters of the brook.

There was one unkind nymph named Echo, whose chief amusement was to play tricks upon, and to tease her companions. "Daphne! Oh, come here! Quick just see!" she would sometimes call, and when Daphne came running to the spot, eager to see what there was to be seen, Echo would have vanished as completely as if she had never been there until finally a stifled laughed showed her hiding place.

Echo was, too, a great chatterer; she never listened long to anyone else but was sure to talk a great deal herself. One day she came upon a shepherd sitting on a rock, and, watching his sheep as they cropped the grass below, she noticed that some of the sheep were beginning to stray from the flock, and, thinking this a fine chance for a bit of fun, she at once began to laugh and talk with the shepherd, to keep him from thinking of his charge.

Finally, not one of the flock was left in sight, and then, with a laugh at the dismayed face of the shepherd, Echo, too, ran away and left him. At first the other nymphs used to laugh at her nonsense, and enjoyed the fun as much as Echo herself did; but as she was continually unkind to others and playing her tricks upon everybody in season and out of season, and as the tricks, like that she played on the shepherd, were often unkind ones, her companions gradually came to leave her out of their sports and plays, and after a time, as she did not mend her ways, avoided her altogether.

One day it happened that Juno (Hera), the queen of the gods, came to the forest, and Echo troubled her so much with her foolish chattering that, finally, Juno declared a just punishment upon the teasing nymph. "Since Echo talks and jokes only to weary everyone," Juno said, "she shall no longer be able to speak unless someone first speaks to her. She shall have power to answer but only repeat what the other had just said and never be able to begin a conversation."

Echo, ashamed and sorry, went away into the deep woods, where there after she dwelt alone. She was seldom seen by men, but a traveler, once, coming out of the wood, told how he had lost his way at nightfall, and had called loudly, hoping someone might hear and come to his aid; he seemed to have a faint answer, he said, but as he could not tell whence it came, he called again, saying "Come here!" "Here," the voice answered. "Where are you?" he called. "Where are you?" replied the voice. Finally, out of patience, "Away with you!" he shouted. "Away with you," came back with an angry sound. After that he heard no more, nor, although he searched the wood, was he able to find a trace of anyone.

Echo's voice is still heard sometimes in lonely places but only when someone calls to her; if the call is a laughing one, she laughs back; if it is sad, she answers mournfully, but, merry or sad, she never shows herself.

Monday Student Lessons – Week Twenty One

(Baking/Cooking – Purple Day)

Language Arts

1. Begin your lesson time by reading (or telling) *The Story of Echo* to your child. Let the children look at the sentences as you read as this visual will aid with their knowledge of letters, words and sentences. If possible, use simple props to accompany the story as we have suggested.

2. When your story is finished, unveil your blackboard drawing that you have prepared ahead of time as suggested at the beginning of this week's curriculum. If your child has his or her own small blackboard and chalk, have them take a few moments to create their own drawing.

3. Review what your child worked on last week in their lesson book. Have them practice writing the capital letter T a few times on their blackboard or an extra piece of paper. Be sure they have a good grasp of this letter before moving onto the next.

4. In your child's lesson book, have them create a similar image of the unkind nymph (or whatever depiction you used) with the letter U revealed inside. On the righthand side, have your child practice writing the capital letter U. Share this poem as you work to form the letter:

    This letter is made just like a cup.
    Start going down,
    And then back up!

5. Today begin to introduce the difference between long U and short U sounds. An easy way to remember if a vowel sound is long is if it sounds exactly like its letter is pronounced.

    For example:

    Long U sounds like (yew) – just like the actual letter U is pronounced
    examples: **unicorn, human, cute**

Short U sound is more like (uhh). It is the sound we hear in words like: **u**mbrella, tr**u**ck, r**u**n

6. This letter is our last vowel to learn (we will not consider Y as a vowel until a later time)! Take some time to go over all the long and short sounds of A, E, I O and U.

7. Practice saying the sounds of both the long U and the short U. Notice how our mouth forms to make the sound. Bringing awareness to the way our body forms sounds and words is very important. This process helps us to notice the use of air and our body muscles as we communicate.

Mathematics

1. In addition to the Roman numeral XXI, write down the number 21 and word TWENTY ONE in all capital letters for your child to see. Say each letter as you write.

2. Have the child draw images of the number TWENTY ONE. They may copy some of the items you made in your blackboard drawing for this week. Your child should then practice writing the number 21, Roman numeral XXI and the word TWENTY ONE in all capital letters on the opposite page of their book. If you feel they need extra time with writing, let them continue to practice as needed. Here is a verse to share when forming the number 21:

   First the number two goes down;
   Then write a one without a sound.

3. Counting Music

   Supplies Needed:
   Plastic Eggs
   Small Pebbles, Beans or Marbles

   Have your child practice their counting skills by adding items into the plastic eggs. Challenge them with some addition and subtraction questions as they do this. When they are finished, close the eggs up tight and shake them to make sounds.

Domestic Arts/Practical Life Skills

Simple Canning – Homemade Grape Jelly

*Please note - The mixture gets extremely hot, so we do not recommend doing this activity with the children but rather surprising them with the result or allowing them to watch from a distance.

Supplies Needed:
3 1/2lbs Grapes
1/2 Cup Water
7 Cups Sugar
1 Package Liquid Pectin
Saucepan with Lid
Cheesecloth
Glass Jars with Metal Lids
Large Pot
Metal Kitchen Tongs

Sort and wash grapes; remove stems, and place in a saucepan. Using kitchen utensil, crush the grapes and add ½ cup of water. Bring to a boil and reduce the heat. Cover and let simmer for 10-15 minutes.

Use cheesecloth to drain the jelly, pressing with another cloth on top to get all the juice out. Save the juice! Cover and let sit for a few hours or even overnight in a cool place.

Combine the juice and sugar in a saucepan stirring constantly and bringing it to a boil. Add pectin stirring for one minute. Remove from heat and use a spoon to take the layer of foam off. Pour hot mixture into hot sterile jars leaving ¼" space on top. Wipe the jar rims and cover with metal lids. Place the jars in a pot of boiling water for 5 minutes. Use tongs or other tool to remove the jars carefully from the water to cool.

Outdoor Time/Nature Walk

Take your children outside each day regardless of the weather. Invest in good rain gear, snow gear and wool undergarments if your location requires it. Do your lessons outdoors whenever possible.

Caregiver Focus

Listening to Live Music

This week take your child to a local musical, concert, band performance or church choir. In an age where most of our entertainment is provided in digital format, many children rarely experience the clarity of sound and voices in a live performance. Going forward, try to seek out opportunities to take your family to live events more often.

Science, Nature Study, Earth Discovery

Learning About Our Senses: Hearing

Spend time today talking to your child about the sense of hearing. Ask the following questions to inspire free discussion and conversation:

What part of our body do we use when we listen? (ears)
Let's be quiet and still for a few minutes and listen very closely.

What did you hear?

Can you name a few sounds that can be very loud?

Can you name sounds that can be very soft?

How do you think someone who cannot hear is able to communicate with others? (sign language)

Some people who are hearing impaired are able to communicate using a special kind of language with their hands. This language is called sign language. This language allows them to use their body and their sense of sight to communicate with others.

Afternoon Lessons

1. Music: Continue Practicing Flute or Recorder

2. Art/Fine Motor Skills: Cutting & Folding

Supplies Needed:
Paper
Popsicle Sticks/Dowels
Glue

One of the old lessons we've lost in our modern day early childhood and early primary grade classrooms is paper cutting. Cutting scenes and decorations out of paper was a daily activity in most early childhood education programs as a way to strengthen fine motor skills, utilize creative thinking and as an art form based on the academic and seasonal lessons being presented.

Be sure your child has a very good quality pair of scissors with pointed ends. Keep in mind this can be quite challenging for children. If you see your child getting frustrated, take a break and work on it again in a bit.

Here are very simple but fun umbrella paper cutting and folding activities for children. These can be made in all different colors and sizes.

Umbrella Silhouette

The following template can be used on white paper. Cut around the black design. Try it the opposite way and cut out the black design. You will need to make a slit to get to the interior silhouette. You can share this little verse while working:

> *The rain is falling all around*
> *It rains on fields and tress*
> *It rains on the umbrellas here*
> *And on the ships at seas*

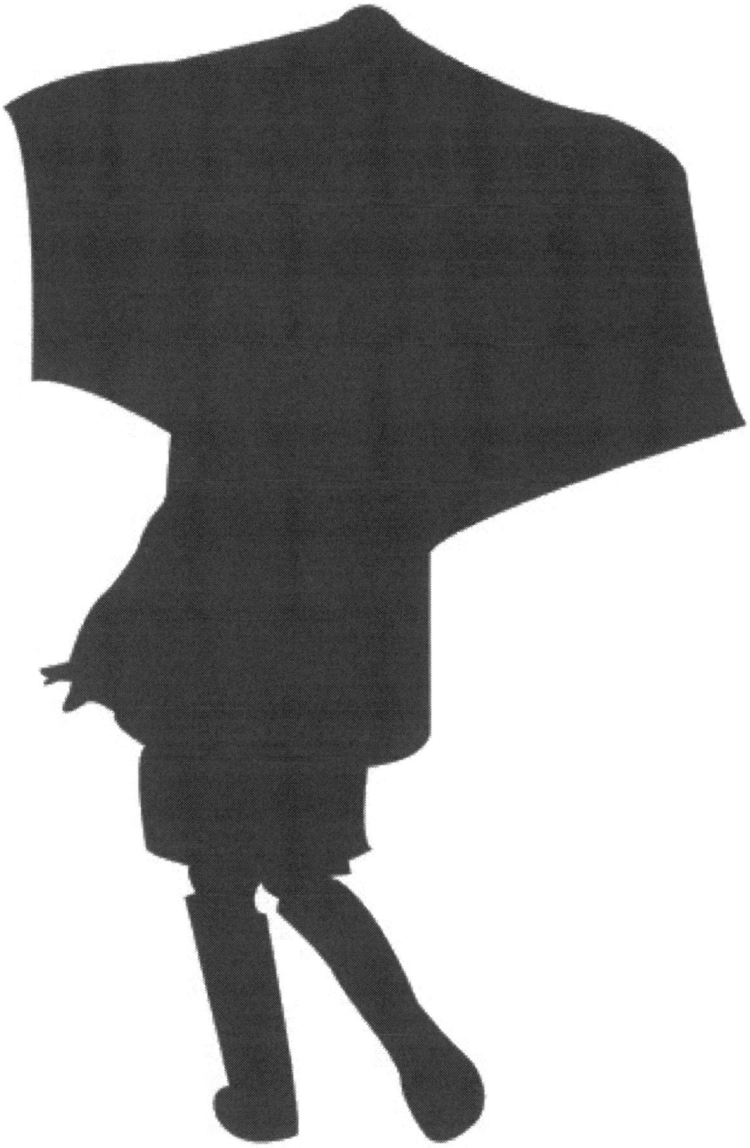

Here is a more simple version of an umbrella for your child to practice cutting. Try different colors, shapes and sizes and display them in your homeschool area.

Lastly, here is a folding activity. Make these beautiful umbrellas out of different colors and styles of paper. First, draw an even circle, then make two lines with a light pencil mark: one from top to bottom and one across. Next, make two more lines diagonal in between those. From each point where your lines meet the circle, draw slight dips/curves to create the affect of the umbrella below.

As shown on the diagram below, cut a triangle shape out of one of the panels. This will be glued to the other later to make the umbrella rounded. Cut out on the solid lines and fold on the dotted lines. Glue one panel to the other and you have your umbrella! The handles can be added with a dowel, twig or popsicle stick. A trick: add a rubber band or tape around the top of the popsicle sticks so they don't slide through.

Enjoy!

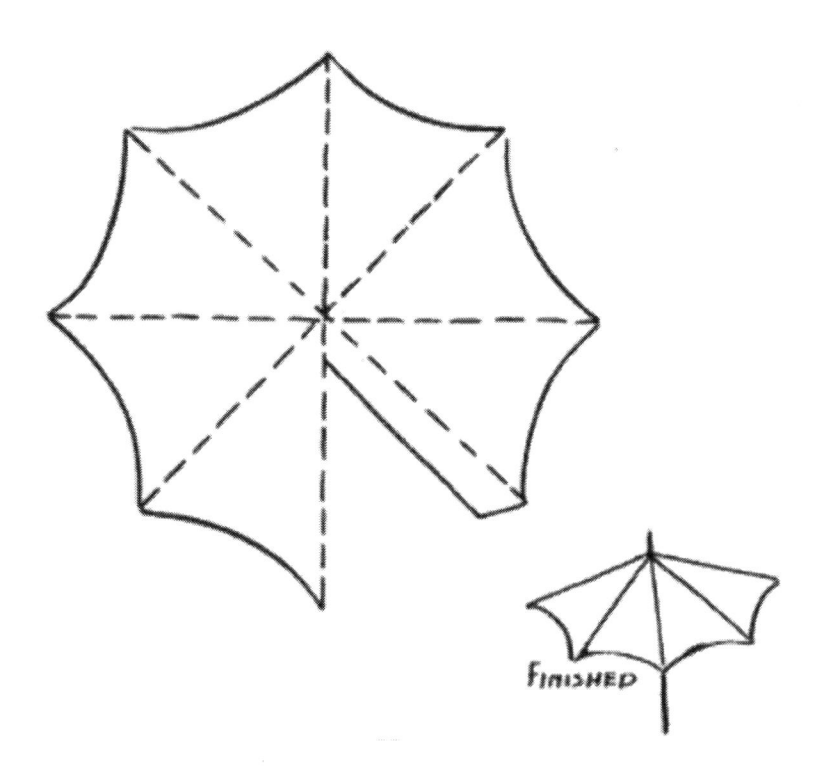

Tuesday Student Lessons – Week Twenty One

(Painting – Red Day)

Language Arts

1. Like yesterday, begin your lesson time by continuing to read (or tell) *The Story of Echo.* Provide your child with a piece of beeswax modeling material as you read. Let them hold this piece of beeswax as they listen, warming it with their hands so it softens.

2. Have your child form the softened beeswax material into the letter U. Roll it into a long snake, form it just so and then put it back together again. Next, have them form it into the number 21.

3. Open your lesson book and review the work you did yesterday. Have your child trace the letter U number 21 and words TWENTY ONE with their fingers.

4. Today we will work on a tongue twister to practice and memorize with your child to help learn the letter U and its sound. Tongue twisters and rhymes are fun ways to learn and help with finding rhythm. As we have begun bringing awareness to syllables, pay careful attention with your child to be sure they get it correctly.

   To begin, say the following tongue twister to your child slowly **and tap one finger on the palm of your other hand to the syllables** to create a pattern for memory:

   Underneath the Ugly Umbrella
   Was an Unkind Nymph
   With A Unique Echo

5. On your blackboard, write some simple sentences with blanks and have your child copy them in their lesson book. Discuss what different options can be used for the missing words and then have your child write one in as well. Here are some examples:

   MY UMBRELLA IS _____
   THE NOISE IS _____
   BANANAS ARE _____
   MY EYES ARE _____

Mathematics

1. Review Counting Backwards

   On your blackboard write down numbers 70 to 1 with some blanks. You're your child copy this into their lesson book and fill in the missing numbers. Continue these types of exercises over the next week or two aiming to be able to have your child confidently count backwards from 100.

2. Review Skip Counting

   Next, write numbers skip counting forward by 2s, 3s, 5s and 10s, leaving some blanks. Have your child copy and fill in any missing numbers.

Outdoor Time/Nature Walk

Take your children outside each day regardless of the weather. Invest in good rain gear, snow gear and wool undergarments if your location requires it. Do your lessons outdoors whenever possible.

Social Studies, Geography, Weather, Time

Learning Sign Language, The Alphabet

Review the discussion you had with your child earlier this week about sign language. Today you can practice and learn various letters of the alphabet together. This is so fun for children and you can work together to spell out vocabulary words or names. Continue working on this for the next few weeks.

a b c d e f g

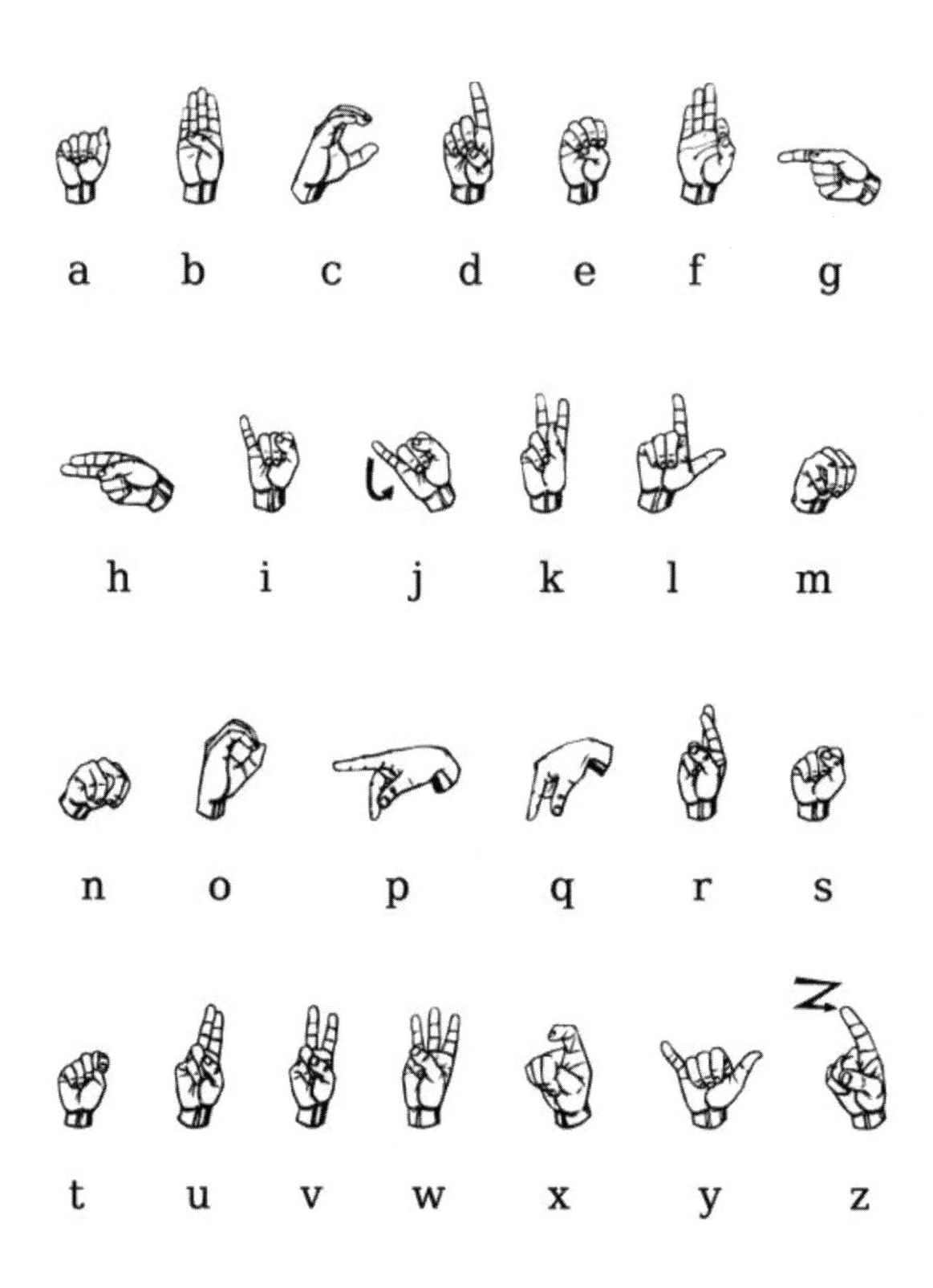

h i j k l m

n o p q r s

t u v w x y z

Afternoon Lessons

1. Music: Continue Practicing Flute or Recorder

2. Art: Painting to Music

   Supplies Needed:
   White Paper
   Paints
   Paint Brushes
   Smocks
   Water
   Cloths/Paper Towels
   Musical Instruments or Recorded Music to Play

   Today talk to your child about how sounds can make us feel. Here are some talking points:

   Sounds can make us feel different. Some sounds can make us feel happy – like listening to our favorite song. Other sounds can make us feel calm – like listening to a running stream outside.

   There are also sounds that can make us feel bad. Can you think of examples of each of these types of sounds and how you feel when you hear them?

   Next set up your workspace to paint with your child to different types of music. You should both paint how the music makes you feel, moving your brush to the sounds or expressing your feelings in color and art on your paper.

Wednesday Student Lessons – Week Twenty One
(Coloring – Yellow Day)

Language Arts

1. Practice our tongue twister again. Keep working on this until you have it memorized together. Say the following tongue twister to your child slowly **and tap one finger on the palm of your other hand to the syllables** to create a pattern for memory:

    Underneath the Ugly Umbrella
    Was an Unkind Nymph
    With A Unique Echo

2. In your child's lesson book have them make a drawing of *The Story of Echo*.

3. Like yesterday, again write some simple sentences with blanks and have your child copy them in their lesson book. Discuss what the missing words could be and then have your child write that in as well.

4. Tonight, at bedtime tell your child of *The Story of Echo*.

5. When out and about, ask your child to find things that begin with the letter U. This can be done while shopping or when driving in the car. Throughout the week, ask your child to think of all the words they can that begin with the letter U. How many can they come up with? Make a list.

6. Keep practicing and reviewing long U short U sounds and words.

Mathematics

Learning Sign Language, Numbers

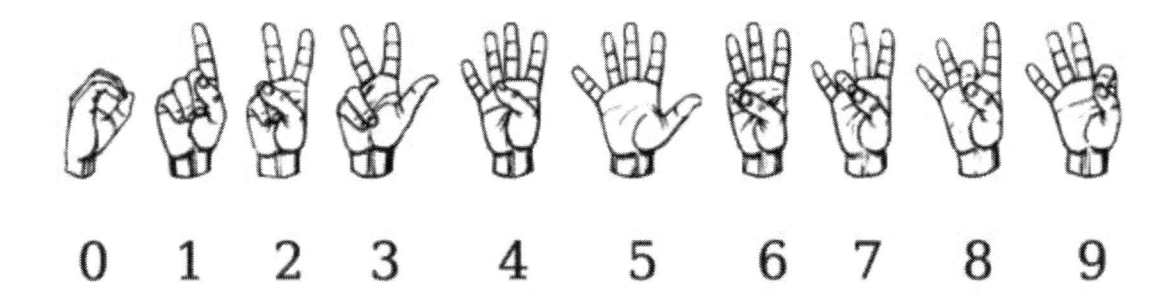

0   1   2   3   4   5   6   7   8   9

Today you can practice and learn various numbers in sign language together. Continue working on this for the next few weeks.

Outdoor Time/Nature Walk

Take your children outside each day regardless of the weather. Invest in good rain gear, snow gear and wool undergarments if your location requires it. Do your lessons outdoors whenever possible.

Science, Nature Study, Earth Discovery

Learning About Sound: Listening Walk

Take a quiet walk outdoors with your children and bring along a journal, art supplies, and pencils. As you walk through various areas tell your child to be very quiet and listen to what sounds they hear. First have them listen with their eyes open. Then have them close their eyes and listen closely. When they open their eyes, give them a few moments to write, draw, or journal what they experience.

Continue walking to different areas and journaling the sounds that they hear. This lesson can be expanded to be done a few times at different hours of the day. When you get back inside, work together to draw pictures, write sentences or words and discuss what you experienced together.

Afternoon Lessons

1. Handwork: Beginner Knitting, Learning to Change Colors

   Supplies Needed:
   Bulky Yarn of Various Colors
   Knitting Needles
   Crochet Hook

   Changing colors is a wonderful way for children to use scrap yarn and create beautiful designs with their knitting projects.

   To begin, cast on and knit two rows in the first color of yarn.

   It is much easier to change colors at the beginning of the right side rows. When you are ready to begin the third row (right side of your work), simply drop your first color yarn and pick up the yarn for the second color and continue knitting. Do not cut the first color until you have knitted with the new color for half of the row. Then, leave a tail of your first color yarn of at least 6-8" that you will weave in later. Here's how:

   Insert your needle into the first stitch and simply hold the end and loop of the new color over the right needle. Knit.

   Continue to knit with new color across the row. When you reach about halfway, you can safely cut the first color, leaving a tail of at least 6-8" to weave in later. Continue to knit with your new color across the row and the entire next row. On the sixth row, change colors again. Cut your new color after getting halfway through and leaving a tail as before.

   Continue this until you have a beautiful striped scarf or washcloth. There are many tutorials online that can help you further if needed. Don't forget to weave in your tails with a crochet hook.

2. Music: Homemade Instruments

   <u>Dried Corn Melody</u>

   Supplies Needed:
   Dried Corn still on the Cob

Plastic Container or Bottle with Lid or Top
Hot Glue

Give your child his or her own dried corn still on the cob. Have the child pick the kernels off the cob and place them into the container. Leave room for the kernels to move around inside the container. Hot glue lid and use these to create interesting rhythms or to play along with music.

Homemade Tambourines

Supplies Needed:
Small Embroidery Hoops
Large Jingle Bells
Zip Ties

Give your child a small embroidery hoop and bunch of jingle bells. Use zip ties or wire to help the children adhere their bells to the hoop. These homemade tambourines can be used during circle time or use them with the other instruments you make this week to make a musical band. A cute variation of this craft is to sew jingle bells to each finger of a child sized glove – let the children wear these and move their fingers to music.

Sandpaper Blocks

Supplies Needed:
Two Flat Blocks or Pieces of Wood
Two Wooden Knobs
Sandpaper
Hot Glue

Using hot glue adhere sandpaper (rough side facing outward) to one side of each flat block or piece of wood. On the opposite side, hot glue a wooden knob to each block. These sandpaper blocks will create a fun sound when your child rubs them together.

Thursday Student Lessons – Week Twenty One
(Crafting/Games – Orange Day)

Language Arts

1. Continue to tell your child *The Story of Echo*.

2. Alphabet Cards

    Supplies Needed:
    Heavy White Cardstock
    Beeswax Stick Crayons
    Scissors

    Spend time cutting cards out of cardstock with your child. Using beeswax crayons, continue to finish drawing each letter we have learned so far and include the letter U. Next to the letter, have your child draw an image that begins with it. Using scissors, round the corners of these cards and keep working on them throughout the year. You can use them in your lessons and for an upper case and lowercase match game later in the curriculum when we learn those as well.

3. Continue reading simple reader books together.

4. Print out or share the following photos and practice saying them together with your child. Your child may be ready to copy these words into their lesson book. Ask your child to sort out the words into piles of long U and short U sounds.

UMBRELLA

UNICORN

SUN

DUCK

MUSIC

Mathematics

Musical Uno

Supplies
Colored Number Cards or Uno Cards

Get ready to have some fun! Put on some music and play a musical card game together. Each time the following colors are played, have your child do the following dances or moves the same amount of times as the card says. If you'd like to create more of a challenge, ask your child to add, subtract or multiply that number by another number you call out to get the card:

Red: Jump
Yellow: Spin
Green: Wiggle
Blue: Clap
Wild: Free Choice

Outdoor Time/Nature Walk

Take your children outside each day regardless of the weather. Invest in good rain gear, snow gear and wool undergarments if your location requires it. Do your lessons outdoors whenever possible.

Social Studies, Geography, Weather, Time

Learning About Music: Cultural, Religious and Geographic Differences

1. Review some of the cultures, religions, and traditions you learned about with your child last week. Explore how different faiths, locations and traditions incorporate music into their culture differently. Take time to listen to different music from these places.

   What similarities do you notice compared to the music you are used to?
   What differences?
   Are the songs in a different language?
   Are they used in a place of worship?
   Does this place have an anthem or song to represent it?

2. Next, find a familiar song or nursery rhyme to listen to in a different language than you are accustomed to. Does the beat and rhythm sound the same?

Movement, Body Awareness & Health

1. Cooperative Musical Chairs

   Supplies Needed:
   Chair for Each Child
   Symbol Drawn on Card for Each Child on Chair
   Musical Instruments or Recorded Music to Play

   For each child, draw his or her name or a symbol on an index card and adhere to a chair. Set chairs up facing outward just like a regular game of musical chairs. Start the game by playing music and having the children circle around the chairs. When the music stops, each child must find their symbol and sit in the chair as quickly as possible. Rearrange the order of chairs and begin again.

2. Hide and Seek the Sound

   Supplies Needed:
   Whistle or Bell

   This game puts a fun twist on the traditional game of hide and seek. Give one child a whistle or a bell and have them hide while the others cover their eyes or go into another room. While hiding, have the child softly blow the whistle or ring the bell. Other children try to find the child by following the sound. The one who finds the child gets to hide next.

Afternoon Lessons

1. Form Drawing/Art – Review, Straight and Curved Lines

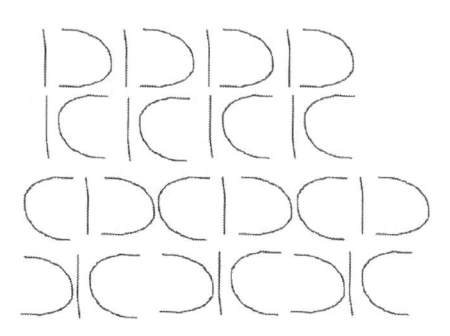

   We are going to begin reviewing the form drawings we've worked on this year. Today, we will review straight and curved lines:

   - To begin have the child stand up tall in a straight line, reaching their arms way up to the sky.

   - Have the child walk a straight line forward and try to walk a straight line backward.

   - If you have a ribbon stick, this is a wonderful tool to express a curved line with. You may also give your child rope or string and ask them to make a curved line in both directions on the floor.

   - Can your child make a curved line with their body on the floor?

   - Next have your child sit and prepare to imitate you as you work to draw and repeat a straight line, then a curved line. This can be done on a blackboard or with a stick crayon in your lesson book.

2. Handwork: Hand Stitching/Embroidery

   Supplies Needed:
   Embroidery Needle
   Embroidery Floss
   White Scrap Fabric
   Embroidery Hoop (optional)
   Scissors

Using our embroidery instructions, work with your child to make a letter U embroidery piece. You can do this with a simple running stitch, or you may choose to learn more complicated stitches together.

Friday Student Lessons – Week Twenty One
(Modeling/Housework – Green Day)

Language Arts

1. Today have your child continue to practice writing the letter U in their lesson book on unlined paper.

2. In your child's lesson book, have them practice writing the alphabet from A-U copying each letter a few times on each line.

3. Ask your child to tell YOU *The Story of Echo.*

4. Begin to introduce your child to poetry and rhymes. There are many beautiful ones to explore. You can get a poetry book from the library or share some of your favorites. Here is one from Longfellow to share.

> I shot an arrow into the air,
> It fell to earth, I knew not where;
> For, so swiftly it flew, the sight
> Could not follow it in its flight.
>
> I breathed a song into the air,
> It fell to earth, I knew not where;
> For who has sight so keen and strong
> That it can follow the flight of song?
>
> Long, long afterward, in an oak
> I found the arrow, still unbroke;
> And the song, from beginning to end,
> I found again in the heart of a friend.
>
> HENRY W. LONGFELLOW

5. After you read the poem, ask your child the following questions:

How did that poem make you feel?

Words rhyme when they have similar sounds at the end. What words do you think rhyme in that poem? (air/where, sight/flight, strong/song, etc.)

When you heard that poem, what images came to your mind? What did you imagine?

6. Have your child draw what they saw after hearing that poem in their lesson book.

7. On your blackboard, write down some rhyming words. Say these together out loud and have your child copy them. Ask your child to think of some other rhyming words of their own. Here are some examples:

BUG : DUG
TRUCK : DUCK
BLUE : GLUE
SNAIL : PAIL
FROG : DOG
CAN : PAN
FOUR : MORE

8. Which of these words have long U and short U sounds? Have your child circle those that do with a different colored pencil.

Mathematics

Review Four Processes

Continue to work with your child on addition, subtraction, multiplication and division work. Try to work toward being able to solve problems up to 100. If there are areas that your child needs to strengthen, go back through the curriculum and review.

Outdoor Time/Nature Walk

Take your children outside each day regardless of the weather. Invest in good rain gear, snow gear and wool undergarments if your location requires it. Do your lessons outdoors whenever possible.

Science, Nature Study, Earth Discovery

Learning About Sound: The Sense of Hearing, Name that Sound

Supplies Needed:
Coins
Cups or Containers with Lids
Pencil or Pen
Books
Paper or Foil
Ball
Stapler
Timer
Other Items to Make Sounds

Prior to this lesson, have various items in a box or area for you to challenge your child to "name that sound". Have them close their eyes and guess what item they think the sound is coming from. Here are some examples to explore:

Coins rattling in a container
Clapping hands
A book falling on floor
Stapler closing
Paper being torn
Foil being crumbled
Ball bouncing
Stomping on the floor
Tapping a pen on table

Domestic Arts/Practical Life Skills

Being a Good Listener

Talk to your child today about the importance of listening. Ask the following questions to inspire free discussion:

Can you tell me reasons why it is important to listen to others?

When we listen to others speak, we let them know that what they are saying is important to us.

Here is a sweet little mouse verse you can share today as you talk about practicing good manners and listening:

Listening Mouse

Only one at a time can we talk and be heard,
So, this is what I'll do.
I'll listen like a little mouse
Until my friend is through!

Afternoon Lessons

Use the afternoon hours today to review areas from this week's afternoon lessons that you feel may need a bit more attention. Bring these into your weekend as you find time.

Week Twenty Two, Winter
First Grade

Theme: Flames & Shadows, Cleansing

This Week's Lessons:

Language Arts:
The Land of The Fire Fairies Story
Letter V
V Sound – Beginning, Middle or End
Poetry and Rhyming

Mathematics:
Number 22
Review Four Processes Math up to 100
Math Fire Extinguisher
Firetruck Division
Division Tricks

Social Studies, Geography, Weather, Time:
Learning About Community Helpers: Firefighters
Learning About Fire Safety & Home Fire Drill

Science, Nature Study, Earth Discovery:
Learning About The Sense of Smell
Learning About Fire and Fuel Sources
Candle Making

Teacher's Classroom Work:
Prepare for Guess That Smell Game
Plan Trip to Candle Factory and/or Fire Department

For the Caregiver:
Caregiver Meditation: Cleansing
Caregiver Focus: Detoxing & Cleansing

Domestic Arts/Practical Life Skills:
Apple Crepes
Cleaning Out the Pantry
Monthly Home Fire Drill

Music:
Flames and Shadows Fingerplays & Songs
Beginning Recorder or Flute

Art/Handwork:
Art: Homemade Pretend Campfire
Handwork: Beginner Knitting, Review Changing Colors
Art: Shadow Animals
Embroidery, Letter V
Alphabet Card Letter V
Art: Watercolor Painting

Form Drawing:
Form Drawing/Art – Review, Circle

Movement, Body Awareness & Health:
Game of the Fire Fairies

Supplies Needed for Week Twenty Two

Cooking List:

<u>For Apple Crepes:</u>
1 Large Tart Apple, Thinly Sliced
2 Tablespoon Melted Butter
2/3 Cup Flour
Dash of Sea Salt
4 Eggs
2/3 Cup Milk
1 Teaspoon Vanilla
Dash Cinnamon

<u>For Detox Smoothie:</u>
1 Medium Apple (skin on, cored and chopped)
1 Cup of Strawberries (frozen or fresh)
1 Cup of Pineapple (frozen or fresh)
1 Cup Kale
1 Cup Coconut Water
1 Small Red Beet
1 Tablespoon Lemon Juice

Homeschooling List:

Blackboard
Chalk
Red Playsilk, Small Figure for Fairy, Large Figure for King
Lesson Book
Stockmar Stick Crayons
Stockmar Block Crayons
Colored Pencils
Stockmar Beeswax Modeling Material
Knitting Needles
Super Bulky Single Ply 100% Wool Yarn
Heavy White Cardstock
Scissors
Embroidery Needle
Embroidery Floss
White Scrap Fabric

Embroidery Hoop (optional)
Cut Lemon
Cut Lime
Shampoo
Garlic
Perfume
Soap
Flower
Fresh Pine
Essential Oils
Coffee Grounds
Flashlight
Tissue Paper in Red, Yellow and/or Orange
Glue
Clear Plastic Cup
Small LED Light

Week Twenty Two Book Recommendations

Visit your local library the weekend before to check out books based on your theme for the week. Older children can help you look up the books by author and title. When setting up your play space for the week ahead, mindfully display these books in baskets for the children to enjoy.

Gretchen Groundhog, It's Your Day! ~ Abby Levine
Gregory's Shadow ~ Don Freeman
The Groundhog Day Book of Facts and Fun ~ Wendie C. Old
Groundhog Stays Up Late ~ Margery Cuyler
My Shadow ~ Robert Louis Stevenson
The Little Book Of Hand Shadows ~ Phila H. Webb
Hand Shadows and More Hand Shadows ~ Henry Bursill
Me and My Shadows ~ Elizabeth Adams
Night and the Candlemaker ~ Wolfgang Somary
The Three Candles of Little Veronica: The Story of a Child's Soul in This World and the Other ~ Manfred Kyber
The Story of the Little Candle: A Book of Inspiration ~ Inshan Meahjohn
Burn: Michael Faraday's Candle ~ Darcy Pattison
Carnival at Candlelight ~ Mary Pope Osborne
The Candle Star ~ Michelle Isenhoff
The Sign of the Twisted Candles (Nancy Drew, Book 9) ~ Carolyn Keene
A Flicker of Hope ~ Julia Cook
Sparky the Fire Dog ~ Don Hoffman
Shadow Castle ~ Marian Cockrell
Ignis ~ Gina Wilson
The Fire Cat (I Can Read) ~ Esther Averill
Big Frank's Fire Truck ~ Leslie McGuire & Joe Mathieu
Our House is on Fire ~ Greta Thunberg's Call to Save the Planet ~ Jeanette Winter
Hill Of Fire (I Can Read) ~ Thomas P. Lewis
A Day in the Life of a Firefighter (Beginning to Read) ~ Linda Hayward
The Fire Station ~ Robert Munsch

Week Twenty Two Circle, Songs & Movement

The following songs and verses should be shared during circle time each day this week after you open your circle.

Shadow Fingerplay

If I walk, my shadow walks.
(use two fingers, in walking motion)

If I run, my shadow runs.
(same fingers in running motion)

And when I stand still, as you can see,
(same fingers, standing still)

My shadow stands beside me.
(use first two fingers on other hand and stand beside the first two fingers)

When I hop, my shadow hops.
(first two fingers, hopping)

When I jump, my shadow jumps.
(same fingers, jump)

And when I sit still, as you can see,
(same fingers, bend at knuckles to sit)

My shadow sits beside of me.
(use as before, both sets of fingers sitting beside each other)

My Shadow
by Robert Louis Stevenson

I have a little shadow that goes in and out with me,
And what can be the use of him is more than I can see.
He is very, very like me from the heels up to the head;
And I see him jump before me, when I jump into my bed.

The funniest thing about him is the way he likes to grow,
Not at all like proper children, which is always very slow;
For he sometimes shoots up taller like an India-rubber ball,
And he sometimes goes so little that there's none of him at all.

He hasn't got a notion of how children ought to play,
And can only make a fool of me in every sort of way.
He stays so close behind me, he's a coward you can see;
I'd think shame to stick to nursie as that shadow sticks to me!

One morning, very early, before the sun was up,
I rose and found the shining dew on every buttercup;
But my lazy little shadow, like an arrant sleepy-head,
Had stayed at home behind me and was fast asleep in bed!

This firefighter rings the bell.
(point to thumb)

This firefighter holds the hose so well.
(point to index finger)

This firefighter slides down the pole.
(point to middle finger)

This firefighter chops a hole.
(point to ring finger)

This firefighter climbs higher and higher.
(point to pinky finger)

And all the firefighters put out the fire!

For the following, have an empty candlestick or other object in the center of your circle that the children can jump over..

Jack, be nimble, Jack, be quick!
Jack, jump over the candlestick!

Week Twenty Two Blackboard Drawing

Drawing Ideas for This Week: Capital letter V as shown in the shape of the Fire Fairy's clothing or wings, Fire King, flame or fire, young child and their shadow, candle with flame, Letter V, words beginning with V, Roman numeral XXII, TWENTY TWO, 22

Week Twenty Two Teacher's Classroom Work

1. Prepare in advance for the Guess That Smell game by preparing the items. Some ideas are listed in the lesson.

2. If you have a candle factory within driving distance of your home, consider taking the children to see how candles are made. Many of these factories hold

demonstrations and offer free products. An alternative would be to visit a local candle shop or make homemade wax candles.

3. Additionally, consider visiting your local fire department with your child to learn more about fire safety and what firefighters in their profession.

4. Review any handwork before working on projects with your children.

Week Twenty Two Caregiver Meditation

This Week's Reflection: Cleansing

"Making resolutions is a cleansing ritual of self-assessment and repentance that demands personal honesty and, ultimately, reinforces humility. Breaking them is part of the cycle." ~ Eric Zorn

Depending on when you are working on this weekly lesson, you may be feeling as if you are stuck in the darkness that comes before spring. If so, rest assured, the light will come. We may also have regrets of resolutions that we have made and broken or maybe we never even got started in the first place. The beauty of life is that we are offered so many chances to begin again.

Being truly honest with yourself and evaluating where you need to grow, or change is the first step. Part of the cycle of living and learning is often realizing that we are struggling to follow through or get started. Sometimes we need to spin our tires a while before we are able put in the strength and effort needed to get ourselves out of the mud.

What is in your life that needs cleansing or renewal? Where can you begin again?

Take time to reflect upon this during your meditation time this week. If this week happens to fall during Lent and you recognize that in your faith and/or traditions, consider giving up old habits or thoughts that are holding you back instead of the more customary things others refrain from.

Week Twenty Two Story

This is a very old fairy story that children enjoy so very much. A red silk bunched up can be placed on the floor ahead of time to symbolize the flames of the fire Ted falls asleep next to. If you have a small figure dressed in red to hide under the silk, this can be the fairy that comes out to tell Ted that the King has sent for him. Now take your red silk and lay it long and narrow for the 'road' that they travel. You can just tell the tale as you move your fairy down the road (or you can really take the time to set up beforehand and have small figures on each side for the other fairies working on logs, houses, etc.). Use a large figure for the King of the Fire Fairies and speak in a deep tone as you tell his part.

The Land of the Fire Fairies

The east wind was blowing the falling snow into drifts against the house, fences, and trees. Colder and colder it grew, and little Ted, who had been out playing snowball, suddenly burst into his grandmother's room, crying: "Oh, I'm so cold" He took off his coat, hat, muffler, and overshoes, stamped his feet and shook off the snow. A bright fire was roaring in the grate, and Ted lay down before it to warm himself. He began to watch the flames dancing up the chimney and disappearing into the darkness above. Picking up a stick, he lit it and held it up the chimney, trying to see whether he could tell where the flame on the end of it went; and he was enjoying himself very much, when his grandmother called to him to put down the stick.

"Why," said Ted, "I am just playing, and want to see what becomes of the flames when they go up the chimney."

"Yes," said Grandmother, "perhaps you do; but the Fire King does not allow people to play with his fairies. They are meant to do work, not to play."

"The Fire King!" said Ted, as he dropped the stick into the fire; "who is he, Grandmother?"

"I've never seen him," she answered; "but he lives in the Land of the Fairies."

With his toes turned toward the fire, lying on his back on the warm hearth, Ted soon dropped off to dreamland, the home of the pixies and fairies. No sooner had he reached that land than straight out of the roaring fire jumped a tiny little fairy clothed all in red, who said to Ted: "The King of the Fire Fairies has sent for you. Will you come with me?"

Ted was up in a moment, and jumping into the fire, followed close behind the tiny little leader. The bright red road along which they traveled was very interesting. On either side was a fringe of gray moss-like ashes, and as they hurried along Ted saw the Fire Fairies at work by the hundreds. In one place they had a large log they were working with, which was sending up great flames and much smoke. All around the log were the blackened remains of the grass they had spoiled. In another place a beautiful house was being torn down and burned up by these little mischief-loving fellows. Again, he came to a large stove in which were many of them were helping a cook get dinner ready and warming the cold fingers and toes of a little boy and girl.

The fairy who was leading Ted went so fast that he did not have a good look at any of these things, and very soon the fairy shouted at the top of his little voice, "Look!"

Ted did look, and straight before him was a larger palace than he had ever supposed could be built. Flames were bursting out of doors and windows, and the roar made Ted hold his ears, it was so loud. On either side of the great front door stood a large giant whom the little fairy said were the giants Heat and Light. Putting Ted safely on the top of a high wall, the fairy disappeared into the palace. And just at that moment a giant greater than either of the others came to the door.

In a voice that sounded like thunder and shook everything around, the giant called: "Where is the little boy I sent for?"

Ted knew then that this was the great Fire King, and was frightened, but answered quickly, "Here I am!"

Then the giant said: "I have sent for you to tell you that my Fire Fairies are not to be played with. They never hurt anyone unless they are played with and taken away from their work; then they are sure to hurt the person who disturbs them."

How frightened little Ted was as he promised faithfully never again to play with fire! He was glad when the giant, satisfied with his promise, shut the great door and disappeared, and his little guide in the bright red suit came skipping toward him, and offered to take him back home.

On the way back he found things changed. The stove was black and cold, and the people who had been warming themselves around it and getting dinner had gone away. The house was burned to the ground, and only a few sleepy fairies were showing their red coats in the gray rubbish. Where the log had been only an ash-heap remained, which the wind was carrying away. The road was no longer red, but dusty, and Ted found that he could walk much more slowly.

How tired he was! His face felt so warm, his body so stiff and what was that noise? How much like the dinner bell it sounded! Was that the fairy who was slinking him? A long stretch and a yawn, and his eyes flew open. There was his dear grandmother trying to get him awake.

"Did you see him, Grandmother," asked Ted.

"See whom?" she answered.

"The Fire Fairy," said Ted; and then began to laugh when he saw his grandmother's eyes twinkle.

"Oh! Grandmother," said he, "I have really been to see the giant King of the Fire Fairies and have seen his palace and the two giants Light and Heat that guard his door."

Monday Student Lessons – Week Twenty Two

(Baking/Cooking – Purple Day)

Language Arts

1. Begin your lesson time by reading (or telling) *The Land of the Fire Fairies* to your child. Let the children look at the sentences as you read as this visual will aid with their knowledge of letters, words and sentences. If possible, use simple props to accompany the story as we have suggested.

2. When your story is finished, unveil your blackboard drawing that you have prepared ahead of time as suggested at the beginning of this week's curriculum. If your child has his or her own small blackboard and chalk, have them take a few moments to create their own drawing.

3. Review what your child worked on last week in their lesson book. Have them practice writing the capital letter U a few times on their blackboard or an extra piece of paper. Be sure they have a good grasp of this letter before moving onto the next.

4. In your child's lesson book, have them create a similar image of the Fire Fairy (or whatever depiction you used) with the letter V revealed inside. On the righthand side, have your child practice writing the capital letter V. Share this poem as you work to form the letter:

> I love to make the letter V
> For everyone to see.
> *(make a V with your fingers)*
>
> Diagonal line down
> And then one up
> Letter V…
> Yippee!
> *(draw letter V)*

Mathematics

1. In addition to the Roman numeral XXII, write down the number 22 and word TWENTY TWO in all capital letters for your child to see. Say each letter as you write.

2. Have the child draw images of the number TWENTY TWO. They may copy some of the items you made in your blackboard drawing for this week. Your child should then practice writing the number 22, Roman numeral XXII and the word TWENTY TWO in all capital letters on the opposite page of their book. If you feel they need extra time with writing, let them continue to practice as needed. Here is a verse to share when forming the number 22:

> *Write a TWO to begin*
> *And then another*
> *It's a twin!*

Domestic Arts/Practical Life Skills

Apple Crepes

Candlemas is a beautiful festival celebrated in many cultures across the world on February 2nd. This also happens to be the day people who live in the United States celebrate Groundhog's Day. It is the midway point of winter when we can look ahead with anticipation of the coming of Spring. It is a festival of candles and the warmth of the hearth.

Candlemas (and Groundhog's Day) both stem from the very ancient festival of Imbolc which is one of the four Celtic fire festivals and the very word means 'in the belly', as in a celebration of the life hidden within that will soon appear to us in Spring. It is also customary to enjoy pancakes or crepes on Candlemas Day and while you may or may not be using this lesson in February, it is always a good time to eat pancakes!

Supplies Needed:
1 Large Tart Apple, Thinly Sliced
2 Tablespoon Melted Butter
2/3 Cup Flour
Dash of Sea Salt
4 Eggs

2/3 Cup Milk
1 Teaspoon Vanilla
Dash Cinnamon

Whisk the eggs by hand, then add the flour. Try to get out as much of the lumps as you can before adding the milk. Add the remaining ingredients and whisk well. Heat some butter in a well-seasoned cast iron skillet (or other non-stick skillet). Add a few slices of apple. Pour about 1/2-1/3 cup of batter in the skillet over the apple slices. Swirl the skillet around so as to cover the bottom of the pan. Cook on medium until the top is set and the bottom golden brown. Flip once and cook the bottom until golden brown as well. Keep warm under a hot towel or in a warm oven. Serve with butter, powdered sugar, honey, jam or, as is traditional in The Netherlands, with some grated sharp cheese.

Outdoor Time/Nature Walk

Take your children outside each day regardless of the weather. Invest in good rain gear, snow gear and wool undergarments if your location requires it. Do your lessons outdoors whenever possible.

Caregiver Focus

Caregiver Focus: Detoxing and Cleansing

It is important to take time to cleanse our body to reset and feel better. This week try to focus more on what you are putting into your body each day. Consider eliminating alcohol, breads, sugars, and dairy for a period of time and give your body the gift of fresh, clean foods and water. Here is a very nice detox smoothie recipe you can try. Blend all ingredients below together, with or without ice:

1 Medium Apple (skin on, cored and chopped)
1 Cup of Strawberries (frozen or fresh)
1 Cup of Pineapple (frozen or fresh)
1 Cup Kale
1 Cup Coconut Water
1 Small Red Beet
1 Tablespoon Lemon Juice

Science, Nature Study, Earth Discovery

Learning About The Sense of Smell

Spend time today talking to your child about the sense of smell. Ask your child what part of our body we use when we smell something. (nose)

Guess That Smell

Next, play a game to test your child's sense of smell! Be very quiet and still and have your child close their eyes. Then bring various items near their nose and have them guess what each item is.

Some ideas:

Cut Lemon
Cut Lime
Shampoo
Garlic
Perfume
Soap
Flower
Fresh Pine
Essential Oils
Coffee Grounds

Afternoon Lessons

1. Music: Continue Practicing Flute or Recorder

2. Art/Fine Motor Skills: Homemade Pretend Campfire

   Supplies Needed:
   Tissue Paper in Red, Yellow and/or Orange
   Glue
   Clear Plastic Cup
   Small LED Light

   Have the children practice their cutting skills by cutting small squares out of the different colored tissue paper. Crumple each square up and glue all over the plastic cup. Place the cup over a small LED light and turn off your lights!

The children can use this pretend fire to be camping, cook marshmallows, have a pretend fireplace and more!

Tuesday Student Lessons – Week Twenty Two

(Painting – Red Day)

Language Arts

1. Like yesterday, begin your lesson time by continuing to read (or tell) *The Land of the Fire Fairies.* Provide your child with a piece of beeswax modeling material as you read. Let them hold this piece of beeswax as they listen, warming it with their hands so it softens.

2. Have your child form the softened beeswax material into the letter V. Roll it into a long snake, form it just so and then put it back together again. Next, have them form it into the number 22.

3. Open your lesson book and review the work you did yesterday. Have your child trace the letter V number 22 and words TWENTY TWO with their fingers.

4. Today we will work on a tongue twister to practice and memorize with your child to help learn the letter V and its sound. Tongue twisters and rhymes are fun ways to learn and help with finding rhythm. As we have begun bringing awareness to syllables, pay careful attention with your child to be sure they get it correctly.

   To begin, say the following tongue twister to your child slowly **and tap one finger on the palm of your other hand to the syllables** to create a pattern for memory:

   The village on vacation
   Had long vines of vegetables
   Up and down the valley

5. On your blackboard, write some simple sentences with blanks and have your child copy them in their lesson book. Discuss what the missing words could be and then have your child write that in as well. Here are some examples:

   THE CAT JUMPS _____
   THE TREE IS _____
   FIRETRUCKS ARE _____
   FIRE IS _____

Mathematics

1. Review Counting Backwards

   On your blackboard write down numbers 80 to 1 with some blanks. Have your child copy this into their lesson book and fill in the missing numbers. Continue these types of exercises over the next week or two aiming to be able to have your child confidently count backwards from 100.

2. Math Fire Extinguisher

   On your blackboard, draw flames with numbers inside no higher than 100. Alternatively, you can use the template we have provided below.

   Next, present your child with an addition, subtraction, multiplication, or division fact that equal an amount listed. Let your child use paper or their own blackboard to use dots, skip counting or other methods to solve the problems.

   When they get the answer, have them erase, strike through or color the correct flame answer accordingly (you may wish to do this with the color red).

   If your child is still working on building these skills up to 100, simplify this game according to their ability.

Math Fire Extinguisher

Present your child with an addition, subtraction, multiplication or division equation that equals the fire numbers.

When your child calculates the correct answer, have them color, erase or cross out the associated fire until all are extinguished.

100 − 5 =	7 x 5 =	30 + 20 =	25 − 20 =
7 + 3 =	60 ÷ 3 =	40 + 30 =	25 x 4 =
85 − 40 =	5 x 3 =	80 ÷ 2 =	60 ÷ 1 =
75 x 1 =	70 − 5 =	100 − 20 =	15 + 15 =
50 ÷ 2 =	11 x 5 =	50 + 35 =	30 x 3 =

Outdoor Time/Nature Walk

Take your children outside each day regardless of the weather. Invest in good rain gear, snow gear and wool undergarments if your location requires it. Do your lessons outdoors whenever possible.

Social Studies, Geography, Weather, Time

<u>Learning About Community Helpers: Firefighters</u>

Try to organize a trip to take your child for a visit to your local Fire Department. Local community helpers such as firefighters are usually very receptive to having visitors and teaching children about fire safety and the profession.

Talk about the clothes and equipment firefighters must have to protect themselves and help them fight fires.

Have your child help you make a list of the equipment and clothing that firefighters use. What does each piece of equipment do?

Some examples:

Hat
Ladder
Fire Extinguisher
Boots
Coat
Hose
Mask
Ax

Afternoon Lessons

1. Music: Continue Practicing Flute or Recorder

2. Art: Shadow Animals

   Supplies Needed:
   Flashlight

   Turn down the lights and use a flashlight to make shadow animals with the children. To make a rabbit hold two fingers up and bunch the others. To make a bird, join thumbs and extend fingers on both hands. To make a dog, place both palms together with fingers extended and touching, keep pinkies down apart from the others for his mouth and then pull thumbs apart a bit to show the ears.

   Experiment and see what other types of animals you can make:

Wednesday Student Lessons – Week Twenty Two
(Coloring – Yellow Day)

Language Arts

1. Practice our tongue twister again. Keep working on this until you have it memorized together. Say the following tongue twister to your child slowly **and tap one finger on the palm of your other hand to the syllables** to create a pattern for memory:

    The village on vacation
    Had long vines of vegetables
    Up and down the valley

2. In your child's lesson book have them make a drawing of *The Land of the Fire Fairies*.

3. Like yesterday, again write some simple sentences with blanks and have your child copy them in their lesson book. Discuss what the missing words could be and then have your child write that in as well.

4. Tonight, at bedtime tell your child the story of *The Land of the Fire Fairies*.

5. When out and about, ask your child to find things that begin with the letter V. This can be done while shopping or when driving in the car. Throughout the week, ask your child to think of all the words they can that begin with the letter V. How many can they come up with? Make a list.

6. Show your child words that include the letter V. Ask them to identify if the V sound is at the beginning, middle or end of each word.

Mathematics

Firetruck Division

A fun way to practice division this week is to play this little firetruck game with the children.

To begin, tape or glue a firetruck to the front of 10 separate containers. During free time, your child may like to color these trucks in before adhering. (template below if needed)

Next, print out or draw 20-40 small fire extinguishers and glue or paste onto pegs or blocks that can easily fit inside the larger containers. You may choose to simplify and use red beads or blocks for these.

Present your child with various scenarios. In each scenario, the firefighters are off to fight a fire. Example:

They have ___ firetrucks to take on this trip and there are ___ fire extinguishers. They must evenly distribute the extinguishers in the firetrucks before they can leave the firehouse.

Continue with this game with various division word problems. If your child is ready, you can continue to explore remainders by seeing how many extinguishers are left out after each truck is full. Be sure to take the time to work with your child and write out the actual division equation in numeric format before proceeding to the next.

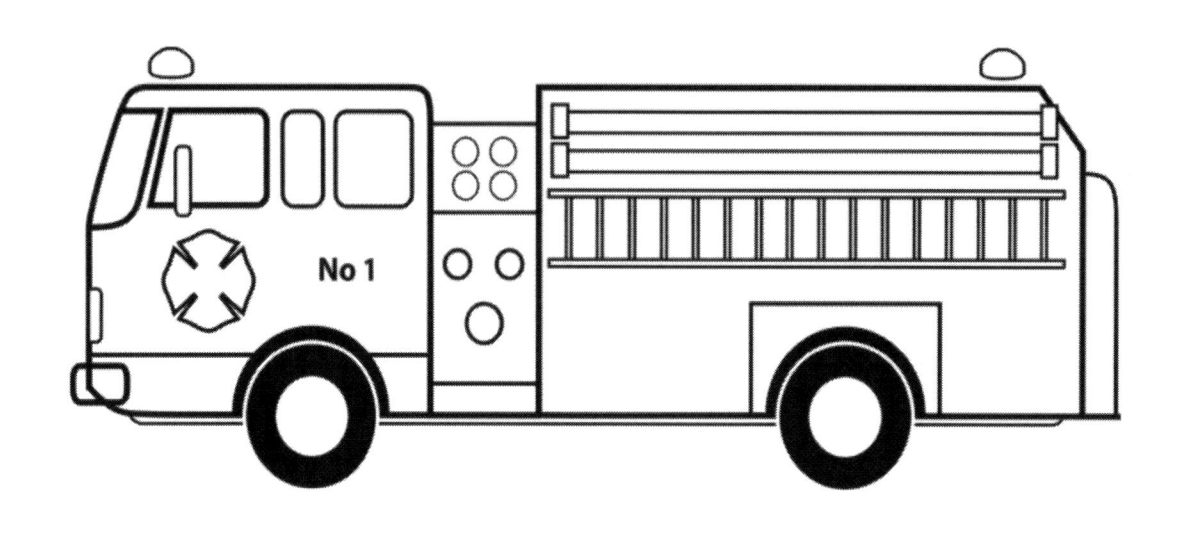

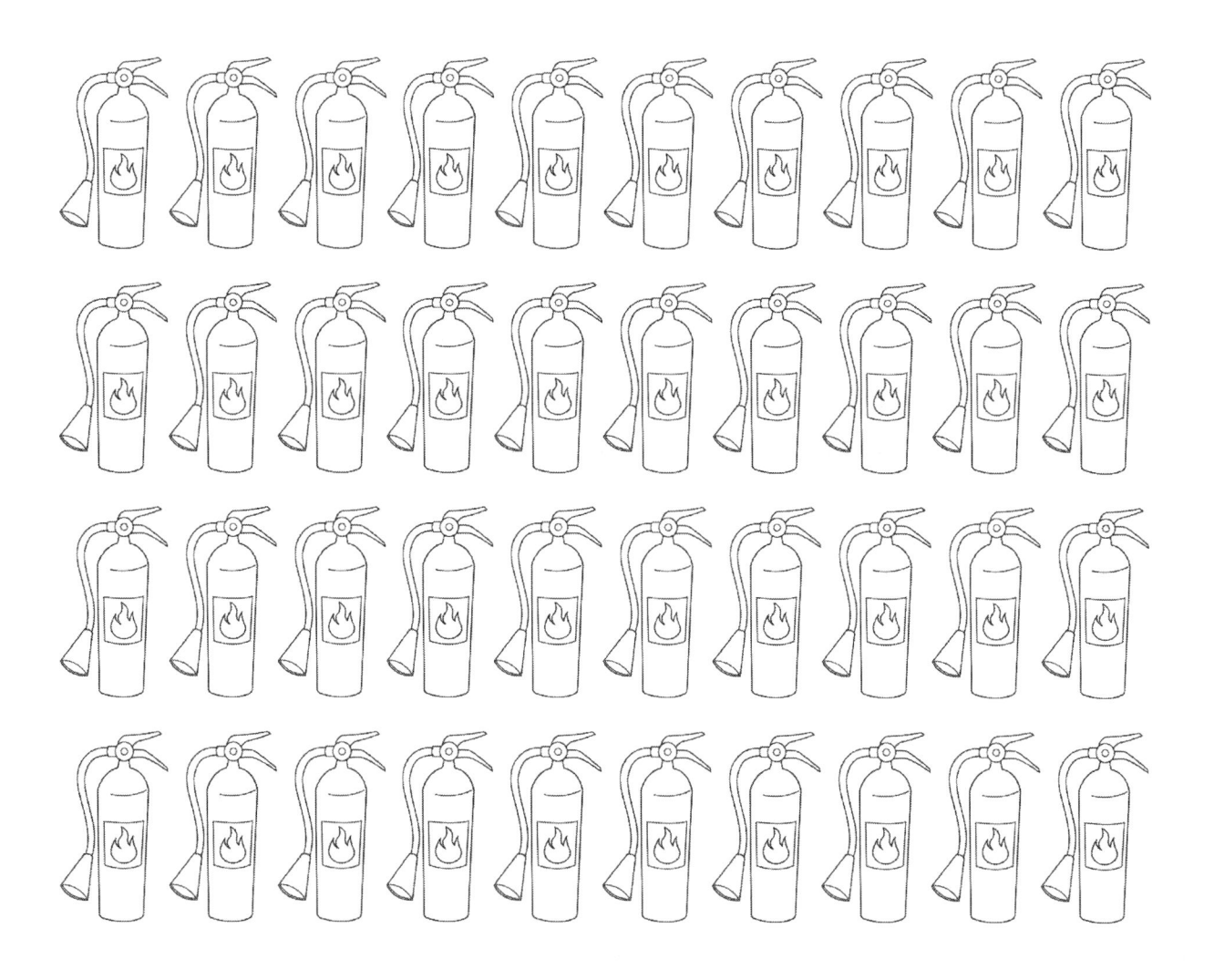

First Grade Curriculum | WINTER | Little Acorn Learning

Outdoor Time/Nature Walk

Take your children outside each day regardless of the weather. Invest in good rain gear, snow gear and wool undergarments if your location requires it. Do your lessons outdoors whenever possible.

Science, Nature Study, Earth Discovery

1. Learning About Fire and Fuel Sources

Today talk to your child about fire.

What is fire?

Fire is a chemical reaction. It happens when heat combines with oxygen in the air and hits a fuel source. Flames are then created and gives off light and smoke.

What is a fuel source?

A fuel source is a material that can be burned by the fire to make energy.

Fires can be indoors and outdoors. Fire can be used for many good purposes. Fire can also be dangerous.

Can you think of an outdoor fire you've seen? What was used as the fuel source? For example, in a campfire the fuel source may have been wood and newspaper.

Can you think of a safe indoor flame or fire you have seen? Candles, fireplaces, some stovetops and matches are some good examples. What was the source of fuel for these? (wax/wick, paper/wood, gas/oil, etc.)

How can fire help us? (provide heat, light, warmth, cook food, roast marshmallows, celebrate birthday parties, etc.)

If a fire is not carefully made and watched by a responsible adult, it can get out of control and be extremely dangerous. That is why is very important never to go near fire or play with it. How are some ways a fire could be dangerous?

When a fire has developed and becomes dangerous, firefighters are trained to try to put them out and keep people safe.

2. In your child's lesson book, have them draw an example of a good fire. On the righthand side, have them write a simple sentence or word depending on their writing progress at this time. For example:

CANDLE
THE FIREPLACE IS WARM

Afternoon Lessons

Handwork: Beginner Knitting, Review Changing Colors

As you did last week, continue practicing changing colors in your knitting with your child.

Thursday Student Lessons – Week Twenty Two
(Crafting/Games – Orange Day)

Language Arts

1. Continue to tell your child *The Land of the Fire Fairies.*

2. Alphabet Cards

   Supplies Needed:
   Heavy White Cardstock
   Beeswax Stick Crayons
   Scissors

   Spend time cutting cards out of cardstock with your child. Using beeswax crayons, continue to finish drawing each letter we have learned so far and include the letter V. Next to the letter, have your child draw an image that begins with it. Using scissors, round the corners of these cards and keep working on them throughout the year. You can use them in your lessons and for an upper case and lowercase match game later in the curriculum when we learn those as well.

3. Continue reading simple reader books together.

4. Print out or share the following photos and practice saying them together with your child. Your child may be ready to copy these words into their lesson book.

VIOLIN

VILLAGE

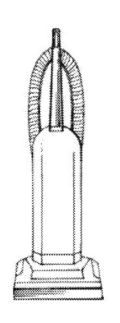

VACUUM

VASE

VINE

First Grade Curriculum | WINTER | Little Acorn Learning

Mathematics

Division Tricks

There are some tricks that can help your child as they learn to master division. A few you likely already know. Your child may or may not be ready to learn all these tricks but keep them handy for when they are.

- By 1: Anytime a number is divided by 1, the answer is the same as the dividend.

  Example:

  $10 \div 1 = 10$
  $55 \div 1 = 55$

- By 2: If the last number of the dividend is even, the entire number can be divided by 2. And, dividing anything by 2 is the same as cutting it in half.

  Example:

  $48 \div 2 = 24$
  $126 \div 2 = 63$

- By 4: When the last two numbers of the dividend are divisible by four, then the entire number is as well.

  Example:

  $432 \div 4 = 108$
  $112 \div 4 = 28$

- By 5: If the dividend ends in a 0 or 5, it is divisible by 5.

  Example:

  $25 \div 5 = 5$
  $10 \div 5 = 2$

- By 10: If the dividend ends in 0, it is divisible by 10.

Example:

$100 \div 10 = 10$
$10 \div 10 = 1$

Outdoor Time/Nature Walk

Take your children outside each day regardless of the weather. Invest in good rain gear, snow gear and wool undergarments if your location requires it. Do your lessons outdoors whenever possible.

Movement, Body Awareness & Health

Game of the Fire Fairies

Talk with your children about how flames seem to dance when they watch a campfire or fire in the fireplace. Discuss the story of *The Land of the Fire Fairies* again and how dangerous it can be to play with fire. Play music and have your children show you with their arms the way that the fire fairies (flames) might dance.

Next have your child use their entire body to be just like the fire fairies. Have them show you how the very tall fire fairies dance and grow upward over the wood. How do the fire fairies shrink down to the ground when the fire starts to dwindle?

Tell them the fire is going out, out, out and it's gone. Have them move to this sequence. Can they lay still on the floor like a pile of ash or heap of coal?

Clap your hands and tell your child you just lit a match and the fire has started again! It starts off so very slow (hands and arms only) and then grows and grows.

Continue to have fun dancing to the music like little fire fairies together.

Afternoon Lessons

1. Form Drawing/Art – Review, Circle

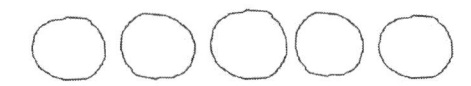

   ○ ○ ○ ○ ○

   This afternoon, we will review form drawing circles with our bodies and in writing format.

   - To begin have your child stand up and make a circle with both arms above their head just like the big yellow sun.

   - Have your child bring the circle down and in front of them.

   - If you have a group of children, have them hold hands in a circle and move to the left for a while and then to the right. If you do not, have your child walk a circle on the floor in one direction and then in the other.

   - Next have your child sit and prepare to imitate you as you work to draw and repeat circles. Take your time and work slowly. This can be done on a blackboard or with a stick crayon in your lesson book.

   - Have your child look for examples around the home or outdoors of circles in nature. What letters and numbers have circles in them?

2. Handwork: Hand Stitching/Embroidery

   Supplies Needed:
   Embroidery Needle
   Embroidery Floss
   White Scrap Fabric
   Embroidery Hoop (optional)
   Scissors

   Using our embroidery instructions, work with your child to make a letter V embroidery piece. You can do this with a simple running stitch, or you may choose to learn more complicated stitches together.

Friday Student Lessons – Week Twenty Two
(Modeling/Housework – Green Day)

Language Arts

1. Today have your child continue to practice writing the letter V in their lesson book on unlined paper.

2. In your child's lesson book, have them practice writing the alphabet from A- V each letter a few times on each line.

3. Ask your child to tell YOU the story of *The Land of the Fire Fairies.*

4. Continue to introduce your child to poetry and rhymes. There are many beautiful ones to explore. You can get a poetry book from the library or share some of your favorites. Here is one from George B. Carpenter from a very long time ago to share.

   <u>Fire-Fairies</u>

   When the fire cracks and sputters
   In defiance to the snow
   And the fire fairies sparkle
   In the ruddy afterglow
   Did you ever ever wonder
   How they happen to be near
   Just to break the wood asunder
   And so quickly disappear

   Through the long and drowsy summer
   Every sunbeam streaming down
   From the azure arch of heaven
   Into forest field and town
   Finds some cozy nook or crevice
   Where the forest watchers creep
   Burrows deep beneath the surface
   Cuddles up and goes to sleep

But when winter steals upon us
And the fender shines again
In the mellow light of hemlock
Oak or maple it is then
That the sunbeams break their bondage
And from woody fiber free
Each becomes a fire fairy
Sparkling there in ecstasy

Leaping laughing in the fire
Casting shadows on the wall
Rising higher higher higher
Till the snowy ashes fall
And they vanished up the chimney
Leaving here within the den
All the fragrant warmth of summer
Which will bring them back again

GEORGE B. CARPENTER

5. After you read the poem, ask your child the following questions:

   How did that poem make you feel?

   Words rhyme when they have similar sounds at the end. What words do you think rhyme in that poem? (snow/afterglow, down/town, wall/fall, etc.)

   When you heard that poem, what images came to your mind? What did you imagine?

6. Have your child watercolor paint what they saw after hearing that poem.

7. On your blackboard, write down some rhyming words. Say these together out loud and have your child copy them. Ask your child to think of some other rhyming words of their own. Here are some examples:

HIVE : DIVE
RED : TED
KING : RING
FIRE : TIRE

Mathematics

Continue to work with your child on addition, subtraction, multiplication, and division work. Try to work toward being able to solve problems up to 100. If there are areas that your child needs to strengthen, go back through the curriculum and review some lessons.

Outdoor Time/Nature Walk

Take your children outside each day regardless of the weather. Invest in good rain gear, snow gear and wool undergarments if your location requires it. Do your lessons outdoors whenever possible.

Science, Nature Study, Earth Discovery

Candle Making

Candle, candle burning bright
Fill us with your shining light

May your flame of joy and love
Glow now in our hearts

Candle, candle burning bright
Share with us your golden light

There are many ways to make candles. You can order simple sheets of beeswax and wicks online and have the children roll candles. You can also buy materials for melting and pouring candles out of beeswax, soy, and glycerin. Take time today to make candles with your children. If you are looking for a way to make a candle out of materials you have around the house, you can even make them out of crayons!

We have put together two crayon candle tutorials for you if you would like to try this method. As always, use extreme caution when working with any fire, hot wax or candles. Only an adult should work with hot wax or fire. Use this as an opportunity to reiterate to your child the fire safety lessons you've gone over this week.

https://littleacornlearning.com/2020/02/03/make-candles-out-of-crayons/

Domestic Arts/Practical Life Skills

1. Cleaning out the Pantry

   Today would be a great day to clean out your pantry and refrigerator. The children can help you wipe down the shelves and organize your space. Use up any perishable foods along with your evening meal tonight (get creative!). Take note of what you have and plan your meals for the upcoming week based on these items. Next, make a list of the things that you need to get from the grocery store to complete your menu.

2. Monthly Home Fire Drill

   Ask your child if people can smell fire. Explain that sometimes our noses can identify the smell of smoke, but we need other tools to help keep us safe from fire as well. When have there been times that your child has smelled smoke or fire?

   Use this time to talk about the importance of smoke alarms, an escape plan and fire safety. Go over your monthly home fire drill:

   Every 83 seconds, the fire department is called to a fire in an American home. Our homes contain our most precious possessions, our children. In addition to having smoke detectors on every level of your house and in every sleeping area, each home and business should have a fire-escape plan. If you do not have a plan, take time to create one prior to doing this drill. Draw an overhead floor plan of your home including all doors and windows. Write 'EXIT' over each location that you can get out of in case of a fire. Draw arrows marking the direction the children can walk to get out of your home. Put a big star on top of your outdoor meeting place. Show your children the escape plan you created for your home. Explain to children that if they hear the fire alarm go off at any time to follow these basic rules: Check any doors before opening them to see if they feel hot. If the door is hot, use another exit or open the window and yell for help. If the room is smoky, get very low and go under the smoke to the closest exit. Do not worry about pets, toys or other belongings. Never go back to get something – the firefighter will get it later and animals have a natural instinct to flee during a fire.

   Go outside to your family meeting place and wait for help. Older children can be instructed to go knock on the door of a trusted neighbor if necessary. To do your drill this morning: Press the 'test' button of your fire alarm and tell the children that you will be having a fire drill. See how quickly and quietly you can bring the children together and get to your meeting place outside.

Afternoon Lessons

Use the afternoon hours today to review areas from this week's afternoon lessons that you feel may need a bit more attention. Bring these into your weekend as you find time.

Week Twenty Three, Winter
First Grade

Theme: Ocean, Waves & Water, Love & Affection

This Week's Lessons:

Language Arts:
The Fisherman and His Wife Story
Letter W
W Sound – Beginning, Middle or End
Poetry and Rhyming
Letter Hunt Game

Mathematics:
Number 23
Review Four Processes Math up to 100
Review Simple Tangible Math
Fishing Math
Multiplication Circle
Times Tables 1x – 4x
Multiplication Tips & Tricks

Social Studies, Geography, Weather, Time:
Learning About How Human Beings Show Affection

Science, Nature Study, Earth Discovery:
Learning About the Sense of Touch
Learning About How Animals Show Affection
Land and Sea Animal Sort
Ocean in a Bottle

Teacher's Classroom Work:
Prepare Love Notes for Your Children
Consider Swimming Lessons and Water Safety Plans

For the Caregiver:
Caregiver Meditation: Spreading Love
Caregiver Focus: Love Notes to Your Children

Domestic Arts/Practical Life Skills:
Discussing Love and Affection
Learning to Wash Our Hair
Homemade Red Playdough
Learning to Swim & Water Safety

Music:
Ocean & Love Fingerplays & Songs
Beginning Recorder or Flute

Art/Handwork:
Art: "Stained Glass" Hearts
Handwork: Knitting
Embroidery, Letter W
Alphabet Card Letter W
Watercolor Painting

Form Drawing:
Form Drawing/Art – Review, Zig Zags

Movement, Body Awareness & Health:
Boat & Rowing Movements

Supplies Needed for Week Twenty Three

Cooking List:

<u>For Homemade Playdough:</u>
2 Cups All Purpose Flour
4 Tablespoons Cream of Tartar
2 Tablespoons Cooking Oil
1 Cup Salt
Few Drops of Red or Pink Food Coloring
2 Cups of Boiling Water

Homeschooling List:

Blackboard
Chalk
Different Colored Scarves Ranging from Lights to Darks, Small Item for Fish
Lesson Book
Stockmar Stick Crayons
Stockmar Block Crayons
Colored Pencils
Stockmar Beeswax Modeling Material
Knitting Needles
Super Bulky Single Ply 100% Wool Yarn
Heavy White Cardstock
Scissors
Embroidery Needle
Embroidery Floss
White Scrap Fabric
Embroidery Hoop (optional)
Bowl of Dry Rice
Paper, Foam or Plastic Alphabet Letters
Large Bag or Container
Various Items for Sensory Bag
Contact Paper
Red, Pink and/or White Tissue Paper
Hole Punch
Blue Food Coloring
Empty Plastic Bottle with Cap
Cooking Oil

Week Twenty Three Book Recommendations

Visit your local library the weekend before to check out books based on your theme for the week. Older children can help you look up the books by author and title. When setting up your play space for the week ahead, mindfully display these books in baskets for the children to enjoy.

Ocean Meets Sky ~ Terri Fan & Eric Fan
Blue on Blue ~ Dianne White
The Snail and The Whale ~ Julia Donaldson
Flotsam ~ David Wiesner
Wave ~ Suzy Lee
Water is Water ~ A Book About the Water Cycle ~ Miranda Paul
Emma and the Whale ~ Julie Case and Lee White
Water Can Be… ~ Laura Purdie Salas
Ocean Sunlight: How Tiny Plants Feed the Seas ~ Molly Bang
Down, Down, Down: A Journey to the Bottom the Sea ~ Steve Jenkins
The Fisherman & The Whale ~ Jessica Lanan
Pond Circle ~ Betsy Franco
Day It Rained Hearts ~ Felicia Bond
I Love You With All My Heart ~ Noris Kern
The Man Who Kept His Heart in a Bucket ~Sonia Levitin
Keep Love in Your Heart, Little One ~Giles Andreae
Heart in the Pocket ~ Laurence Bourguignon
In the Heart ~ Ann Turner
The Room In My Heart ~ Beverly Evans
The Crystal Heart: A Vietnamese Legend ~ Aaron Shepard
The Biggest Valentine Ever ~ Steven Kroll & Jeni Bassett
The Story of Valentine's Day~ Nancy Skarmeas
Saint Valentine ~ Robert Sabuda
The Very Special Valentine ~ Kneen
Hearts, Cupids, and Red Roses: The Story of the Valentine Symbols ~ Edna Barth

First Grade Curriculum | WINTER | Little Acorn Learning

Week Twenty Three Circle, Songs & Movement

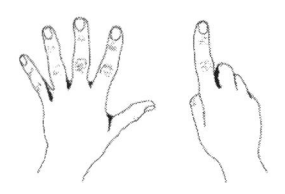

The following songs and verses should be shared during circle time each day this week after you open your circle.

Once I Caught a Fish Alive

1, 2, 3, 4, 5,
(raise one finger at a time until all five fingers on one hand are raised)
Once I caught a fish alive,

6, 7, 8, 9, 10,
(raise fingers on your second hand one at a time)
Then I let him go again.

Why did you let him go?
Because he bit my finger so.

Which finger did he bite?
This little finger on my right.
(wiggle right pinky finger)

Like a Fish Finger Play

I hold my fingers like a fish
(place hands together to form a fish)

And I wave them as I go
(swim hand fish up and down)

See them swimming with a swish
(swish hands through the air)

So swiftly to and fro
(weave hands back and forth)

Whoosh goes the wind,
(sway arms back and forth)
Sniff goes my nose,
(sniff)

Crash goes the waves,
(clap)
Splish splash go my toes,
(move feet)

I'll hunt for seashells,
(gather shells)
You sift the sand,
(gather on ground)

Let's build a castle,
As high as we can!
(place one fist on top of the other going higher and higher)

For lunch we'll have crackers
Some juice and a peach
(pretend to eat)

Oh my! What fun
Is this day at the beach.
(clap)

Heart
(make shape of heart with two hands)

I put my hands together,
This is how I start.
I curve my fingers right around,
And I can make a heart!

The Love Bug

It begins with a grin
(smile)
It turns to giggle
(put both hands on mouth and giggle)

You start to laugh
(pretend to laugh)
Your legs start to wiggle
(wiggle legs)

You look all around for someone to hug
(move eyes back and forth)
What can you do?
(shrug shoulders)

You've caught the love bug
(hug another child or yourself)

Week Twenty Three Blackboard Drawing

Drawing Ideas for This Week: Capital letter W as shown in the WAVES of the sea, the flounder from our story, husband by the sea, Letter W, words beginning with W, Roman numeral XXIII, TWENTY THREE, 23

Week Twenty Three Teacher's Classroom Work

1. Prepare the love notes for your children.

2. Consider options for swimming lessons and water safety for your child.

3. Review any handwork before working on projects with your children.

Week Twenty Three Caregiver Meditation

This Week's Reflection: Love & Affection

"You can search throughout the entire universe for someone who is more deserving of your love and affection than you are yourself, and that person is not to be found anywhere. You yourself, as much as anybody in the entire universe, deserve your love and affection." ~ Gautama Buddha

There are many ways we show our love to those around us. These gestures of love can do such amazing things. Showing love when it is not easy is a wonderful way to change the dynamic of difficult situations and it feels good to care for others. As caregivers, our time, love and affection are a wonderful gift we give daily to those around us and the positive effects of children being raised in such a caring environment will last a lifetime.

While we work so hard to show our love and affection toward others, we must never forget that we are just as worthy and deserving of our own love. Listen to your needs, forgive yourself, be kind to your body and have patience with yourself when you are struggling. Think of yourself as just as deserving and worthy of the gentleness and affection you give your children.

Week Twenty Three Story

For this story use any small item for the flounder and keep him tucked under different colored scarves ranging from lights to darks as the waves grow more furious over each visit. This fairy tale carries us through the desires and greed of always wanting more and not being content with what we have. The husband's love for his wife keeps him going back to the sea against his wishes. Do not explain the moral to the children, rather let the story sit with them.

The Fisherman and His Wife
~ Brothers Grimm

Part One

There was once upon a time a fisherman who lived with his wife close by the sea, and every day he went out fishing. And he fished, and he fished. And once he was sitting with his rod, looking at the clear water, and he sat, and he sat. Then his line suddenly went down deep under the waves, far down below, and when he drew it up again, he brought out a large flounder. Then the flounder said to him, "Hark, you fisherman, I pray you, let me live, I am no flounder really, but an enchanted prince. What good will it do you to kill me. I should not be good to eat, put me in the water again, and let me go." "Come," said the fisherman, "there is no need for so many words about it - a fish that can talk I should certainly let go, anyhow." And with that he put him back again into the clear water under the waves, and the flounder went to the bottom.

Then the fisherman got up and went home to his wife. "Husband," said the woman, "have you caught nothing today?" "No," said the man, "I did catch a flounder, who said he was an enchanted prince, so I let him go again." "Did you not wish for anything first?" said the woman. "No," said the man, "what should I wish for?" "Ah," said the woman, "it is surely hard to have to live always in this hut which stinks and is so disgusting. You might have wished for a better home for us. Go back and call him. Tell him we want to have a little house; he will certainly give us that."

"Ah," said the man, "why should I go there again?" "Why?" said the woman, "you did catch him, and you let him go again. He is sure to do it. Go at once." The man still did not quite like to go, but did not like to oppose his wife either, and he went to the sea.

When he got there the sea was all green and yellow, and no longer so smooth, so he stood still and said,

> *"Flounder, flounder in the sea,*
> *Come, I pray thee, here to me.*
> *For my wife, good Isabel,*
> *Wills not as I'd have her will."*

Then the flounder came swimming to him and said, "Well what does she want, then." "Ah," said the man, "I did catch you, and my wife says I really ought to have wished for something. She would like to have a better home." "Go, then," said the flounder, "she has it already." When the man went home, his wife was sitting on a bench before the door of a nice little house.

Then she took him by the hand and said to him, "Just come inside. Look, now isn't this a great deal better?" So, they went in, and there was a small porch, and a pretty little parlor and bedroom, and a kitchen and pantry, with the best of furniture, and fitted up with the most beautiful things made of tin and brass, whatsoever was wanted. And behind the home there was a small yard, with hens and ducks, and a little garden with flowers and fruit.

"Look," said the wife, "is not that nice?" "Yes," said the husband, "and so it shall remain - now we will live quite contented." "We will think about that," said the wife. With that they ate something and went to bed.

Everything went well for a week or a fortnight, and then the woman said, "Hark you, husband, this house is far too small for us, and the garden and yard are little. The flounder might just as well have given us a great stone castle with a much bigger yard. Go to the flounder and tell him to give us a castle."

"Ah, wife," said the man, "the home is quite good enough. Why would we live in a castle?" "What?" said the woman. "Just go there, the flounder can always do that." "No, wife," said the man, "the flounder has just given us the house, I do not like to go back so soon, it might make him angry." "Go," said the woman, "he can do it quite easily, and will be glad to do it. Just you go to him."

The man's heart grew heavy, and he would not go. He said to himself, it is not right, and yet he went. And when he came to the sea the water was quite purple and dark-blue, and grey and thick, and no longer so green and yellow, but it was still quiet, and the waves were still. And he stood there and said,

*"Flounder, flounder in the sea,
Come, I pray thee, here to me.
For my wife, good Isabel,
Wills not as I'd have her will."*

"Well, what does she want, now?" said the flounder. "Alas, said the man, half scared, "she wants to live in a great stone castle." "Go to it, then, she is standing before the door," said the flounder. Then the man went away, intending to go home, but when he got there, he found a great stone palace, and his wife was just standing on the steps going in, and she took him by the hand and said, "Come in."

So, he went in with her, and in the castle was a great hall paved with marble, and many servants, who flung wide the doors. And the walls were all bright with beautiful hangings, and in the rooms were chairs and tables of pure gold, and crystal chandeliers hung from the ceiling, and all the rooms and bedrooms had carpets, and food and wine of the very best were standing on all the tables, so that they nearly broke down beneath it.

Behind the house, too, there was a great courtyard, with stables for horses and cows, and the very best of carriages. There was a magnificent large garden, too, with the most beautiful flowers and fruit trees, and a park quite half a mile long, in which were stags, deer, and hares, and everything that could be desired.

"Come," said the woman, "isn't that beautiful?" "Yes, indeed," said the man, "now let it be, and we will live in this beautiful castle and be content." "We will consider about that," said the woman, "and sleep upon it." Thereupon they went to bed.

Part Two

Next morning the wife awoke first, and it was just daybreak, and from her bed she saw the beautiful country lying before her. Her husband was still stretching himself, so she poked him in the side with her elbow, and said, "Get up, husband, and just peep out of the window. Look you, couldn't we be the king over all that land. Go to the flounder, we will be the king."

"Ah, wife," said the man, "why should we be king? I do not want to be king." "Well," said the wife, "if you won't be king, I will. Go to the flounder, for I will be king."

"Ah, wife," said the man, "why do you want to be king? I do not like to say that to him." "Why not?" said the woman. "Go to him this instant. I must be king."

So, the man went, and was quite unhappy because his wife wished to be king. It is not right, it is not right, thought he. He did not wish to go but he went. And when he came to the sea, it was quite dark-grey, and the waves heaved up from below, and smelt putrid. Then he went and stood by it, and said,

> *"Flounder, flounder in the sea,*
> *Come, I pray thee, here to me.*
> *For my wife, good Isabel,*
> *Wills not as I'd have her will."*

"Well, what does she want, now?" said the flounder. "Alas, said the man, she wants to be king." "Go to her. She is king already." So, the man went, and when he came to the palace, the castle had become much larger, and had a great tower and magnificent ornaments, and the sentinel was standing before the door, and there were numbers of soldiers with kettledrums and trumpets.

And when he went inside the house, everything was of real marble and gold, with velvet covers and great golden tassels. Then the doors of the hall were opened, and there was the court in all its splendor, and his wife was sitting on a high throne of gold and diamonds, with a great crown of gold on her head, and a scepter of pure gold and jewels in her hand, and on both sides of her stood her maids-in-waiting in a row, each of them always one head shorter than the last. Then he went and stood before her, and said, "Ah, wife, and now you are king."

"Yes," said the woman, "now I am king." So, he stood and looked at her, and when he had looked at her thus for some time, he said, "And now that you are king, let all else be, now we will wish for nothing more."

"No, husband," said the woman, quite anxiously, "I find time passes very heavily, I can bear it no longer. Go to the flounder - I am king, but I must be emperor, too."

"Oh, wife, why do you wish to be emperor?"

"Husband," said she, "go to the flounder. I will be emperor." "Alas, wife," said the man, "he cannot make you emperor. I may not say that to the fish. There is only one emperor in the land. An emperor the flounder cannot make you. I assure you he cannot."

"What?" said the woman, "I am the king, and you are nothing but my husband. Will you go this moment? Go at once. If he can make a king, he can make an emperor. I will be emperor. Go instantly."

So, he was forced to go. As the man went, however, he was troubled in mind, and thought to himself, it will not end well. It will not end well. Emperor is too shameless. The flounder will at last be tired out. With that he reached the sea, and the sea was quite black and thick, and the waves began to boil up from below, so that it threw up bubbles, and such a sharp wind blew over it that it curdled, and the man was afraid. Then he went and stood by it, and said,

"Flounder, flounder in the sea,
Come, I pray thee, here to me.
For my wife, good Isabel,
Wills not as I'd have her will."

"Well, what does she want, now?" said the flounder. "Alas, flounder," said he, "my wife wants to be emperor." "Go to her," said the flounder. "She is emperor already." So, the man went, and when he got there the whole palace was made of polished marble with alabaster figures and golden ornaments, and soldiers were marching before the door blowing trumpets, and beating cymbals and drums. And in the house, barons, and counts, and dukes were going about as servants. Then they opened the doors to him, which were of pure gold. And when he entered, there sat his wife on a throne, which was made of one piece of gold, and was quite two miles high. And she wore a great golden crown that was three yards high, and set with diamonds and carbuncles, and in one hand she had the scepter, and in the other the imperial orb. And on both sides of her stood the yeomen of the guard in two rows, each being smaller than the one before him, from the biggest giant, who was two miles high, to the very smallest dwarf, just as big as my little finger. And before it stood several princes and dukes.

Then the man went and stood among them, and said, "Wife, are you emperor now." "Yes," said she, now I am emperor. Then he stood and looked at her well, and when he had looked at her thus for some time, he said, "Ah, wife, be content, now that you are emperor."

Part Three

"Husband," said she, "why are you standing there? Now, I am emperor, but I will be pope too. Go to the flounder."

"Oh, wife, said the man, what will you not wish for? You cannot be pope. There is but one in the world. He cannot make you pope."

"Husband, said she, I will be pope. Go immediately, I must be pope this very day."

"No, wife," said the man, "I do not like to say that to him. That would not do, it is too much. The flounder can't make you pope."

"Husband," said she, "what nonsense! If he can make an emperor, he can make a pope. Go to him directly. I am emperor, and you are nothing but my husband. Will you go at once."?

Then he was afraid and went, but he was quite faint, and shivered and shook, and his knees and legs trembled. And a high wind blew over the land, and the clouds flew, and towards evening all grew dark, and the leaves fell from the trees, and the waves rose and roared as if it were boiling and splashed upon the shore.

And yet in the midst of the sky there was still a small patch of blue, though on every side it was as red as in a heavy storm. So, full of despair, he went and stood in much fear and said,

"Flounder, flounder in the sea,
Come, I pray thee, here to me.
For my wife, good Isabel,
Wills not as I'd have her will."

"Well, what does she want, now?" said the flounder. "Alas," said the man, "she wants to be pope." "Go to her then," said the flounder, "she is pope already."

So, he went, and when he got there, he saw what seemed to be a large church surrounded by palaces. He pushed his way through the crowd. Inside, however, everything was lighted up with thousands and thousands of candles, and his wife was clad in gold, and she was sitting on a much higher throne, and had three great golden crowns on, and round about her there was much ecclesiastical splendor. And on both sides of her was a row of candles the largest of which was as tall as the very tallest tower, down to the very smallest kitchen candle, and all the emperors and kings were on their knees before her, kissing her shoe.

"Wife," said the man, and looked attentively at her, "are you now pope?"

"Yes," said she, "I am pope."

So, he stood and looked at her, and it was just as if he was looking at the bright sun. When he had stood looking at her thus for a short time, he said, "Ah, wife, if you are pope, do let well alone." But she looked as stiff as a post and did not move or show any signs of life.

Then said he, "Wife, now that you are pope, be satisfied, you cannot become anything greater now."

"I will consider about that," said the woman.

Thereupon they both went to bed, but she was not satisfied, and greediness let her have no sleep, for she was continually thinking what there was left for her to be.

The man slept well and soundly, for he had run about a great deal during the day. But the woman could not fall asleep at all and flung herself from one side to the other the whole night through, thinking always what more was left for her to be, but unable to call to mind anything else.

At length the sun began to rise, and when the woman saw the red of dawn, she sat up in bed and looked at it. And when, through the window, she saw the sun thus rising, she said, "Cannot I, too, order the sun and moon to rise?" "Husband," she said, poking him in the ribs with her elbows, "wake up. Go to the flounder, for I wish to be even as God is."

The man was still half asleep, but he was so horrified that he fell out of bed. He thought he must have heard amiss, and rubbed his eyes, and said, "Wife, what are you saying?"

"Husband," said she, "if I can't order the sun and moon to rise and have to look on and see the sun and moon rising, I can't bear it. I shall not know what it is to have another happy hour, unless I can make them rise myself." Then she looked at him so terribly that a shudder ran over him, and said, "Go at once. I wish to be like unto God."

"Alas, wife," said the man, falling on his knees before her, "the flounder cannot do that. He can make an emperor and a pope. I beseech you, go on as you are, and be pope."

Then she fell into a rage, and her hair flew wildly about her head, she tore open her bodice, kicked him with her foot, and screamed, "I can't stand it, I can't stand it any longer. Will you go this instant.?"

Then he put on his trousers and ran away like a madman. But outside a great storm was raging and blowing so hard that he could scarcely keep his feet. Houses and trees toppled over, the mountains trembled, rocks rolled into the sea, the sky was pitch black, and it thundered and lightened, and the sea came in with black waves as high as church-towers and mountains, and all with crests of white foam at the top. Then he cried, but could not hear his own words,

*"Flounder, flounder in the sea,
Come, I pray thee, here to me.
For my wife, good Isabel,
Wills not as I'd have her will."*

"Well, what does she want, now?" said the flounder. "Alas," said he, "she wants to be like unto God." "Go to her, and you will find her back again in the hut." And there they are still living to this day and the wife has not asked for anything again.

Monday Student Lessons – Week Twenty Three

(Baking/Cooking – Purple Day)

Language Arts

1. Begin your lesson time by reading (or telling) Part One of *The Fisherman and His Wife* to your child. Let the children look at the sentences as you read as this visual will aid with their knowledge of letters, words and sentences. If possible, use simple props to accompany the story as we have suggested.

2. When your story is finished, unveil your blackboard drawing that you have prepared ahead of time as suggested at the beginning of this week's curriculum. If your child has his or her own small blackboard and chalk, have them take a few moments to create their own drawing.

3. Review what your child worked on last week in their lesson book. Have them practice writing the capital letter V a few times on their blackboard or an extra piece of paper. Be sure they have a good grasp of this letter before moving onto the next.

4. In your child's lesson book, have them create a similar image of the waves (or whatever depiction you used) with the letter W revealed inside.

    On the righthand side, have your child practice writing the capital letter W. Share this poem as you work to form the letter:

    > Down and up goes the sea
    > Down and up
    > Then let it be

5. Letter Hunt Game

    Fill a large container or bowl with rice. In your container hide alphabet letters of all types (these can be printed pieces of paper or foam or plastic letters). Each time your child finds a letter, have them put it in place to form the alphabet on the table next to them.

Mathematics

1. In addition to the Roman numeral XXIII, write down the number 23 and word TWENTY THREE in all capital letters for your child to see. Say each letter as you write.

2. Have the child draw images of the number TWENTY THREE. They may copy some of the items you made in your blackboard drawing for this week. Your child should then practice writing the number 23, Roman numeral XXIII and the word TWENTY THREE in all capital letters on the opposite page of their book. If you feel they need extra time with writing, let them continue to practice as needed. Here is a verse to share when forming the number 23:

> *A two for you*
> *A three for me*
> *Now we have a 23*

3. Fishing Math

    Draw or cut out fish (like the flounder from our story!) with various equations on them. Label containers or draw buckets with some of the answers. Have your child place each fish into the bucket or draw a line from the correct fish to the bucket.

    Example:

Buckets: 15, 25, 50, 100

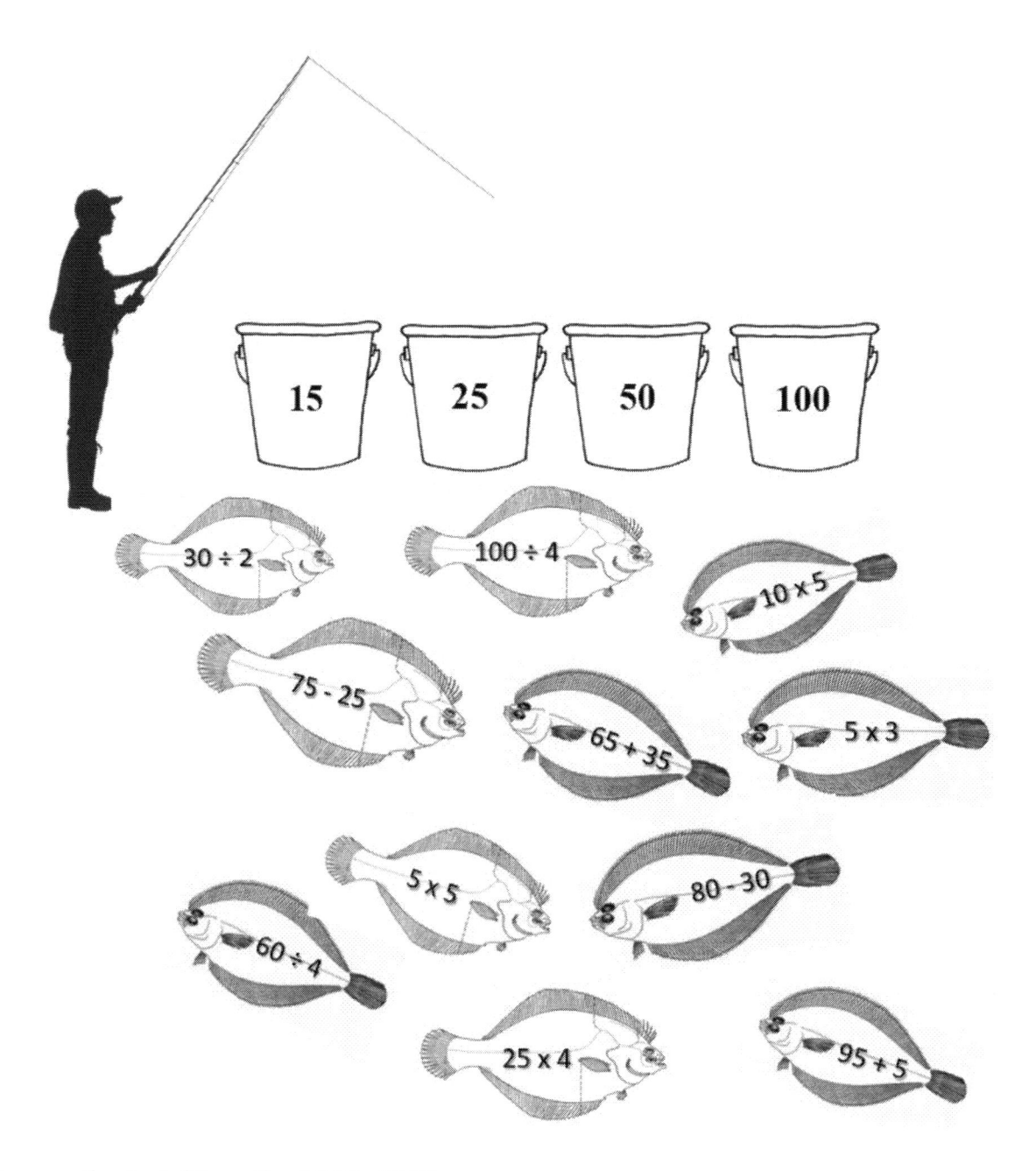

Fish:
- 30 ÷ 2
- 100 ÷ 4
- 10 × 5
- 75 - 25
- 65 + 35
- 5 × 3
- 5 × 5
- 80 - 30
- 60 ÷ 4
- 25 × 4
- 95 + 5

Domestic Arts/Practical Life Skills

1. Talk to your child today about love. Ask the following questions to inspire free discussion:

   Can you tell me something special that you love about your family or friends?

   I can tell you something special I love about you.

   When we tell people why we love them we make them feel good inside.

   First Grade Curriculum | WINTER | Little Acorn Learning

What other things do you love? (pets, schoolwork, church, friends, etc.)

How do you show your love for those things?

Today we will make special red playdough to celebrate our love and affection!

2. Homemade Red Playdough

    Supplies Needed:
    2 Cups All Purpose Flour
    4 Tablespoons Cream of Tartar
    2 Tablespoons Cooking Oil
    1 Cup Salt
    Few Drops of Red or Pink Food Coloring
    2 Cups of Boiling Water

    Put all ingredients into large bowl except for boiling water. Pour boiling water over the mixture and stir it up with a large spoon. Sprinkle your surface with flour and lift warm dough out of your bowl and knead until texture is right. Play dough can be stored in an airtight container. Enjoy!

Outdoor Time/Nature Walk

Take your children outside each day regardless of the weather. Invest in good rain gear, snow gear and wool undergarments if your location requires it. Do your lessons outdoors whenever possible.

Caregiver Focus

Caregiver Focus: Love Notes to Your Children

Create heart shaped love notes for your children to be left all over the house. On each little heart, write a message of love to your child. This activity is not limited by age or time of year. You would be quite surprised how special this would make a teenager feel and much a young child will understand you as you read each heart to them. Some ideas:

I love your bright blue eyes.
I love being your mommy.

I love the way you listen at story time.
I love how kind you are to animals.

These sweet notes can be left with the child's name on the opposite side in places they will find them throughout the day. Another idea would be to make a treasure hunt out of this activity and have the child follow clues to find each heart.

Science, Nature Study, Earth Discovery

Learning About the Sense of Touch

1. Spend time today talking to your child about the sense of touch. Ask your child if they can describe different ways that things feel (rough, smooth, cold, hot, wet, etc.) How do they use their sense of touch in everyday life?

2. Touch Sensory Bag

   Supplies Needed:
   Large Bag or Container
   Various Items to Touch (soft, smooth, bumpy, pointy, rough, etc.)

   Blindfold your child or have them close their eyes. Have them reach into your sensory bag and use their sense of touch only to guess what each item is. When they have guessed correctly have them describe how the item felt and how they knew what it was.

Afternoon Lessons

1. Music: Continue Practicing Flute or Recorder

2. Art/Fine Motor Skills: Stained Glass Hearts

   Supplies Needed:

   Contact Paper
   Red, Pink and/or White Tissue Paper
   Scissors
   Hole Punch
   Yarn or Ribbon

Have children cut tissue paper into small pieces. Lay out contact paper sticky side up. Have children place colored tissue all over contact paper covering surface. Remove backing from another piece of contact paper and push it down on top of the tissue covered piece. Press flat and use scissors to cut out heart shapes.

Use hole punch to place hole at the top of each heart. Tie loop with yarn through the hole. These can be given to loved ones and hung in the window to catch sunlight like stained glass.

Tuesday Student Lessons – Week Twenty Three

(Painting – Red Day)

Language Arts

1. Like yesterday, begin your reading (or tell) Part Two of *The Fisherman and His Wife*. Provide your child with a piece of beeswax modeling material as you read. Let them hold this piece of beeswax as they listen, warming it with their hands so it softens.

2. Have your child form the softened beeswax material into the letter W. Roll it into a long snake, form it just so and then put it back together again. Next, have them form it into the number 23.

3. Open your lesson book and review the work you did yesterday. Have your child trace the letter W number 23 and words TWENTY THREE with their fingers.

4. Today we will work on a tongue twister to practice and memorize with your child to help learn the letter W and its sound. Tongue twisters and rhymes are fun ways to learn and help with finding rhythm.

   To begin, say the following tongue twister to your child slowly and **clap your hands to the syllables for the words that begin with W** and pause for the other words. Note that this is difficult so go very slowly:

   Waves *(clap)* and water *(clap, clap)* in the sea,

   Come, I wonder *(clap, clap)*, wildy *(clap, clap, clap)*.

   The wife *(clap)* and woman *(clap, clap)* waits *(clap)* so still.

   For the words *(clap)* I do not will *(clap)*.

   Say it again but **stomp alternate feet to the syllables for the words that begin with W** and stop stomping for the other words:

   Waves *(stomp)* and water *(stomp, stomp)* in the sea,

   Come, I wonder *(stomp, stomp)*, wildy *(stomp, stomp, stomp)*.

The wife *(stomp)* and woman *(stomp, stomp)* waits *(stomp)* so still.

For the words *(stomp)* I do not will *(stomp)*.

5. On your blackboard, write some simple sentences with blanks and have your child copy them in their lesson book. Discuss what the missing words could be and then have your child write that in as well. Here are some examples:

TODAY I ATE _____
MY HAIR IS _____
WATER IS _____
I LOVE _____

Mathematics

Multiplication Circle

This is a wonderful way to help your child learn their multiplication tables from 1x – 4x. You can create this with sidewalk chalk, crayons in your lesson book or with yarn, a board and nails.

Using different colored yarn or chalk, always start at 0 to begin.

As you will see, the answer to each equation ends with the number you go to next. This may be confusing at first but once it is mastered, it will be one of the most fun ways your child has to remember their multiplication facts.

Here is a video tutorial as well: https://youtu.be/ArCIrn2pDO8

For 1x:

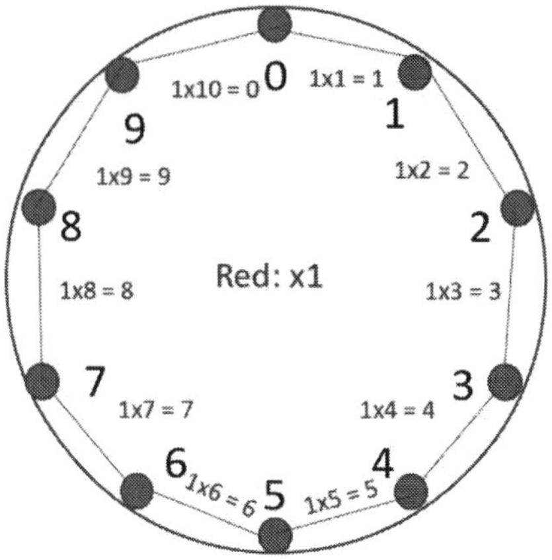
0
1
2
3
4
5
6
7
8
9
1x1 = 1
1x2 = 2
1x3 = 3
1x4 = 4
1x5 = 5
1x6 = 6
1x7 = 7
1x8 = 8
1x9 = 9
1x10 = 0
Red: x1

1x1 = 1 Draw a line from 0 to 1

1x2 = 2 Draw a line from 1 to 2

1x3 = 3 Draw a line from 2 to 3

1x4 = 4 Draw a line from 3 to 4

Continue this all the way around, ending with 1x10 = 10 Draw a line from 9 to 0 (for 10).

For 2x:

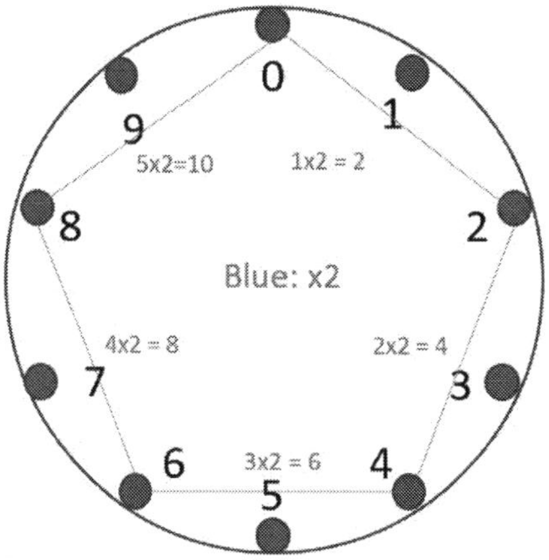
0
1
2
3
4
5
6
7
8
9
1x2 = 2
2x2 = 4
3x2 = 6
4x2 = 8
5x2=10
Blue: x2

1x2 = 2 Draw a line from 0 to 2

2x2 = 4 Draw a line from 2 to 4

2x3 = 6 Draw a line from 4 to 6

Continue this all the way around, ending with 2x10 = 20 Draw a line from 8 (for 18) to 0 (for 20).

For 3x:

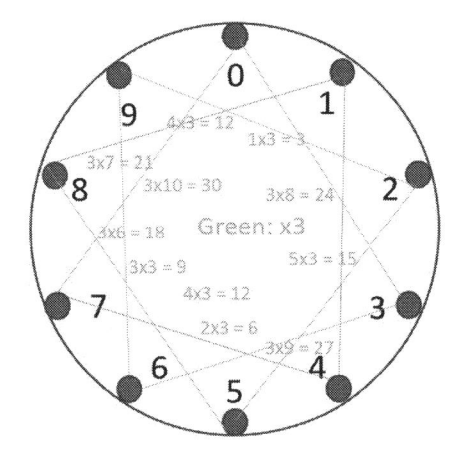

1x3 = 3 Draw a line from 0 to 3

3x2 = 6 Draw a line from 3 to 6

3x3 = 9 Draw a line from 6 to 9

Continue this all the way around up until 3x10 = 30 Draw a line from 7 (for 27) to 0 (for 30).

For 4x:

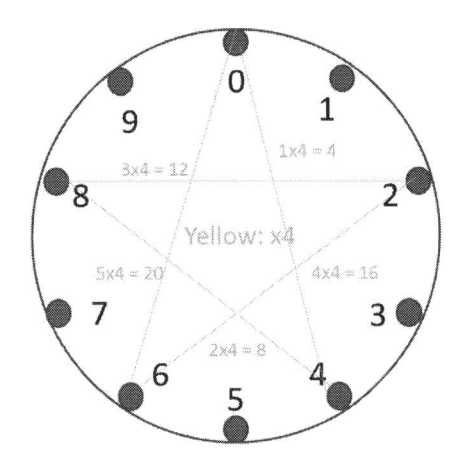

1x4 = 4 Draw a line from 0 to 4

4x2 = 8 Draw a line from 4 to 8

4x3 = 12 Draw a line from 8 to 2 (for 12)

Continue this all the way around up until 5x4 = 20 Draw a line from 6 (for 16) to 0 (for 20).

We can also do this with more times tables, but the direction varies so we will learn that at a later time.

The end result is quite beautiful if done on top of one another:

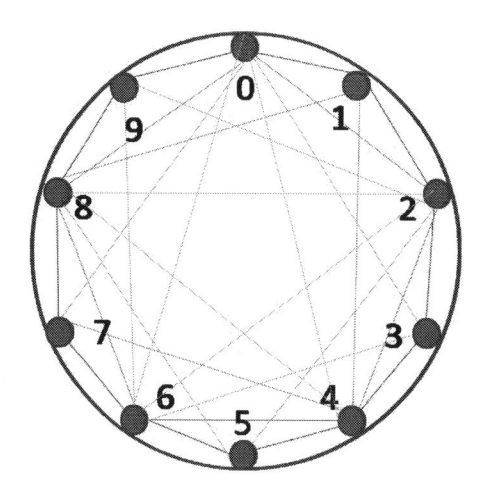

Outdoor Time/Nature Walk

Take your children outside each day regardless of the weather. Invest in good rain gear, snow gear and wool undergarments if your location requires it. Do your lessons outdoors whenever possible.

Social Studies, Geography, Weather, Time

1. Learning About How Human Beings Show Affection

Here are some questions and discussion points you can bring up with your child today to learn more about how human beings show affection to one another:

What are some ways that human beings show affection? (hugging, kissing, taking care of one another, holding hands, sharing, etc.)

Human beings and especially babies and young children need affection and love to develop in a healthy way. When you were little, what were some ways that people showed affection toward you?

2. Today watercolor paint a piece of artwork that expresses love and affection between humans in some way.

Afternoon Lessons

Music: Continue Practicing Flute or Recorder

Wednesday Student Lessons – Week Twenty Three
(Coloring – Yellow Day)

Language Arts

1. Practice our tongue twister again. Keep working on this until you have it memorized together.

   To begin, say the following tongue twister to your child slowly and **clap your hands to the syllables for the words that begin with W** and pause for the other words. Note this is difficult so go very slowly:

   Waves *(clap)* and water *(clap, clap)* in the sea,

   Come, I wonder *(clap, clap)*, wildy *(clap, clap, clap)*.

   The wife *(clap)* and woman *(clap, clap)* waits *(clap)* so still.

   For the words *(clap)* I do not will *(clap)*.

   Say it again but **stomp alternate feet to the syllables for the words that begin with W** and stop stomping for the other words:

   Waves *(stomp)* and water *(stomp, stomp)* in the sea,

   Come, I wonder *(stomp, stomp)*, wildy *(stomp, stomp, stomp)*.

   The wife *(stomp)* and woman *(stomp, stomp)* waits *(stomp)* so still.

   For the words *(stomp)* I do not will *(stomp)*.

2. In your child's lesson book have them make a drawing of *The Fisherman and His Wife*.

3. Like yesterday, again write some simple sentences with blanks and have your child copy them in their lesson book. Discuss what the missing words could be and then have your child write that in as well.

4. Tonight, at bedtime tell your child the story Part Three of *The Fisherman and His Wife*.

5. Take your child to the grocery store with you and have them search the store for items that begin with the letter W. This letter is hard to find in many foods, so we listed some ideas to help. Bring the list with you and add to it as you find more.

   Watermelon
   Wheat Bread
   Waffles
   Walnut
   Wafers
   Water
   Worcestershire
   Watercress
   White Rice
   White Wine Vinegar
   Wasabi
   Wonton
   Whey
   Wild Rice
   Whipped Cream

6. Show your child words that include the letter W. Ask them to identify if the W sound is at the beginning, middle or end of each word.

Mathematics

1. Have your child put popsicle sticks, pasta or toothpicks together to make the Roman numeral XVIII. Make sure they count each line and have them trace it with their fingers. The more they incorporate their senses and body into a lesson, the more they will absorb it and become one with it.

2. Next use these tangible items to review some simple math together. You can do simple addition and subtraction. Be sure to also practice repetitive addition and discuss how it translates to multiplication. For example:

   $5 + 5 + 5$ is the same as 5×3

   Additionally, demonstrate division by beginning with a large group of items and grouping them by a certain amount. For example:

20 pasta divided by 5
5 groups of 4 pasta
$20 \div 5 = 4$

Outdoor Time/Nature Walk

Take your children outside each day regardless of the weather. Invest in good rain gear, snow gear and wool undergarments if your location requires it. Do your lessons outdoors whenever possible.

Science, Nature Study, Earth Discovery

1. Learning About How Animals Show Affection

    We have learned that human beings need affection to grow into healthy adults and that parents often show their babies affection in many ways. Ask your child if they think it is possible that other animals show affection too? They do!

    Here are some examples:

    Dogs show affection by making eye contact with their human and wagging their tails.

    Cats show affection by purring.

    Science has proven that mice and rats become attached to one another and care for their family. They also show affection toward the humans that take care of them.

    Mother elephants caress their calves and often make a soft soothing noise to them.

    Chimpanzees take care of their babies similarly to how we do. They also use gentle touch, face expressions and sounds to communicate.

2. Learning About Land and Sea Animals

    Cut out photos or words of various land and sea animals. Alternatively, you can write the names of these animals on your blackboard.

Working together, have your child determine if each is a land or sea animal. If you have cut out photos or words, have your child sort these into the appropriate group.

Afternoon Lessons

Handwork: Knitting

Continue to practice knitting skills during afternoon time and completing any unfinished handwork projects.

Thursday Student Lessons – Week Twenty Three
(Crafting/Games – Orange Day)

Language Arts

1. Continue to tell your child the story of *The Fisherman and His Wife* if you haven't completed it.

2. Alphabet Cards

   Supplies Needed:
   Heavy White Cardstock
   Beeswax Stick Crayons
   Scissors

   Spend time cutting cards out of cardstock with your child. Using beeswax crayons, continue to finish drawing each letter we have learned so far and include the letter W. Next to the letter, have your child draw an image that begins with it. Using scissors, round the corners of these cards and keep working on them throughout the year. You can use them in your lessons and for an upper case and lowercase match game later in the curriculum when we learn those as well.

3. Continue reading simple reader books together.

4. Print out or share the following photos and practice saying them together with your child. Your child can also copy these words into their lesson book.

WAVES

WIND

WINDOW

WOMAN

WHALE

Mathematics

Little by little, your child will begin to pick up on some of the more obvious multiplication tricks with memorization. Here is a list of various tricks for you to keep handy as you work with your child throughout the year.

Multiplication Tricks

0 – Any time times zero equals zero

Example:

10 x 0 = 0
100 x 0 = 0

1 – Any number times one stays the same

Example:

15 x 1 = 15
100 x 1 = 100

2 – To get the answer, add the number to itself (double it)

Example:

20 x 2 = 40
20 + 20

3 – To get the answer, double the other number (not 3), then add it to itself

Example:

4 x 3 = 12
4 + 4 = 8 + 4 = 12

4 – Double it once, then double the result

Example:

12 x 4 = 48
12 + 12 = 24   24 + 24 = 48

5 – Count by fives (repetitive addition)

Example:

5 x 5 = 25
5 + 5 + 5 + 5 + 5 = 25

Outdoor Time/Nature Walk

Take your children outside each day regardless of the weather. Invest in good rain gear, snow gear and wool undergarments if your location requires it. Do your lessons outdoors whenever possible.

Science, Nature Study, Earth Discovery

<u>Ocean in a Bottle</u>

Supplies Needed:
Water
Blue Food Coloring
Empty Plastic Bottle with Cap
Cooking Oil

Fill the plastic bottle with ¾ cup of water and add 3 drops of blue food coloring. Pour 1 cup of cooking oil into the bottle and tighten the cap. Lay the bottle on its side and you should see that the oil rises to the top. Have your child move the bottle to create waves like the ocean. Point out how the waves are bigger on one end and smaller at the other.

Movement, Body Awareness & Health

Boat & Rowing Movements

Face your child or have your child and another friend or sibling face one another in a crisscross sitting position.

Reach out and hold hands in front of your bodies and take turns pushing and pulling so you rock back and forth like a boat.

Share the following well-known song as you go:

Row, row, row your boat
Gently down the stream
Merrily, merrily, merrily, merrily
Life is but a dream

For smaller children, you can place them on your lap facing forward. Start by moving backward and then forward as you sing.

Afternoon Lessons

1. Form Drawing/Art – Review, Zig Zag

   This afternoon, we will review form drawing zig zag lines.

   - To begin, have your child practice drawing zig zag lines both horizontally and vertically in their lesson book.

   - Next, using tape, string or just on their own, have your child walk a zig zag line on the ground. Practice this forward and backward.

   - Lastly, with a marker draw various zig zag lines on paper. Have your child practice cutting these lines with scissors.

2. Handwork: Hand Stitching/Embroidery

   Supplies Needed:
   Embroidery Needle

Embroidery Floss
White Scrap Fabric
Embroidery Hoop (optional)
Scissors

Using our embroidery instructions, work with your child to make a letter W embroidery piece. You can do this with a simple running stitch, or you may choose to learn more complicated stitches together.

Friday Student Lessons – Week Twenty Three
(Modeling/Housework – Green Day)

Language Arts

1. Today have your child continue to practice writing the letter W in their lesson book on unlined paper.

2. In your child's lesson book, have them practice writing the alphabet from A- W each letter a few times on each line.

3. Ask your child to tell YOU the story of *The Fisherman and His Wife.*

4. Continue to introduce your child to poetry and rhymes. There are many beautiful ones to explore. You can get a poetry book from the library or share some of your favorites. Here is one from Nathaniel Hawthorne from a very long time ago.

> The Ocean has its silent caves,
> Deep, quiet, and alone;
> Though there be fury on the waves,
> Beneath them there is none.
> The awful spirits of the deep
> Hold their communion there;
> And there are those for whom we weep,
> The young, the bright, the fair.
>
> Calmly the wearied seamen rest
> Beneath their own blue sea.
> The ocean solitudes are blest,
> For there is purity.
> The earth has guilt, the earth has care,
> Unquiet are its graves;
> But peaceful sleep is ever there,
> Beneath the dark blue waves.
>
> NATHANIEL HAWTHORNE

5. After you read the poem, ask your child the following questions:

How did that poem make you feel?

Words rhyme when they have similar sounds at the end. What words do you think rhyme in that poem? (caves/waves, deep/weep, care/there etc.)

When you heard that poem, what images came to your mind? What did you imagine?

6. Have your child draw a picture after they heard the poem.

7. On your blackboard, write down some rhyming words. Say these together out loud and have your child copy them. Ask your child to think of some other rhyming words of their own. Here are some examples:

WAVE : BRAVE
LOVE : DOVE
TOUCH : MUCH
RED : SAID

Note how rhyming words do not have to have the same exact spelling at the end of each word. It is the sound that matters.

Mathematics

1. Review Counting Backwards

   On your blackboard write down numbers 90 to 1 with some blanks. Have your child copy this into their lesson book and fill in the missing numbers. Continue these types of exercises over the next week or two aiming to be able to have your child confidently count backwards from 100.

2. Review Four Processes

   Continue to work with your child on addition, subtraction, multiplication and division work. Try to work toward being able to solve problems up to 100. If there are areas that your child needs to strengthen, go back through the curriculum and review some lessons. As previously learned:

   The simplest way to begin teaching multiplication is by leveraging your child's understanding of addition.

For example:

    5 apples PLUS 5 apples PLUS 5 apples EQUALS 15 apples

    $5 + 5 + 5 = 15$

Continue to practice these types of equations with your child.

Be sure that your child has a good understanding of repetitive addition then have your child go back and take a closer look at the equations.

For example, in the above equation, we see that there are THREE groups of 5.

Explain to your child that our friend TIMES has a fun way of grouping items to get the answer.

So, there are 3 groups with 5 apples in them.

FIVE TIMES THREE (circle the three groups one at a time) EQUALS…

Ask your child to count all the apples.

15 APPLES

Outdoor Time/Nature Walk

Take your children outside each day regardless of the weather. Invest in good rain gear, snow gear and wool undergarments if your location requires it. Do your lessons outdoors whenever possible.

Domestic Arts/Practical Life Skills

1. Washing Our Hair

If your child does not yet know how to wash their own hair without your assistance, spend time teaching them the steps and allowing them to practice shampooing, conditioning (if you do), and rinsing their hair on their own. Rinsing can be hard for young children and may require some patience and practice to learn how to do it properly.

2. Swimming

   Additionally, if your child does not yet know how to swim start considering how and when you will teach them. If the weather does not allow for this now, look into lessons in indoor facilities or take a trip to the local YMCA to practice with your child. Water safety and learning how to swim are very important for all children to know.

Afternoon Lessons

Use the afternoon hours today to review areas from this week's afternoon lessons that you feel may need a bit more attention. Bring these into your weekend as you find time.

Week Twenty Four, Winter
First Grade

Theme: Seeds, Self-Reflection

This Week's Lessons:

Language Arts:
The Little Seed Story
Letter X, Y & Z
Write Simple Sentence
Poetry and Rhyming

Mathematics:
Number 24
Seed Sorting/Identification and Math
Math Seed Word Problems & Measuring Seedlings
Seed Estimating & Calculating Differences
Multiplication Circle, Times Tables 5x-9x

Social Studies, Geography, Weather, Time:
Learning About the Sense of Sight, Braille
Learning About the Sense of Sight, The Braille Alphabet

Science, Nature Study, Earth Discovery:
Learning About the Sense of Sight
Learning About Seeds, Germination
Learning About Seeds, Lima Bean Sprouts
Pin the Vegetables in the Garden Game (Sight)

Teacher's Classroom Work:
Prepare to Start Seeds Indoors
Prepare Pin the Vegetables Game

For the Caregiver:
Caregiver Meditation: Self-Reflection
Caregiver Focus: Self-Reflecting on How to Find Purpose in Life

Domestic Arts/Practical Life Skills:
Oat and Seed Breakfast Jars
Learning to Zipper

Music:
Seeds & Growing Fingerplays & Songs
Beginning Recorder or Flute

Art/Handwork:
Art: Seed & Bean Mosaics
Handwork: Knitting, The Seed Stitch
Embroidery, Letters X, Y & Z
Alphabet Card Letters X, Y & Z

Form Drawing:
Form Drawing/Art – Review, Spiral

Movement, Body Awareness & Health:
Sowing Seeds Circle Game
Nature Tic Tac Toe (Letter X)

Supplies Needed for Week Twenty Four

Cooking List:

<u>For Oat & Seed Breakfast Jars:</u>
Glass Jars with Lids
Vanilla Greek Yogurt
Flax Seed
Granola
Fresh Cut Fruit
Rolled Oats
Organic Milk

<u>For Sweetener Options:</u>
Vanilla Extract
Organic Applesauce
100% Maple Syrup
Cinnamon
Brown Sugar

Homeschooling List:

Blackboard
Chalk
Silk or Cloths in Brown, Yellow and Blue, Rocks or Beads, Small Seedling or Artificial Stem
Lesson Book
Stockmar Stick Crayons
Stockmar Block Crayons
Colored Pencils
Stockmar Beeswax Modeling Material
Knitting Needles
Super Bulky Single Ply 100% Wool Yarn
Heavy White Cardstock
Scissors
Embroidery Needle
Embroidery Floss
White Scrap Fabric
Embroidery Hoop (optional)

First Grade Curriculum | WINTER | Little Acorn Learning

Packets of Seeds
Dry Seeds, Beans & Pasta
Glue
Garden Chalkboard Drawing or Print Out
Cut Out Vegetables
Tape
Plate
Paper Towel
Water
Beeswax or Other Wax-Like Material (Wiki Sticks, etc.)
Paper
Large Sticks and Branches
Rocks, Seeds & Other Nature Items
Clear Plastic Cups
Potting Soil
Lima Beans
Water
Sunlight
Ruler
Seedlings or Lima Bean Sprouts

Week Twenty Four Book Recommendations

Visit your local library the weekend before to check out books based on your theme for the week. Older children can help you look up the books by author and title. When setting up your play space for the week ahead, mindfully display these books in baskets for the children to enjoy.

From Seed to Plant ~ Gail Gibbons
One Bean ~ Anne Rockwell
Max's Magic Seeds ~ Geraldine Elschner
Thumbelina ~ Hans Christian Andersen and Brad Sneed
Planting a Rainbow ~ Lois Ehlert
The Tiny Seed ~ Eric Carle
How a Seed Grows ~ Helene J. Jordan
A Seed Is Sleepy ~ Dianna Hutts Aston
The Dandelion Seed ~ Joseph P. Anthony
Berries, Nuts, And Seeds ~ Diane Burns
In a Nutshell ~ Joseph Anthony
Glenna's Seeds ~ Nancy Edwards
The Trellis and the Seed ~ Jan Karon
What Kinds of Seeds Are These? ~ Heidi Bee Roemer
What Do Roots Do? ~ Kathleen V Kudlinski
A Seed Is Sleepy ~ Diana Aston & Sylvia Long
Pumpkin Cycle: The Story of a Garden ~ George Levenson & Shmuel Thaler
Miss Maple's Seeds ~ Eliza Wheeler
The Empty Pot ~ Demi
The Watermelon Seed ~ Greg Pizzoli
Plant the Tiny Seed ~ Christie Matheson
If You Plant a Seed ~ Kadir Nelson
Ten Seeds ~ Ruth Brown
The Seed Who Was Afraid to Be Planted ~ Anthony DeStefano
A Handful of Quiet: Happiness in Four Pebbles ~ Thich Nhat Hanh
The Reason for a Flower ~ Ruth Heller
Lilla's Sunflowers ~ Colleen Rowan Kosinski
Who Will Plant a Tree? ~ Jerry Pallotta
If You Hold a Seed ~ Elly MacKay

Week Twenty Four Circle, Songs & Movement

The following songs and verses should be shared during circle time each day this week after you open your circle.

'The Baby Seed' - A Fingerplay
~Eileen Foley

A baby seed fell from above and landed in my hand
(left palm up – right finger starting high and swirling down onto left palm)

It asked if I could tuck it in, deep down within the sand
(close left fingers over palm enclosing right finger inside)

Each morning on my walk back home I stopped to say hello
(make walking motion with right hand and wave hello)

One day it popped its head out high and asked if it could go
(left hand open palm down – bring right finger up through bottom and out through left finger spaces)

I took a pot and dug it up and carried it along
(make cup with left hand and pretend to shovel with right)

And planted it in front of home and sung to it this song:
(pretend to pick up pot and move it and place it down to the side)

My little seed you spoke to me in words that have no sound
(place finger to lips to make 'quiet' gesture)

I heard your wish and cared for you and placed you in the ground
(cup ear with hand and tap ground or flat surface)

And now you've come to brighten up the lives of all who see
(motion arms up and around to symbolize 'sun')

The little seed that grew so strong into a great big tree
(outstretch arms with fingers hanging downward like a 'tree')

In my little garden bed
(place two fists together)
Raked so nicely over,
(make raking motion with one hand)

First the tiny seeds I sow,
(pretend to pinch seeds with one hand)
Then with soft earth cover.
(pat softly with both hands)

Shining down, the great round sun
(hands over head like a circle)
Smiles upon it often;
Little raindrops, pattering down,
(drum fingers against a surface)
Help the seeds to soften.

Then the little plant awakes!
Down the roots go creeping.
(creep fingers down and down)
Up it lifts its little head
(move thumb facing upward on one hand)
Through the brown mold peeping.

High and higher still it grows
(move thumb up and up)
Through the summer hours,
Till some happy day the buds
Open into flowers.
(open fist exposing palm)

There's a strange wee cradle in each little flower,
Where the wee seed children are sleeping.
Though so small, they are growing hour by hour,
And the nurse-flower watch is keeping.

A little sun
(hold arms above head)

A little rain
(wiggle fingers in the air in a downward motion)

Now pull up all the weeds
(pretend to pull weeds)

Our flowers grow all in a row
(hold up all ten fingers lined up like flowers)

From tiny little seeds
(hold thumb and finger to show size of seeds)

This is my garden
(extend one hand forward, palm up)

I'll rake it with care,
(make raking motion on palm with 3 fingers of other hand)

And then some flower seeds
(plant motion)
I'll plant in there.

The sun will shine
(make circle with hands)

And the rain will fall,
(let fingers flutter down to lap)

And my garden will blossom
(cup hands together; extend upward slowly)
And grow straight and tall.

A little seed for me to sow.
A little earth to make it grow.
A little hole, a little pat,
A little wish, and that is that.
A little sun, a little shower,
A little while, and then, a flower!

Week Twenty Four Blackboard Drawing

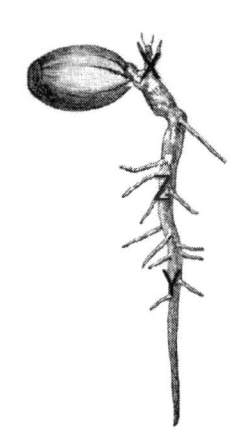

Drawing Ideas for This Week: Capital letters X, Y and Z. You can depict these letters in various ways. Some ideas would be the roots of a seed sprouting underground, in a small plant growing in a pot, in beans sprouting, in a tree with roots, etc. Roman numeral XXIV, TWENTY FOUR, 24

Week Twenty Four Teacher's Classroom Work

1. Starting Seeds Indoors

   This may be the time for you when you can begin to plan your outdoor garden and think about starting some seedlings indoors. Be sure to check your seed packages and plan accordingly. It is important to make sure the last frost has passed before you transplant your tender plants. Starting your seeds indoors is a wonderful activity to do with the children as winter begins to fade. It will create anticipation and excitement for the coming of spring. If this activity does not correlate to the season where you live, plan ahead or use it as a lesson and discussion with your child instead.

2. Pin the Vegetables in the Garden

   Prepare this activity ahead of time by drawing out or printing the garden and creating cut outs to stick on.

3. Review any handwork before working on projects with your children.

Week Twenty Four Caregiver Meditation

This Week's Reflection: Self-Reflection

"It is when you lose sight of yourself, that you lose your way. To keep your truth in sight you must keep yourself in sight and the world to you should be a mirror to reflect to you your image; the world should be a mirror that you reflect upon."
~ C. JoyBell

Caring for young children can be very rewarding but difficult work. We must remember to also be the caregivers of our own souls and bodies. A wonderful way to connect with our source of energy is to find moments of silence and time to absorb the natural world around us. Be sure to take at least 15 minutes each day for yourself without noise or distractions.

If this is a difficult task, ask a loved one or friend to help so you can go for a short evening walk or take a bath in quiet. Use these simple caregiver meditations to reflect on the important things in your life. When we take the time to care for ourselves, we have more to give to those that we love.

Week Twenty Four Story

This story is so sweet and timely if you are heading into spring while using this lesson. Regardless of the time of year, it is a beautiful lesson to teach your child about life and nature.

Use small beads or rocks as the seeds with one being your special little seed from this story. Cover the seeds with a brown play silk or cloth. Using a string, bring out the earthworm and uncover your seeds. You can use a yellow silk to lay over the seeds when the sunbeam speaks and then a blue silk to lay over for the raindrops. If you would like to show the seed turning into a plant, bring out a real or artificial stem or small seedling at the end of the story.

The Little Seed

Far down in Mother Earth a tiny seed was sleeping safely wrapped in a warm brown jacket. The little seed had been asleep for a very long time and now somebody thought it was time for him to wake up.

This somebody was an earthworm that lived close by. He had been creeping about and found that all the seeds in the neighborhood had roused themselves and were pushing their roots deep down into the earth and lifting their heads up through the soil into the bright sunshine and fresh air. So, when the worm saw this little seed still sleeping, he cried, "Oh you lazy little fellow wake up! All the seeds are awake and growing and you have slept long enough." "But how can I grow or move at all in this tight brown jacket?" said the seed in a drowsy tone. "Why push it off! That's the way the other seeds have done it. Just move about a little and it will come off." said the earthworm.

The little seed tried but the tough jacket wouldn't break and all the time the worm was telling him how happy the other seeds were now that they had lifted their heads into the sunshine. "Oh dear, oh dear!" said the seed "What shall I do? I can't break this jacket and I shall never see the beautiful sunshine. Besides, I'm so sleepy I can't keep awake any longer." and he fell asleep again. "The lazy little fellow." thought the earthworm "It is strange that the other seeds shed their jackets so easily. Who could have helped them? I wonder."

The little seed slept soundly for a long while but at last he awoke and found his jacket soft and wet instead of hard and dry and when he moved about it gave way entirely and dropped off! Then he felt so warm and happy that he cried "I really believe I am going to grow after all! Who could have helped me take off my jacket and who woke me, I wonder? I don't see any one nearby."

"I woke you." said a soft voice close by "I'm a sunbeam and I came down to wake you and my friends the raindrops moistened your jacket so that you might find it ready to slip off." "Oh, thank you!" said the seed "You're all very kind. Will you help me to grow into a plant too?" "Yes." said the sunbeam "I'll come as often as I can to help you and the raindrops will come too and then if you work hard with our help you will become a beautiful plant I'm sure."

So, the seed grew into a beautiful vine that climbed higher and higher toward the sky into a beautiful plant.

Monday Student Lessons – Week Twenty Four

(Baking/Cooking – Purple Day)

Language Arts

1. Begin your lesson time by reading (or telling) *The Little Seed* story to your child. Let the children look at the sentences as you read as this visual will aid with their knowledge of letters, words and sentences. If possible, use simple props to accompany the story as we have suggested.

2. When your story is finished, unveil your blackboard drawing that you have prepared ahead of time as suggested at the beginning of this week's curriculum. If your child has his or her own small blackboard and chalk, have them take a few moments to create their own drawing.

3. Review what your child worked on last week in their lesson book. Have them practice writing the capital letter W a few times on their blackboard or an extra piece of paper. Be sure they have a good grasp of this letter before moving onto the next.

4. This week we will work on three letters and finish our work with the capital letters of the alphabet in preparation for learning lowercase letters and word families in our last semester. If you feel your child needs extra time, be sure to spread things out accordingly. Education is not one size fits all. You know your child the best.

   In your child's lesson book, have them create a similar image of the seeds or plants sprouting (or whatever depiction you used) with the letters X, Y & Z revealed inside.

   On the righthand side, have your child practice writing the capital letters X, Y & Z repetitively.

   Here are some letter formation poems you can use as you work:

Letter X

A criss and a cross
and in case you forgot,
Where is the treasure?
X marks the spot!

Letter Y

Capital Y has a V in the air.
The pole at the bottom holds it there.

Letter Z

The alphabet ends with the letter Z;
Zig and zag along with me
A line across the top
A zig down low
A zag on the ground
And now you know!

Mathematics

1. In addition to the Roman numeral XXIV, write down the number 24 and word TWENTY FOUR in all capital letters for your child to see. Say each letter as you write.

2. Have the child draw images of the number TWENTY FOUR. They may copy some of the items you made in your blackboard drawing for this week. Your child should then practice writing the number 24, Roman numeral XXIV, and the word TWENTY FOUR in all capital letters on the opposite page of their book. If you feel they need extra time with writing, let them continue to practice as needed. Here is a verse to share when forming the number 24:

Write a two
And now what's more?
You should write
the number four!

3. Seed Estimating & Calculating Differences

   Supplies Needed:
   Packets of Seeds

   Provide your child with a few packets of seeds. Without opening the packets, let your child feel and look at each one and guess (estimate) how many seeds are inside each one.

   Next, open each packet of seeds and have your child count the contents. Ask your child if their estimate was less than or greater than the actual number of seeds inside.

   In your child's lesson book, have them draw a picture of each packet of seeds on the left side of the spread. On the right hand side, have them write down their estimate and the actual amount of seeds inside each packet.

   Have your child find the difference between their estimate and the actual amounts by subtracting the larger number from the smaller number. Have them record these equations and differences in their lesson books.

Domestic Arts/Practical Life Skills

Oat and Seed Breakfast Jars

Supplies Needed:
Glass Jars with Lids
Vanilla Greek Yogurt
Flax Seed
Granola
Fresh Cut Fruit
Rolled Oats (chia seeds also work)
Organic Milk

For Sweetener Options:

Vanilla Extract
Organic Applesauce
100% Maple Syrup
Cinnamon
Brown Sugar

Whenever children are a part of the process of making food, they tend to like it a lot more! These yummy breakfast jars are the perfect cooking activity for this week's lessons and will encourage healthy eating. Remember to let your child do much of the work and use math skills during the process.

Begin by filling each jar with about 1/3 yogurt. Next add 2-3 tablespoons of milk and the same amount of flax seed. For each jar, have your child include one or two sweeteners next. There is no wrong or right amount but be modest. Hold off on adding your oats and fruit. Put the lid on your jars and have the children shake, shake, shake!

Open your jars back up and have your child add one or two tablespoons of oats. Choose and cut up your fruit into small pieces and add it to the top of your jar as far as you can while still being able to close the lid.

These can stay well in the fridge for 4-5 days. Banana does not last as long so eat those first!

Outdoor Time/Nature Walk

Take your children outside each day regardless of the weather. Invest in good rain gear, snow gear and wool undergarments if your location requires it. Do your lessons outdoors whenever possible.

Caregiver Focus

Caregiver Focus: Self- Reflecting on Purpose

During the week, find alone time to either journal or meditate and explore what you find deep purpose in and what you want to change or see happen in your life.

Begin by asking yourself some of the following questions:

What do you want to change or do?
WHY do you want this?
What brings you joy?
If money weren't an issue, what would you do with your time?
What gifts or talents do you wish to share with the world?
What makes you lose track of time?
What is preventing you from doing more of that?

Science, Nature Study, Earth Discovery

Learning About the Sense of Sight

1. Spend time today talking to your child about the sense of sight. Ask your child if they can describe different ways that things look (circular, square, colorful, dull, tall, short, pretty, ugly, etc.) How do they use their sense of sight in everyday life?

2. Pin the Vegetables in the Garden

   Supplies Needed:
   Garden Chalkboard Drawing or Print Out
   Cut Out Vegetables
   Tape

   This is a fun twist on the old favorite game of Pin the Tail on the Donkey and is a great activity to do as your child learns more about their sense of sight. Create a drawing of a garden bed with various vegetables. Let your child take a good look at the placement of the items. Blindfold your child or have them close their eyes. Hand them a cut out of the same vegetable with tape on the back and have them work to pin it to the right place in the garden. Depending on your child's age and ability, you can let them look after each turn to see how they did or have them wait until the end to see how close they came! We have provided a template for inspiration or for actual use:

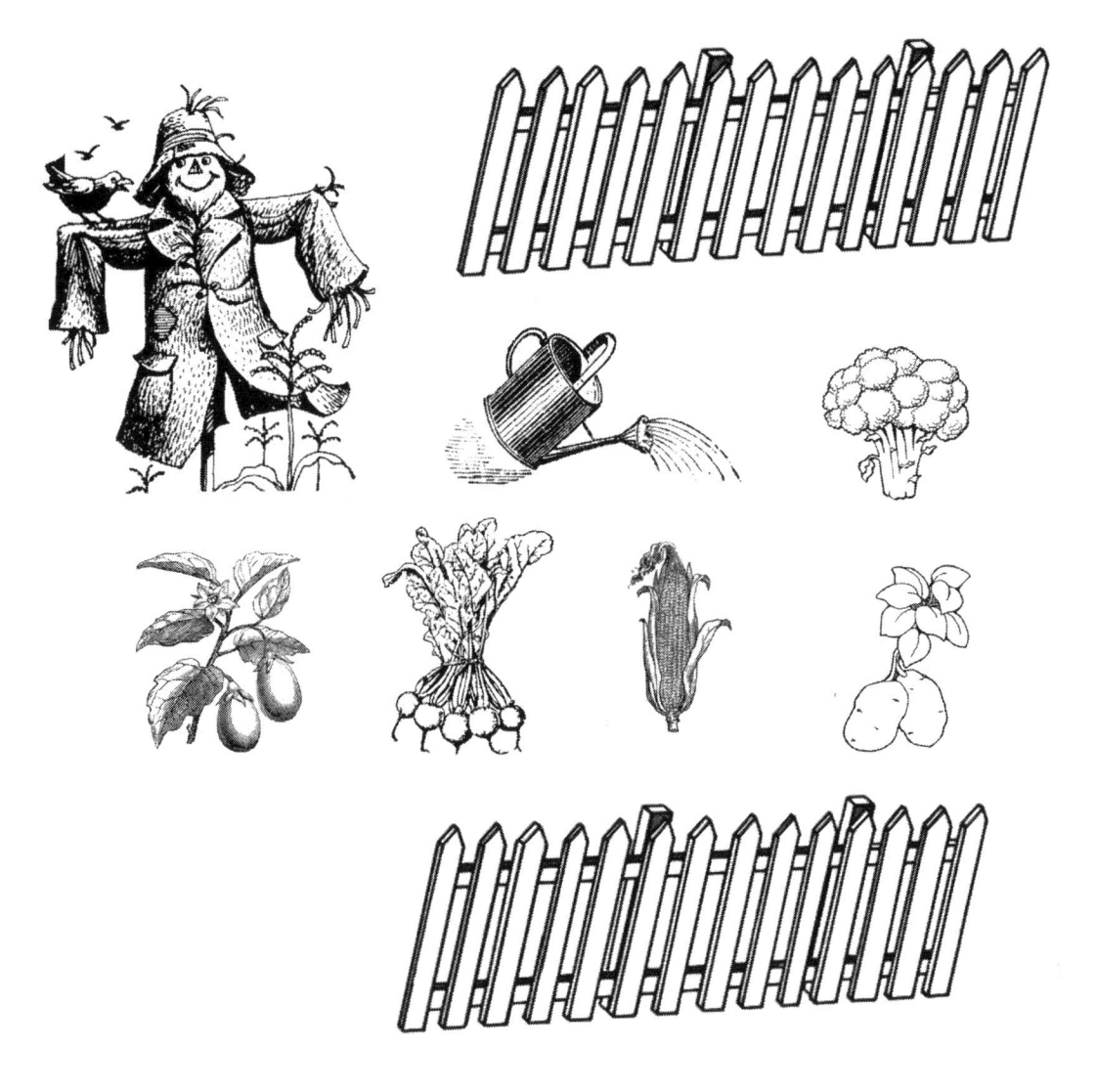

Vegetable Cut Outs
(put tape on back)

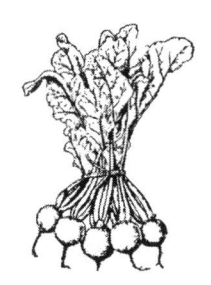

First Grade Curriculum | WINTER | Little Acorn Learning

Afternoon Lessons

1. Music: Continue Practicing Flute or Recorder

2. Art/Fine Motor Skills: Seed and Bean Mosaics

   Supplies Needed:
   White Cardstock
   Dry Seeds, Beans and Pasta
   Glue

   Have the children draw their own design on the cardstock, cut, add glue to the design and choose which seeds, beans or pasta pieces to add to fill up the mosaic. It may be nice to do this with this week's letters X, Y & Z. Let dry and add to your homeschool area.

   Some questions you can ask your children:

   What type of tree do you think would grow from an apple seed?
   What type of tree would grow from an acorn?
   What type of tree would grow from an orange seed?
   There are many different types of seeds. Can you name a few more?

Tuesday Student Lessons – Week Twenty Four

(Painting – Red Day)

Language Arts

1. Like yesterday, read your child the story of *The Little Seed.* Provide your child with a piece of beeswax modeling material as you read. Let them hold this piece of beeswax as they listen, warming it with their hands so it softens.

2. Have your child form the softened beeswax material into the letters X, Y and then Z. Roll it into a long snake, form it just so and then put it back together again. Next, have them form it into the number 24.

3. Open your lesson book and review the work you did yesterday. Have your child trace the letters X, Y and Z, number 24, and words TWENTY FOUR with their fingers.

4. On your blackboard, write some simple sentences with blanks and have your child copy them in their lesson book. Discuss what the missing words could be and then have your child write that in as well.

   Here are some examples:

   OUTSIDE IT IS _____
   I SEE _____
   MY EYES ARE _____
   SEEDS ARE _____
   PLANTS COME FROM _____

Mathematics

Multiplication Circle, 5x-9x Times Tables

Like last week, we will continue using our multiplication circles to learn our times tables 5x-9x. You can create this with sidewalk chalk, crayons in your lesson book or with yarn, a board, and nails.

Using different colored yarn or chalk, always start at 0 to begin. The following times tables will not follow the clockwise rule like 1x-4x did but are just as fun and simple as the others.

As you will see, the answer to each equation ends with the number you go to next. This may be confusing at first but once it is mastered, it will be one of the most fun ways your child has to remember their multiplication facts. Here is a video tutorial as well: https://youtu.be/ArCIrn2pDO8

For 5x:

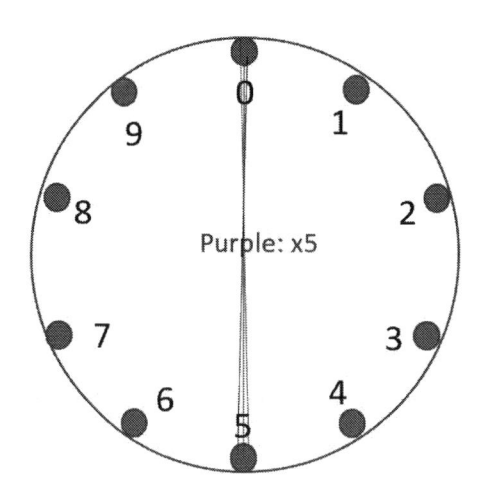

[Circle diagram with numbers 0-9 around the perimeter, labeled "Purple: x5", with a line drawn from 0 to 5]

5x1 = 5 Draw a line from 0 to 5

5x2 = 10 Draw a line from 5 to 0 (for 10)

5x3 = 15 Draw a line from 0 (for 10) to 5 (for 15)

You will soon see that all x5 answers go to either the 0 or 5 spot!

For 6x:

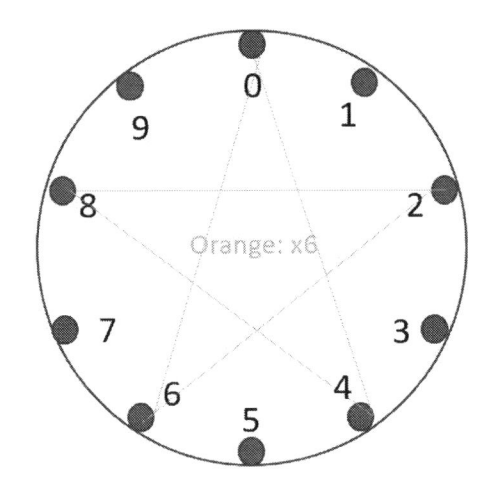

6x1 = 6 Draw a line from 0 to 6

6x2 = 12 Draw a line from 6 to 2 (for 12)

6x3 = 18 Draw a line from 2 (for 12) to 8 (for 18)

Continue this all the way around. You made a star!

For 7x:

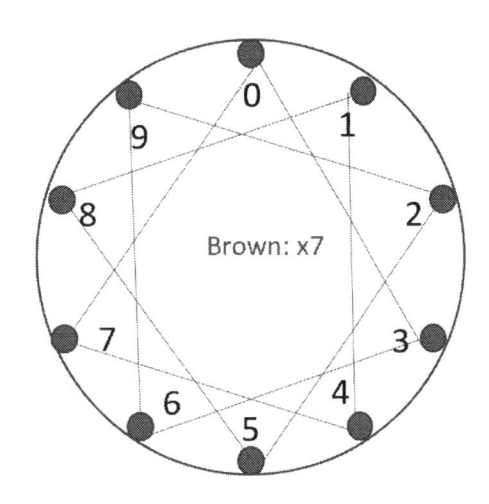

7x1 = 7 Draw a line from 0 to 7

7x2 =14 Draw a line from 7 to 4 (for 14)

7x3 = 21 Draw a line from 4 (for 14) to 1 (for 21)

Continue this all the way around up until 7x10 = 70. You made a 9 pointed star!

For 8x:

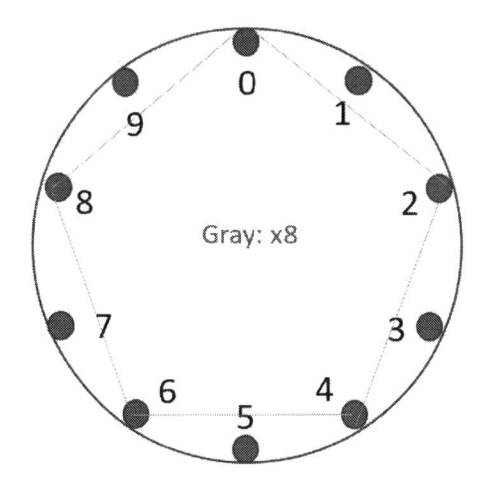

Gray: x8

8x1 = 8 Draw a line from 0 to 8

8x2 = 16 Draw a line from 8 to 6 (for 16)

8x3 = 24 Draw a line from 6 (for 16) to 4 (for 24)

Continue this all the way around.

For x9:

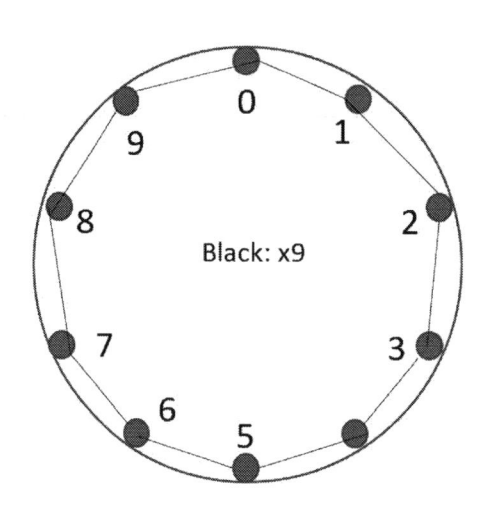

Black: x9

The end result is quite beautiful if done on top of one another:

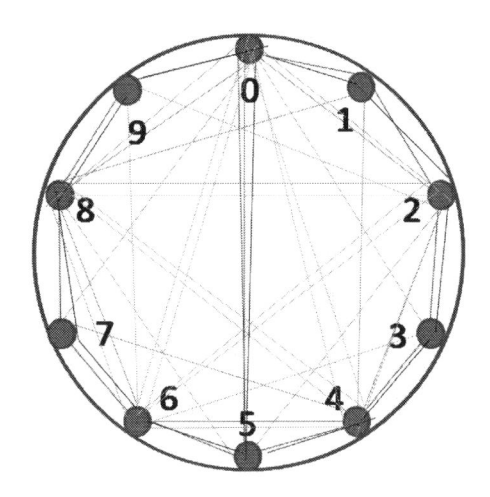

Outdoor Time/Nature Walk

Take your children outside each day regardless of the weather. Invest in good rain gear, snow gear and wool undergarments if your location requires it. Do your lessons outdoors whenever possible.

Social Studies, Geography, Weather, Time

Learning About the Sense of Sight, Braille

Continue talking to your child about the sense of sight. Share the following questions and information to inspire free discussion and conversation:

Some people do not see as well as others. Do you know anyone who uses eyeglasses? Eyeglasses help make vision clearer for people who have trouble seeing.

Other people cannot see at all. When someone's sense of sight is not working, they are blind.

How do you think someone who is blind is able to read? (Braille)

Some people who are blind can read using a special kind of code called Braille. Braille is a system of raised dots on paper that blind people can feel with their fingers to "read" words. These raised dots are symbols that represent numbers, letters, punctuation marks and words.

What sense would someone be using to read Braille instead of their sense of sight? (touch)

Afternoon Lessons

Music: Continue Practicing Flute or Recorder

Wednesday Student Lessons – Week Twenty Four
(Coloring – Yellow Day)

Language Arts

1. In your child's lesson book have them make a drawing of *The Little Seed* story.

2. Like yesterday, again write some simple sentences with blanks and have your child copy them in their lesson book. Discuss what the missing words could be and then have your child write that in as well.

3. Tonight, at bedtime tell your child the story of *The Little Seed*.

4. Take your child to the grocery store with you and have them search the store for items that begin with the letters X, Y & Z. These letters are hard to find, so we listed some ideas to help. As you can see, we do not have any items for the letter X but your child can look for the letter X as they search the store. Bring the list with you and add to it as you find more.

   Yams
   Yogurt
   Yellow Cake
   Yeast
   Yellow Squash
   Yellow Pepper
   Yuca
   Ziploc
   Zucchini

5. Show your child words that include the letter X, Y & Z. Ask them to identify the sounds at the beginning, middle or end of each word.

6. Nature Tic Tac Toe (Letter X)

   Supplies Needed:
   Large Sticks and Branches
   Rocks, Seeds & Other Nature Items

   Using large sticks or branches create an extra large Tic Tac Toe with your child.

Using more sticks and rocks or other nature items, create X and Os each time you choose a square.

Challenge your child and ask them to think of or spell a word that begins with one of this week's letters.

Mathematics

Seed Sorting/Identification and Math

Supplies Needed:
Various Seeds
Plate
Paper Towel
Water

Have your child count out 100 seeds of their choice. Save the packets for later. On a plate, place a damp paper towel and have your child group these seeds into various combinations. Use math skills to make equations out of these groupings (i.e. 4 groups of 25 seeds is 25 x 5 = 100, etc.) Cover your seeds with another damp paper towel.

Create a chart with each type of seed categorized. This can be in your child's lesson book or on your blackboard. Each day have your child count the seeds that have begun to sprout and germinate and mark them on the chart.

After 5 days, record how many seeds did not germinate. Which types of seeds did not? Each type of plant needs a different amount of time to do so. Have your child look on the packets of seeds and find the amount of days required for each type. Did any sprout before they should have? Did any miss the target? How many and which ones?

Outdoor Time/Nature Walk

Take your children outside each day regardless of the weather. Invest in good rain gear, snow gear and wool undergarments if your location requires it. Do your lessons outdoors whenever possible.

Science, Nature Study, Earth Discovery

1. Learning About Seeds, Germination

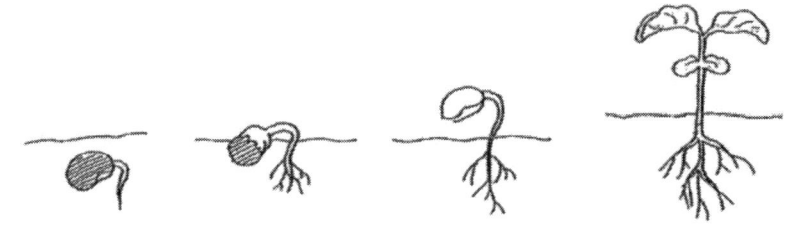

   Spend time discussing seeds with your children today. Here are some questions and thoughts to review as you learn together:

   Even though plants have many seeds, it only takes one seed for a new plant to grow.

   What do you think a seed needs in order to grow into a plant? (sun, soil, water, etc.)

   Just like you wear a coat when it's cold outside, seeds also have a "coat" or a layer to protect them. Deep inside the seed is what we call an embryo. The embryo of the seed is basically a very tiny plant just waiting to come out and grow!

   In order for a seed to grow into a plant, it needs to go through what is called germination. Germination is when a seed goes through many things in order to sprout. All seeds are different with how they germinate.

   Today we will try to sprout our own Lima Bean seeds.

2. Lima Bean Sprouts

Supplies Needed:
Clear Plastic Cups
Potting Soil
Lima Beans
Water
Sunlight

Fill cup 2/3 full of potting soil. Drop in one lima bean and cover with more soil. Water lightly. Make sure the cups are placed in a warm, sunny area. Wait for sprouts to show.

When your plant begins to grow, be sure to talk more about the process and parts of a plant. Some questions you can ask:

Do you know what the roots of a plant do?
The roots absorb water and nutrients from the soil so the plant can grow.

Do roots grow up or down? (down)
What types of plants can you name that have roots?

What do you think the leaves of a plant do?
The leaves of a plant absorb the sunlight and turn it into food so the plant can grow.

Are the leaves above the soil or below? (above)

Afternoon Lessons

1. Handwork: Knitting, The Seed Stitch

    Today you can practice a new stitch with your child. The Seed Stitch is a simple combination of the knit and purl stitches.

    Cast on a row.

    Row 1: *K1, P1, repeat from * to the end of the row.
    Row 2: *P1, K1, repeat from * to the end of the row.
    Repeat rows 1 and 2 for the pattern. Be sure to keep alternate stitches on top of one another to get the seed stitch pattern.

Thursday Student Lessons – Week Twenty Four
(Crafting/Games – Orange Day)

Language Arts

1. Continue to tell your child the story of *The Little Seed.*

2. Alphabet Cards

   Supplies Needed:
   Heavy White Cardstock
   Beeswax Stick Crayons
   Scissors

   Spend time cutting cards out of cardstock with your child. Using beeswax crayons, continue to finish drawing each letter we have learned so far and include the letters X, Y & Z to complete the set. Next to the letters, have your child draw an image that begins with it. Using scissors, round the corners of these cards and keep working on them throughout the year. You can use them in your lessons and for an upper case and lowercase match game later in the curriculum when we learn those as well.

3. Continue reading simple reader books together.

4. Print out or share the following photos and practice saying them together with your child. Your child can also copy these words into their lesson book.

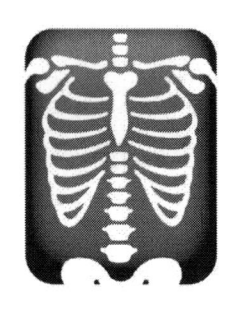

X-RAY

YAM

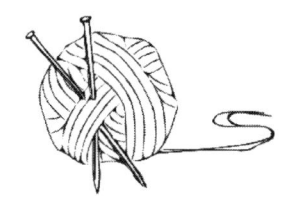

YARN

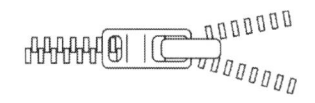

ZIPPER

ZEBRA

First Grade Curriculum | WINTER | Little Acorn Learning

Mathematics

Math Seed Word Problems

Now that your child is well versed in the four processes, this is a wonderful time to introduce word problems.. Tailor these word problems to your child's level and ability. Build upon this skill in the coming weeks and ask your child to create some word problems for you to solve!

For example:

1. A little girl blew a dandelion puff and the seeds flew through the air. As her sister looked up, she saw 10 seeds floating. 4 seeds landed in front of her onto the ground. How many seeds are still floating in the air?

    $10 - 4 = 6$

2. A grandfather and his grandson decided to plant a garden together. The grandfather took out 3 of his seed packets from the previous year. Each packet has 20 seeds inside of them. How many seeds do they have to plant?

    $20 + 20 + 20 = 60$
    $20 \times 3 = 60$

3. The garden nursery is selling plants. They only have 10 tomato plants left in little pots. Two friends walk in and decide to buy them all and split them in half, so it is fair. How many tomato plants will each person get to take home?

    $10 \div 2 = 5$

Outdoor Time/Nature Walk

Take your children outside each day regardless of the weather. Invest in good rain gear, snow gear and wool undergarments if your location requires it. Do your lessons outdoors whenever possible.

Social Studies, Geography, Weather, Time

<u>Learning About the Sense of Sight, The Braille Alphabet</u>

Spend time today with your child, exploring the Braille alphabet and spelling out some familiar words.

Supplies Needed:
Beeswax or Other Wax-Like Material (Wiki Sticks, etc.)
Paper
Scissors

Review your discussion from the other day about Braille. Explain again that people who cannot see, use their fingertips to feel patterns of dots on the paper to read.

Following the chart below, take small pieces of wax and form them into small balls. You may need to use scissors to do this ahead of time. Have your child write a word or their name on the paper. Below each letter, copy the Braille pattern for each. Next, have your child close their eyes and practice feeling the letters and word with their fingertips.

Ask your child how they felt using their sense of touch to read? Did the dots have different patterns that they could notice easily?

A B C D E F G H I
J K L M N O P Q R
S T U V W X Y Z

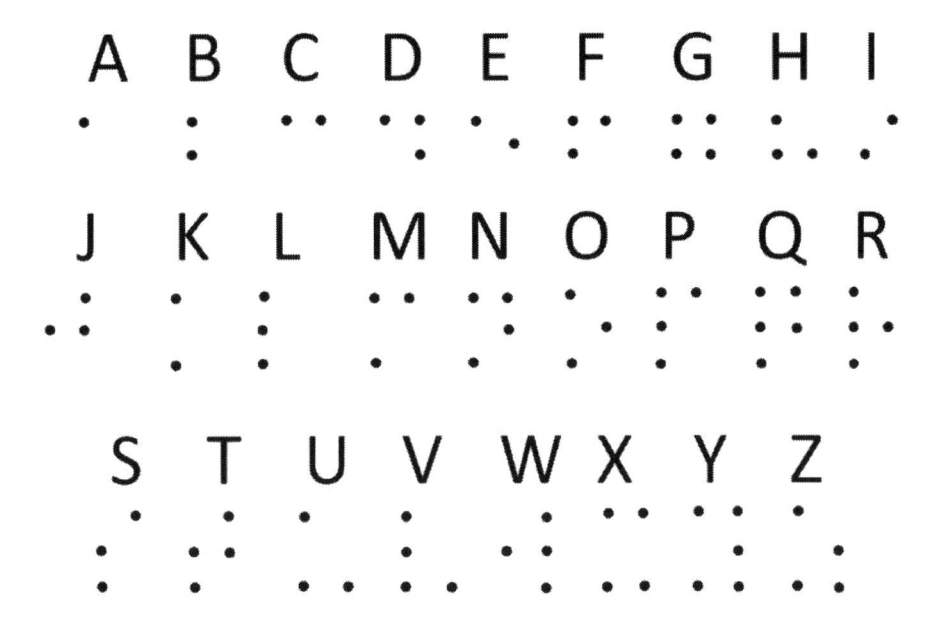

Movement, Body Awareness & Health

Sowing Seeds Circle Game

Let your child act out the various movements and gestures after you share each verse:

First, we'll plough and rake the field
Smooth the ground for harvest yield.
(ploughing: let children tug, guide, push, turn corners, good shoulder and back movements, smooth ground with hands)

Then dig the ditches long and deep,
And pile the bank up high and steep;
(digging: place foot on shovel, push, stoop, throw, up and down through aisles or furniture)

Now scatter seed from side to side,
Across the field, out far and wide,
(sowing: to right, left with both hands alternating, through aisles or furniture, free and broad shoulder movements, arm swung outward, shoulders high)

Open the gates, pour water in
To cover the shoots so tender and green.
(opening gates: pushing slowly and steadily downward, count 1, 2, 3; repeat four times)

Upon the banks now let us walk
And see how grows each tiny stalk.
(walking on banks: through aisles and furniture, around the room, arms back of head, looking from side to side)

When these have grown up high, just so
The water back to the pond must go.

When water and sun have done their best
Then comes our turn to do the rest.

With sickle sharp, then, row on row.
All around the field we mow.
(mowing with sickle: stoop, give sharp clip with right arm, through one aisle; repeat with left arm)

The sheaves now bind and shock the grain
To save from storm and wind and rain;
(binding: stoop, twist, throw; repeat)

Then to the barn, not one will fail,
To thresh it out with swinging flail.
(threshing: two rows of children flail together, alternating down stroke, good shoulder and back movement)

Our bags we now will quickly fill,
Then hasten to the busy mill.
(fill sacks: lift, carry on back to boat, bend under sense of weight)

Here in the mortars shake and pound
The-husks from off the seed around;

Then fans will blow the chaff away,
And here is rice for lunch today.
(*milling: turning wheels, pounding in mortar, blowing or fanning chaff, insist on good realistic work, making the movements strong, yet rhythmically reactionary*)

Afternoon Lessons

1. Form Drawing/Art – Review, Spiral

    This afternoon, we will review form drawing spirals.

    - Using a jump rope or sidewalk chalk, make a spiral for your child to see. Have your child walk on it from the outside to the inside and from the inside to the outside. Continue with various movements such as hopping, skipping and trying to walk backwards.

    - In your child's lesson book, have them draw a picture of the dragon living inside his cave. On the opposite side of the book, have them practice making spirals both starting from the center and outward and also trying to begin outward and going into the center. Continue these forms until your child can create them with confidence.

2. Handwork: Hand Stitching/Embroidery

    Supplies Needed:
    Embroidery Needle
    Embroidery Floss
    White Scrap Fabric
    Embroidery Hoop (optional)
    Scissors

    Using our embroidery instructions, work with your child to make the letters X, Y & Z embroidery piece. You can do this with a simple running stitch, or you may choose to learn more complicated stitches together.

Friday Student Lessons – Week Twenty Four
(Modeling/Housework – Green Day)

Language Arts

1. Today have your child continue to practice writing the letters X, Y & Z in their lesson book on unlined paper.

2. In your child's lesson book, have them practice writing the alphabet from A- Z each letter a few times on each line.

3. Ask your child to tell YOU the story of *The Little Seed*.

4. Continue to introduce your child to poetry and rhymes. There are many beautiful ones to explore. You can get a poetry book from the library or share some of your favorites. Here is one from Robert Kingery, who was only 10 years old when he wrote this a very long time ago.

>Winter time has gone away
>Spring took its place the other day
>
>Spring has come there is no doubt
>For the leaves are coming out
>
>Now the days are getting long
>And the birds begin their song
>
>Every noon the sound we hear at dawn
>Comes from places they are on
>
>Robin redbreast bluebird sweet
>Have their coats decked nice and neat
>
>The grass is getting long and green
>The nicest you have ever seen
>
>Showers have begun to fall
>Not so very hard at all

Spring is well on by this day
And good bye is what I say

ROBERT KINGERY

5. After you read the poem, ask your child the following questions:

    How did that poem make you feel?

    Words rhyme when they have similar sounds at the end. What words do you think rhyme in that poem? (away/day, long/song, green/seen, etc.)

    When you heard that poem, what images came to your mind? What did you imagine?

6. Have your child draw a picture after they heard the poem.

7. On your blackboard, write down some rhyming words. Say these together out loud and have your child copy them. Ask your child to think of some other rhyming words of their own. Here are some examples:

    SEED : FEED
    PLANT : CAN'T
    RAKE : BAKE
    SOW : TOE

    Note how rhyming words do not have to have the same exact spelling at the end of each word. It is the sound that matters.

Mathematics

1. Measuring Seedlings

    Supplies Needed:
    Ruler
    Seedlings or Lima Bean Sprouts

    Show your child a ruler. Have them look at the numbers and lines. Point out the beginning and end of the ruler. Next, show them the inch lines. If your child is understanding this well, show them the centimeters. Explore measuring various things in your home. You can round up to the nearest inch if your child is still learning. When they further understand, you can expand to measuring more accurately.

Every few days, have your child measure a seedling or the Lima Bean Sprout that you planted. How much has it grown? Journal this is your lesson book along with a drawing of the seedling.

2. Review Counting Backwards

On your blackboard write down numbers 100 to 1 with some blanks. Have your child copy this into their lesson book and fill in the missing numbers. Continue these types of exercises over the next week or to aiming to be able to have your child confidently count backwards from 100.

Outdoor Time/Nature Walk

Take your children outside each day regardless of the weather. Invest in good rain gear, snow gear and wool undergarments if your location requires it. Do your lessons outdoors whenever possible.

Domestic Arts/Practical Life Skills

Learning to Zipper

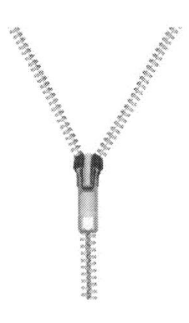

Zipper begins with Z!

If your child has not yet learned how to zipper, spend time today teaching them. Begin by showing your child to hold the zipper between their thumb and index finger. Model inserting the tongue into the zipper pull opening and move it upward with the other hand. Once your child begins to get the hang of this, lay out various coats, clothing and accessories for them to practice on.

If your child already knows how to do this well, have them teach a younger sibling, a friend, or present the instructions to you as if they were teaching another child.

Afternoon Lessons

Use the afternoon hours today to review areas from this week's afternoon lessons that you feel may need a bit more attention. Bring these into your weekend as you find time.

About Eileen Foley

Little Acorn Learning was born out my lifelong love for children and my desire to protect their inherent right to experience childhood as many of us remember it to be. For over 25 years, I have applied my love of nature-based learning and mindful caregiving drawing from my experience as a mother, as owner and teacher of my own home-based Waldorf inspired school, and as my role as Kindergarten Teacher at Housatonic Valley Waldorf School in Connecticut.

Based on seasonal themes and festivals, Little Acorn Learning inspires a love of nature and the home arts while supporting the caregiver's soul. I help parents, teachers, and caregivers find true meaning in their very important work with children through curriculum, courses and mentorship.

In my spare time, I enjoy backyard gardening, beekeeping, chicken and rabbit raising, maple syrup making, cooking, crochet and spending time outdoors with my children, pets and loved ones.

I have been a writer all of my life and had poetry published at a very young age. More recently my work has been published in various sources such as Relevant Times Magazine, Primal Parenting Magazine, Rhythm of the Home Online Magazine, the Simple Kids Website and others. I have also spoken on various media outlets including The Waldorf Connection Radio Show, the Joyfull Parenting Podcast and others.

I look forward to supporting you on this very sacred journey of parenting, educating and guiding the children in your care.

Made in the USA
Middletown, DE
30 September 2020